W9-CZA-323

The Rise of an
American Architecture

The Rise of an American Architecture

Henry-Russell Hitchcock
Albert Fein
Winston Weisman
Vincent Scully

Edited with an introduction and exhibition notes by
Edgar Kaufmann, jr.

Published in Association with The Metropolitan Museum of Art by

PRAEGER PUBLISHERS
New York · Washington · London

PRAEGER PUBLISHERS
111 Fourth Avenue, New York, N.Y. 10003, U.S.A.
5, Cromwell Place, London S.W.7, England

Published in the United States of America in 1970
by Praeger Publishers, Inc., in Association with
The Metropolitan Museum of Art, New York, N.Y. 10028

Library of Congress Catalog Card Number: 70–116442

Design by Robert Fabian
Layout by Paul and Barbara Bodin

On the jacket: View of Brooklyn Bridge,
New York City. Engraving, 1883. Courtesy
Museum of the City of New York.

Printed in the United States of America

Foreword

This important book of essays on the contribution of nineteenth-century America to the history of architecture and city planning appears at a time when this country already has lost many examples of its architectural heritage. Across the land, cities have seen their churches, hotels, homes, and commercial buildings knocked down and bulldozed away in favor of high-rise apartment houses and parking lots. Until recently, a freeway threatened New Orleans's French Quarter and, in fact, Overton Park in Memphis might actually succumb to that fate. Hundreds of fine old Federal homes have been mutilated by new façades and interiors or left to rot in slums. The fantasy of the Harrall-Wheeler House in Bridgeport, Connecticut—one of the country's best Gothic Revival buildings—has been shattered for all time. Detroit has lost its 1871 City Hall and, with it, a piece of its history and a part of its image of itself.

These sad examples merely introduce the story. Many structures that, although uncelebrated, record the emergence of a distinctive American architecture are now in grave danger. This obliteration of our architectural history is not a sinister plot; it is simply heedless, mindless destruction in the service of highway building, urban renewal, industrialization, and other needs that confront our society. It must be stopped; and now is the time to do it.

In 1924, The Metropolitan Museum of Art opened its American Wing devoted to Colonial art and architecture, and it was one of the first museums to install American period rooms. The American Wing fostered a new appreciation for the work of the Colonial period and a concern for its preservation that has since grown into a nationwide movement. The Museum's 1970 Centennial exhibition *The Rise of an American Architecture* was prepared in cooperation with the National Trust for Historic Preservation, and will be seen in museums throughout the country after it closes in New York. The purpose of the show is twofold: to enliven the appreciation of nineteenth-century American architecture and, before it is too late, to dramatize the imminent threat to its preservation. It is being presented at the Metropolitan in conjunction with another Centennial exhibition planned with the same crusading spirit, *19th-Century America*, the first comprehensive exhibition of the paintings, sculpture, and decorative arts of the century.

The concept of historic preservation has changed greatly in recent years. Preservationists—no longer merely content to enshrine pieces of the past—are today as deeply concerned about environment as are conservationists and city planners. Their interest is not directed solely toward the preservation of isolated landmarks; rather, they are concerned with entire historic districts, with the character of neighborhoods, with the quality and texture of cities and towns. They contend that the disfiguration of cities—the neglect or destruction of beautiful old buildings—impairs the total environment as much as the pollution of air and water or the thoughtless extermination of wildlife.

This view of historic preservation as an instrument in shaping total environment is winning increasing acceptance.

v

Many cities throughout the country—San Francisco, Philadelphia, Denver, Savannah, Providence, Richmond—have recognized that historically or culturally important buildings can contribute to the beauty and to the economic and social stability of the community. Such buildings are not employed as museums but, through imaginative adaptation, serve as homes, offices, business establishments, restaurants, and community centers. Their preservation and use can counteract—and prevent—the rootlessness and spiritual alienation that result from living in degrading circumstances and among amorphous structures to which one cannot possibly relate.

Concern for preservation of America's historic landmarks is not new; but the means for channeling and implementing that concern have only recently evolved—and, in many cases, are just now coming about. All too often, cities have created legislation to protect their landmarks after suffering irreparable loss. For example, Grand Rapids lost its 1888 City Hall before its citizens alerted themselves to the need for legal protection of their architectural heritage. In Savannah, an old city market was razed in favor of a blacktop parking lot before the citizenry were sufficiently aroused to prevent further loss. The residents of Savannah have since become one of the most active and successful groups of preservationists in the country. The demolition of Pennsylvania Station in New York City was one of the events that helped to bring about the formation of the New York City Landmarks Commission. As this splendid example of the classical style was being leveled, many architects and other concerned citizens who were trying desperately to save it were astounded to discover that they had no effective legal means of doing so. In fact, a national framework for historic preservation on a broad scale was not created until the passage of the National Historic Preservation Act in 1966. In this act, Congress declared that significant physical evidence of our national patrimony must be preserved, and it authorized the means, through matching grants-in-aid, for state and local governments and the National Trust for Historic Preservation through private preservation organizations to undertake the necessary measures. The act also provides for expansion of The National Register of Historic Places, a growing list of properties worthy of preservation, and assures that these places will not be destroyed without due process.

The National Preservation Act also speaks of the psychological effects of landmarks and of the need for giving "a sense of orientation to the American people." This is a primary concern of both the Metropolitan Museum and the National Trust. The historic landmarks that still surround us, many of them largely unnoticed, can greatly enrich our lives. This is not simply a nice thing. It is a crucial thing. In the midst of the dislocations of today's life, landmarks can help provide emotional security and sanity. America came of an age and established an architectural identity in its nineteenth-century past. Today, in the twentieth century, it has attained an age when it must realize that its national past is an indispensable part of its present.

James Biddle
President
National Trust for Historic
Preservation

Thomas P. F. Hoving
Director
The Metropolitan Museum
of Art

Contents

Introduction

The essays that form this book were written by four scholars, each outstanding for original and comprehensive research in his field. By uniting the essays in one volume, we hoped to present a current report on the understanding of nineteenth-century American architecture in those special areas that represent advances valid today: buildings for commerce, small homes, and city parks. It seemed pedantic, in our time, to separate parks from skyscrapers—landscape architecture from architecture proper—since they are complementary aspects of the city as man's habitat.

Furthermore, in the centenary year of The Metropolitan Museum of Art, it seemed appropriate to consider what the United States had contributed to architecture at large during the fertile century in which the museum was launched.

The essayists were aware, of course, that an exhibition structured in tandem with this book was being prepared for the museum, and that this exhibition would cover the years 1815 to 1915. Contributors were free to determine their own retrospective time spans.

The results of this plan were surprising and heartening, for they revealed that this was a moment of general re-evaluation. Furthermore, none of these scholars was content to consider the past without close links to the present. The famous ivory towers, if ever they were more than mirages, are no longer considered habitable.

HENRY-RUSSELL HITCHCOCK, who opens the sequence, has been famous as a historian and critic of architecture through-out the Western world, covering the eighteenth, nineteenth, and twentieth centuries. It is fair to say that his works, beginning with the synoptic volume on *Modern Architecture, Romanticism and Reintegration,* published forty years ago, have provided basic, solid insights indispensable to all prospectors in these wide fields, and that he has inspired and guided younger talents with unflagging generosity. Professor Hitchcock's recent move to New York City and his assumption of duties at the Institute of Fine Arts of New York University—close to The Metropolitan Museum of Art—are bright events for this area. Professor Hitchcock has, in this volume, followed American architectural contributions to the European scene from the present moment backward to the earliest traces. His statement permits a clear overview of terrain hitherto known best from scattered, probative investigations. It is now evident that, for a century at least, the United States has enriched the composition of modern architecture significantly and consistently.

ALBERT FEIN, a younger scholar, has quickly risen to eminence as historian of landscape and environmental planning in this country, largely through his remarkable and sympathetic command of the whole range of ideas, relationships, and practices that center around Frederick Law Olmsted, Sr., one of the great Americans beginning to be reappreciated today. Olmsted's creative mind perceived the modern urban situation in depth, and his programs for dealing with it humanely and positively are still ahead of practice. The presentation of these vital concepts and of the masterful implementation of them initiated by Olmsted has been made by Dr. Fein in a way that interlocks effectively with the goals and practices of modern city life. He has used history to light our endeavors and our hopes.

WINSTON WEISMAN for some years has been engaged in enlarging and strengthening our understanding of the most famous, the most questioned, and the most far-flung American innovation in architecture, the skyscraper. With the patience and care of an experienced Alpinist, he has explored this massif and here presents a remarkably complete and trustworthy chart of its constituent features. The whole area is more complex and fascinating—more revealing of human cultural processes—than was hitherto believed. The values of architectural practice and criticism are bound to be affected by the knowledge he makes available here.

VINCENT SCULLY'S first well-known publications were concerned with the nineteenth-century American house. Since then, his interests have ranged far and deep, but he has returned occasionally to his early topic with a broad understanding. He closes the quartet of essays with a flaming, almost Blakean vision centered on the development of homes as those artifacts nearest man's heart and instincts. He considers the course and significance of this development at the same time that he discourses on the development and values of architectural history. At once commentator and protagonist, the Master of Morse College at Yale has presented a dramatic sequence on modern architecture as the expression of human goals. The roots that invisibly tie the dweller to his hearth, the designer to his duty as symbolizer of life, and the teacher-critic as monitor (or *DEW* system) to his fellow men, these are the strands that Scully skillfully interlaces in his essay on the American home.

To say that such writings call forth gratitude and pride on the part of those presenting them to the public is an obvious understatement. These four men have brought treasures to the centennial celebration of The Metropolitan Museum of Art in essays that deepen and clarify our understanding of American architecture and its ideals.

EDGAR KAUFMANN, JR.
Editor

American Influence Abroad

1   American Influence Abroad

Henry-Russell Hitchcock

In the D.D.R. *(Deutsche Demokratische Republik*—East Germany), there is, just outside Dresden, a motel—actually called, incidentally, Motel Dresden—that has lately been built, despite the fact that there are very few East Germans who travel by car, as in most Communist countries of Europe, and that motorists from the West are discouraged from crossing the interzonal frontier. This provides rather striking evidence of American architectural influence today in a state where everything from the United States is nominally condemned as decadent if not, indeed, fascist.

Motels are, of course, no novelty in Western Europe. In Italy and Holland, at least, motels of local design *(Fig. 1-1)* rival those that American chains are beginning to provide in Europe *(Fig. 1-2)*. One of the facilities specifically evolved for a motorized civilization, motels came into being first in the United States and now proliferate everywhere. Other such are supermarkets, shopping centers, and parking garages. In the design and building of these last, Europeans are by this time well up to, if not ahead of, the United States. This general influence from organizational and technical developments

1-1. Euromotel near Amsterdam.

3

1-2. Holiday Inn near Leiden, Holland.

in America—for none of these structures represent fully architectural building types, though some involve structural innovations leading to particular sorts of design—is a very old story.[1] It goes back at its beginning a generation and more before The Metropolitan Museum of Art was founded in 1870. Before Willis Carrier's development of air-conditioning, now a felt need throughout much of the world, in underdeveloped tropical countries as much as in those in the temperate zones, the most important instance of this influence has been the skyscraper. The early evolution of that major building type, which began seriously in New York in the Museum's earliest years, is discussed here at length in Winston Weisman's article (pp. 115 – 60).

But balancing the motels and the shopping centers, the latest of novel American building types to be emulated, two individual works by American architects, both completed in 1968, deserve particular attention: the Museum of Modern Art in West Berlin by Ludwig Mies van der Rohe (Fig. 1-3) and the City Gallery of Bielefeld in Westphalia (Fig. 1-4) by Philip Johnson are monumental works of architecture of individual distinction, and

of a kind—or, indeed, two kinds—of distinction that may be considered twentieth-century American.

Of course, Mies was German-born and practiced in Germany, if not very actively, in the 1920's and early 1930's. But the last thirty years of his career, the most productive and the most influential, were spent in America. Like so many earlier immigrants of high talent in various fields, he died an American citizen of whom America became—and this is somewhat exceptional—even formally and governmentally[2] proud. Coincidentally, Philip Johnson was a disciple of Mies's[3] and, on one notable occasion, his collaborator on the Seagram Building in 1956–58, though the development of the two architects diverged rather sharply thereafter.[4]

Not surprisingly, most Germans prefer Mies's museum. He himself, moreover, seems to have considered it the culmination of his career, a career that was so soon to be terminated by his death in the summer of 1969. But it is, all the same, more particularly Mies's later American career that the Berlin museum culminated, crowning the long line of steel-framed and fully glazed buildings he had first begun to build in Chicago more than a quarter-

4

1-3. Museum of Modern Art. Berlin. 1967—68. Ludwig Mies van der Rohe.

1-4. City Gallery. Bielefeld (Westphalia), West Germany. Completed 1968. Philip Johnson.

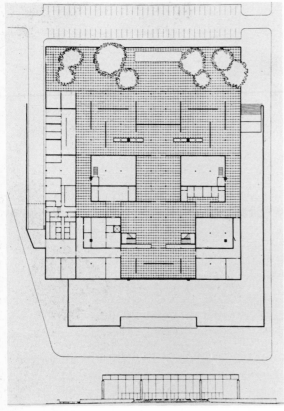

1-5. Museum of Modern Art. Berlin. Plan.

century ago. These were, first, a major influence on American architectural design in the 1950's and soon, partly indirectly via the work of younger American architects who were then becoming leaders, a major international influence that has since become ubiquitous. Thus, even Karl-Marx-Stadt (formerly Chemnitz) in the *D.D.R.,* as now rebuilding after wartime bombing, is little different visually from the results of urban renewal in various American cities; and the skyscrapers along Kalinin Avenue in Moscow in their spacing and general design resemble Wilshire Boulevard in Los Angeles quite as much as they do Le Corbusier's *Ville de 3 Millions* of 1922.[5]

Aesthetically one need not choose between the two new museums. Their more obvious differences, particularly that between the light, open cage of Mies's Berlin gallery, reminiscent of his favorite earlier work, Crown Hall at the Illinois Institute of Technology (IIT) in Chicago, which housed his own architectural school, and the massive concrete piers faced with pink sandstone of Johnson's gallery in Bielefeld *(Fig. 1-4),* boldly articulated inside and out, are as much generational as personal. But functionally there are rather more significant differences that deserve detailed comment.

Mies's museum is predominantly an exhibition gallery, or, more accurately, two stories of galleries *(Fig. 1-5),* one of them within the podium below the glazed cage, and little else. Though Johnson's building has three stories of galleries for the exhibition of works of art *(Fig. 1-6),* it resembles, as his clients[6] wished, the art centers that have been developed in the United States both independently and in relation to existing museums. To mention only a few of the elements provided and the various artistic needs of the community served, there is a large lecture hall—more

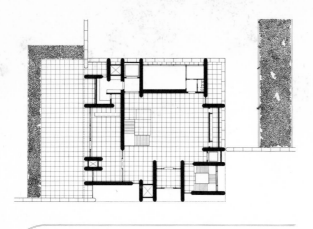

FIRST FLOOR PLAN

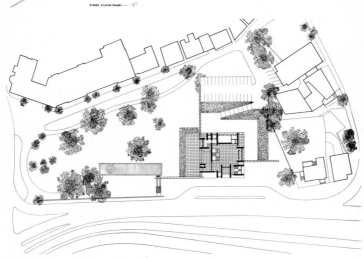

1-6. City Gallery. Bielefeld (Westphalia), West Germany. Plans and section.

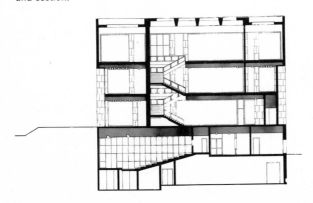

satisfactory functionally than the ones architects who design college buildings are usually able to provide for art departments; a library that is not restricted to the needs of the staff, but is the art library of the city; a print study room; and other reserved study areas such as a university museum might aspire to. There is also a room where young children can work with art materials; a café with garden terrace facing a good-sized park *(Fig. 1-4)*, not to speak of the special workrooms, the large storage spaces, and the suites of offices for the director and his assistants. All of these amenities indicate that the younger, and American-born, architect

here brought to Europe—in the special field of art service to the community—organizational and technical aspects of architecture that had long been developed in the United States, much as Albert Kahn's firm[7] once brought what he had developed in the factories he was building for Detroit's automobile manufacturers to European factory-owners and builders in all the world's continents *(Fig. 1-7)*.

Johnson's contribution at Bielefeld, while more fully architectural than Kahn's, represents, like the motel, the exportation of a concept hitherto somewhat inadequately developed outside the United States except in J. L. Sert's Musée Fon-

1-7. Location in Europe and Africa of factories designed by Albert Kahn Associated Architects. 1968.

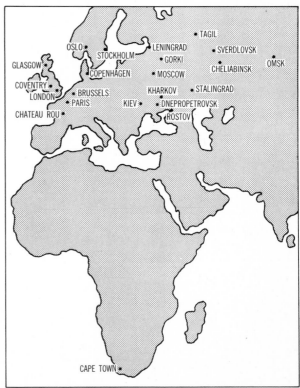

dation Maeght on the Riviera or Frederick Kiesler's Shrine of the Book in Israel.[8] Despite their foreign birth, both those American architects had, even more than Mies since they were younger, learned to employ in the field of museum design functional ideas that had earlier been developed in the United States.

From the first, indeed, it would seem that the outside world has looked to the United States—once we had become truly a nation and not merely a cluster of ex-colonies—for architectural ideas that were organizational and technical, truly functional in their relation to the modern civilization that was evolving already in the second quarter of the nineteenth century, though often by European standards aesthetically *retardataire*. Even earlier, there is at least one instance of foreign interest in American building practice.

The domestic piazza or extended porch was certainly not an American invention. In an etymological sense, it was initiated by Inigo Jones at Covent Garden since, for the novel open arcades that fronted the houses around that first English square, the Italian word that properly applied to the square itself was employed. The other, and perhaps more usual, name for the feature, when, in the later eighteenth century, it began to be widely employed both in England and America, that is, "verandah," suggests the true origins in Asia.[9] Thence, it came directly to England and also to the North American colonies via the West Indies. That the use of verandahs developed more rapidly in America than in Britain, much less on the Continent, was noted very early. A plate (*Fig. 1-8*) in one of the most popular cottage books of the end of the eighteenth century, John Plaw's *Ferme Ornée*,[10] was labeled "American Cottages," and they were thus described: "These double cottages are built (in the

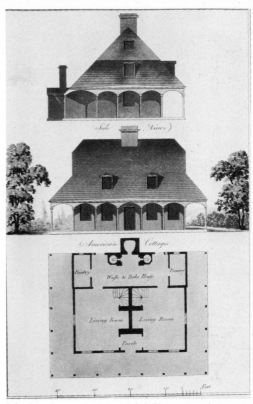

1-8. American cottages. John Plaw. Aquatint, published 1795.

9

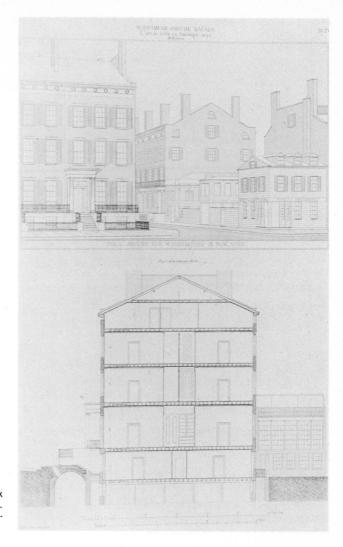

1-9. Residences. New York City, Washington Square. Elevations and section. Engraving, published 1846.

plan and in the style of some in America) . . . in Kent . . . for their extreme singularity [I] have introduced them in this work: the East, West and South aspects have a piazza round them; and the major part of the external appearance, together with the roof, is covered with plain tiles. . . ."

Evidently, not only were the circumambient piazzas considered specifically American but so was the tile-hanging on the walls, doubtless in imitation of the common use of wooden shingles to cover walls as well as roofs in America. This was originally either a continuation of an obsolescent English custom or an imitation of English tile-hanging. Thus, one of the most important visual characteristics of the American "Shingle Style" of the last quarter of the nineteenth century was

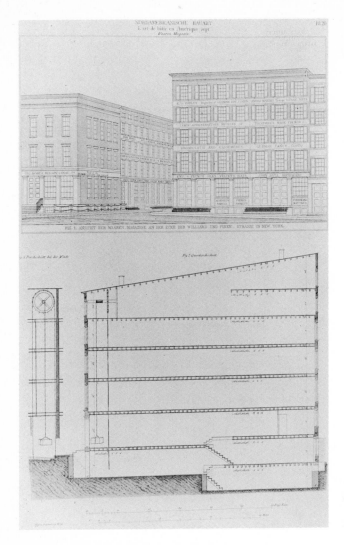

1-10. Commercial buildings. New York City, corner of Williams and Pine streets. Elevations and section. Engraving, published 1846.

already noted 100 years earlier as of "extreme singularity" abroad. To the considerable evidence of foreign interest in the Shingle Style,[11] not only in England but on the Continent, especially in Scandinavia, we will return later.

The next American buildings to be published abroad under professional auspices were of quite a different order from these piazza-surrounded cottages, however. American houses of quite a different sort, the standard New York row houses of the 1830's (*Fig. 1-9*), as well as comparable business buildings (*Fig. 1-10*), were published as late as 1846 in the *Allgemeine Bauzeitung*[12] in Vienna, a building journal that was very active in presenting structural and aesthetic innovations—from England, notably, J. B. Bunning's London Coal Exchange of

1-11. Girard College. Philadelphia. 1833–47. Thomas U. Walter.

1-12. University of the Ruhr. Bochum, West Germany. Under construction. Hentrich-Petschnigg & Partner.

1846–49 and Joseph Paxton's Crystal Palace of 1850–51—as thoroughly or, actually, more thoroughly than the professional press of the countries responsible for them.

But when the English technical publisher Peter Nicholson illustrated Thomas U. Walter's Girard College in Philadelphia, an educational institution for male orphans, in one of the early Victorian editions of his treatise on carpentry,[13] the college's Grecian design, coming a generation after William Wilkins's Downing College at Cambridge, must have seemed quite out-of-date in England. It was the organizational aspects of the institution, so different from an Oxford or Cambridge college, that were of interest in England. Walter, moreover, upon his election to the Institute of British Architects, presented to the Institute's library[14] drawings of the Philadelphia college that are still preserved there (*Fig. 1-11*), reflecting his hope that they would be studied, if not emulated, in Britain.

Today, such newly founded institutions as the Twente Technical University near Enschede in Holland[15] and the vast University of the Ruhr[16] at Bochum (*Fig. 1-12*), still in construction, certainly reflect, in their organization, American colleges and universities. But the nearest approaches to Girard College abroad, which may have been functionally—though certainly not at all stylistically—influenced from that American source, are certain Scottish institutions of the 1840's and 1850's, such as two outside Edinburgh: Donaldson's Hospital for 300 children, 100 of them deaf and dumb, designed by W. H. Playfair in 1842 though built considerably later; and Stewart's Hospital of 1849–53 by David Rhind.[17] Even in the "Athens of the North," by this date, these were not like Walter's Grecian in style, but Jacobean.

13

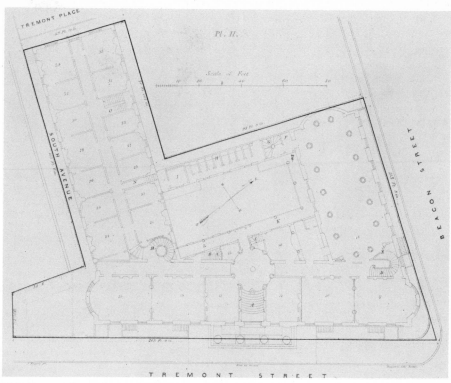

1-13. Tremont House. Boston. 1828–29. Isaiah Rogers. Plan.

1-14. Tremont House. Elevation.

Another, more certain, influence, but one also hard to pin down to surviving foreign examples earlier than the late 1850's, is that of Isaiah Rogers's hotels, particularly the Tremont House in Boston and the Astor House in New York, the former published in a monograph by W. H. Eliot,[18] so that its plans could be readily studied abroad *(Fig. 1-13)*. Grecian in style—though, in the case of the Astor House, including one very elaborate English Perpendicular interior—these were no more aesthetically advanced than the Philadelphia orphans' college *(Fig. 1-14)*. But their monumental character was then rivaled only in a few hotels[19] in watering places—at Cheltenham and at Bristol Hotwells, for example—and their facilities and amenities were of a completeness hardly known up to this time in foreign hostelries. The evidence of this influence is as clear as the current international use of the term "motel": The great hotels of the building boom of the 1860's in England were no more complete without a "grand American bar" than they would be today. Among other ideas from America was the inclusion of a barbershop, or "hair-cutting saloon," described in the account in the *Illustrated London News* of the International Hotel[20] in London in 1858 as "another American luxury," there fifty feet long.

Here, as in the case of motels a century later, Americans had been quicker than Europeans to respond to a change in the usual mode of travel, though the station hotel, incorporated in or contiguous to the new railroad stations,[21] was an English rather than an American innovation, first appearing at the same time as, or a little before, the Boston and New York hotels by Rogers.

The best documented example of early

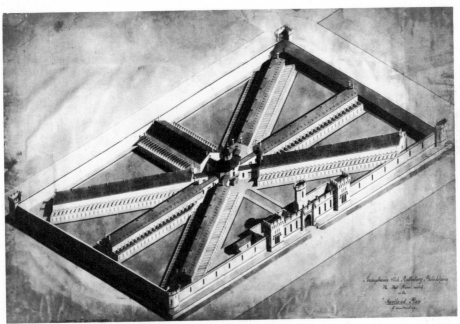

1-15. Eastern Penitentiary. Philadelphia. 1823–25. John Haviland.

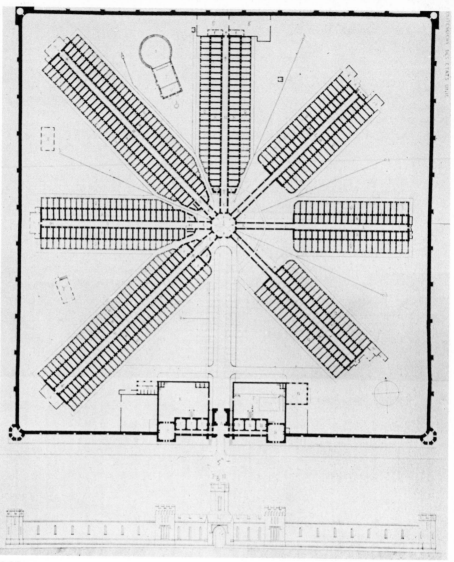

1-16

1-16. Eastern Penitentiary. Philadelphia. Plan.

1-17. Pentonville Prison. London. 1841–42. Sir Charles Barry. Plan.

1-18. Pentonville Prison. London. Interior view from the hub.

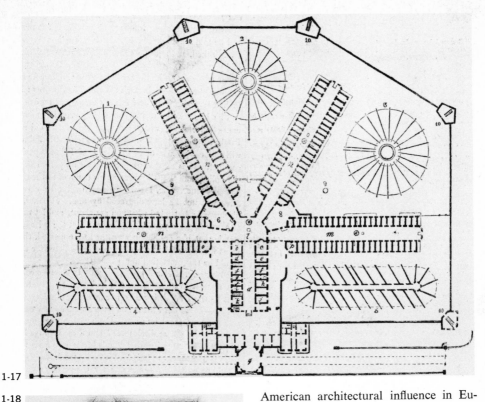

1-17

1-18

American architectural influence in Europe is not stylistic but strictly social and organizational. Even more than in the case of the Tremont House, concerning which Eliot's book provided visual information—elevations and a perspective as well as the plan—Europeans were impressed by the radial cellular plan of John Haviland's Eastern Penitentiary (*Fig. 1-15*) in Philadelphia. Several foreign commissions[22] came to this country to study the building, and detailed reports were published on their return home. The most elaborate of these was the French one by Demetz and Blouet (*Fig. 1-16*).[23] Almost at once, in an age when the reform of prisons was a new social goal—more actively pursued, ironically, than the housing of noncriminals—plans of Haviland's type were employed in England by no less an architect than Sir Charles Barry at Pentonville Prison (*Figs. 1-17 and 1-18*)[24] in London in 1841–42,

17

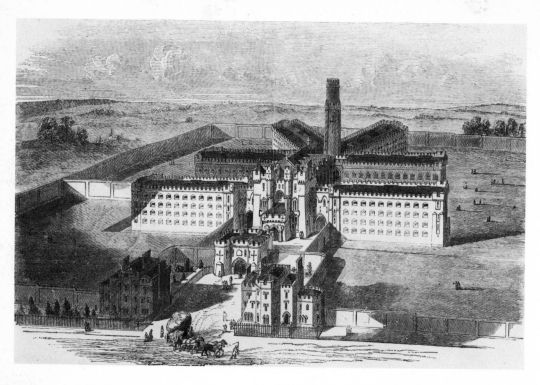

1-19. New City Prison. Holloway, London. 1851–52. J. B. Bunning.

1-20. Suspension bridge at Niagara Falls, New York. 1852. John A. Roebling.

and on the Continent in a major new one in Paris: La Nouvelle Force. E.-J. Gilbert,[25] the architect of La Nouvelle Force, though less well known today than Barry, was the leading institutional architect of the period. This Paris prison was commissioned as early as 1836 but was not erected until 1843–50. Several more English prisons followed in the 1840's and 1850's; two of them, Scott & Moffatt's at Reading[26] of 1842–44—Oscar Wilde's Reading Gaol—and J. B. Bunning's Holloway Gaol *(Fig. 1-19)* of 1851–52 were even "castellated" in style like Haviland's.

So complicated and intertwined is the history of the introduction and early development in the nineteenth century of the important new structural materials and methods of using them that it is rarely possible to assign credit for their original "invention" to any one country.[27] Neither the cable suspension bridge[28] nor the elevator, much less the metal-framing of buildings—which could profitably rise to a height that led to their being called "skyscrapers" only with the developing use of the elevator—were American inventions. Yet, in all three cases, their evolution and exploitation in America proceeded at a more rapid pace than abroad. Evident American leadership, moreover, usually led to significant American influence abroad. In the last case, at least, this was of major importance for world architecture, once that influence could be fully digested and successfully acclimated, though this really came about only in the postwar decades of this century.

As regards suspension bridges, the first great example in metal was Thomas Telford's Menai Bridge in Wales of 1819–24. This was a road bridge, with the roadbed hung from chains. It was supplemented in 1845–50 by the nearby Brittania Tubular Bridge across the Menai Strait, of which the engineer was Robert

Stephenson using certain ideas of Sir William Fairbairn, whose major contribution hitherto had been the substitution in metal-framed buildings of rolled (i.e., wrought) iron beams for cast-iron ones. On the Britannia Bridge, trains were carried inside a rectangular tube of rolled iron that constituted a continuous box-girder. Twenty years earlier, in France, Marc Séguin had spanned the Rhone near Tournon with a suspension bridge hung from cables—that is, ropes spun from wire—instead of chains. In the same years during which Stephenson was building the Britannia Bridge, the German immigrant John A. Roebling, a cable-spinner, was developing further, at Wheeling, West Virginia, and Cincinnati, Ohio, the principle of Séguin's bridge. In 1852, his Niagara Falls Bridge, thanks to its dramatic site, attracted international attention *(Fig. 1-20)*. But it was even more notable to contemporaries that Roebling's bridge successfully carried railroad trains, for no one had dared to send trains across chain-bridges lest the vibration break a link in the chains. Henceforth, the international future of the suspension bridge was assured. But American achievements, from Roebling's final work (which led to his death), the Brooklyn Bridge of 1869–83, to the Verrazano Bridge of the 1960's, though often emulated, have rarely been matched. It is worth recalling also that this major development was the work of a man born abroad, but no more than Mies should Roebling be omitted from the roster of great American builders.

In 1844, when Solomon Willard's Bunker Hill Monument[29] was completed in Charlestown, Massachusetts, a steam-operated hoist, or elevator, was available and capable of carrying six people to the top of the great obelisk of Quincy granite. Already, however, hoists, primarily for lifting bales of cotton but able to carry

1-21. Latting Observatory Tower. New York City. Exposition of 1853.

1-22. Eiffel Tower. Paris. 1887–89. Gustave Eiffel. Section of Otis elevator car.

people as well, were being installed in the handsome cotton warehouses of Manchester in England, built by Edward Walters and others[30] at a time when Manchester's commercial architecture was generally recognized as finer and more advanced than that of London. Then, in 1853, beside the New York Crystal Palace, a rather different obelisk from Willard's rose as a tall metal skeleton containing a passenger elevator (*Fig. 1-21*). Riding in it was one of the real excitements of the exposition, like going to the top of the Empire State building a century later.

The crucial importance of elevator service in tall buildings became evident, however, only with its inclusion in the Haughwout Store on Broadway (*see Fig. 3–21*) built in 1857 by J. P. Gaynor. This elevator was of an improved type lately developed by Elisha G. Otis. Another, not made by Otis, was installed a few months later in the Fifth Avenue Hotel. There was also a lift in the Westminster Palace Hotel in London, built by the Moseley Brothers in Victoria Street in 1860,[31] but it failed to work. To this day, moreover, a large proportion of the world's elevators are provided by foreign branches of the company Otis founded.

In the late 1880's, when the great French engineer Gustave Eiffel was building for the Paris Exposition of 1889 his

20

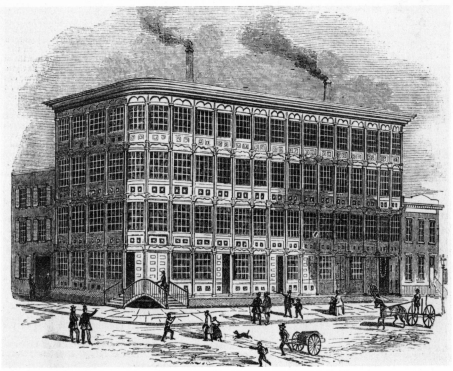

1-23. Eccentric Mill Works. New York City, Centre Street. 1848–49. James Bogardus.

Tour de 300 Mètres—which would henceforth carry his name, and which continued to rank as the world's tallest structure until the Empire State Building was erected in the early 1930's—he called on Otis to provide the specifications for the elevators (*Fig. 1-22*).[32] This was just after William Le Baron Jenney had introduced in the Home Life Insurance Building of 1884–85 in Chicago (*see Fig. 3-12*) what is usually considered, quite specifically, to be "skyscraper construction." Here, for the first time, the outer cladding of masonry was carried by the interior metal skeleton, not erected as a self-supporting wall. But we are getting ahead of the story.

In 1847, *The Builder*[33] in London quoted from a Cincinnati newspaper the information that "a block of three-story buildings are to be erected in this city [and] the entire front is to be of cast-iron! The plates for the same are already being cast." If these were in fact carried to completion, no trace of them survives. But the next year, James Bogardus began to build in New York on Centre Street a factory for his own use with the exterior entirely of iron; even before this was finished, he was erecting two other such structures— one of which survives—for others. Upon the completion of Bogardus's factory, the *Illustrated London News*[34] published a view of it on their front page (*Fig. 1-23*).

21

Because of restrictions in the London building code of 1844, it was impossible to emulate this in the English metropolis. But in Glasgow in Scotland, the second city of the United Kingdom—the Chicago, so to say, of the British Isles—the first of several commercial buildings[35] with exteriors entirely, or at least predominantly, of cast iron was erected by John Baird in 1856 (*Fig. 1-24*). As those who composed the London building code had foreseen, cast-iron fronts in narrow city streets were dangerous, for they often collapsed from the heat of fires in nearby or facing structures, even though the material itself was, of course, noninflammable. The cast-iron front was important in the United States down to the great urban fires in Chicago and Boston of the early 1870's, but not thereafter; and it was never much employed—at least in anything like Bogardus's way—elsewhere. The French use of iron in façades in the later decades of the century[36] was apparently not influenced by the earlier American work that still happily survives in profusion along lower Broadway and nearby streets.

A far more pregnant event in the development of the skyscraper came a decade after the building of the Haughwout Store and the Fifth Avenue Hotel, at the height of the building boom that followed the Civil War when so many cast-iron fronts were being erected. When the Equitable Life Assurance Building in New York (*see Fig. 3-6*) was completed in 1870 it was the first office building to be provided with an elevator. This novel amenity so evidently made it possible to charge as high—or, indeed, often higher—rents for the upper stories as for the lower ones that there was an immediate rush to install elevators in existing New York office buildings of four or five stories, and even to add one or two extra stories in mansards on top of them. Their usual construction, with interior skeletons of cast and rolled iron and outer walls still of self-supporting masonry, made this quite feasible.

Next came the building of the first two skyscrapers, both approximately twice the four- or five-story height of existing commercial buildings in American and European cities. The Tribune Building on Park Row in New York (*see Fig. 3-7*), which survived until it was demolished in 1966 to make way for Pace College, was the first. It was erected in 1873–75 to the design of the Paris-trained Richard Morris Hunt. Post, architect as well as engineer by this time, was not far behind with the Western Union Building (*see Fig. 3-8*), which was completed almost as early. Ironically, as was to be the case again in the 1930's, when the Empire State Building was completed at the bottom of the Depression, these mammoth new structures were begun just at the time of the financial crash of 1873, so that their upper portions stood out all but alone for some years above the nearly flat roof-line of the city that only church steeples had broken through before. Foreign visitors could hardly help noting these striking features of the *Stadbild*, but they were not inclined to approve, much less to emulate, them.

Although the relative importance of Chicago as compared with New York in the architectural developments of the later decades of the nineteenth century has undoubtedly been exaggerated, it was considerably later that the new tall buildings of Chicago, as seen by the foreign visitors to the World's Fair there in 1893, eventually made a strong and not unfavorable impression. That impression was not rivaled by that of New York's skyscrapers before the early years of this century. Then the Flatiron Building rose in 1902 —built, incidentally, by a Chicago architectural firm, Daniel H. Burnham & Com-

22

1-24. Jamaica Street Warehouse. Glasgow, Scotland. 1856. John Baird.

1-25. Ritz Hotel. London. Mewès & Davis. 1905–6.

pany—and the Metropolitan Tower in 1909 (*see Fig. 3-5*), by the sons who were the professional heirs of a Philadelphia architect, Napoleon Le Brun. When the Anglo-French architectural team of Mewès & Davis introduced the steel frame for the first time outside the United States in the Ritz Hotel (*Fig. 1-25*)[37] in London in 1905–6, however, the distinctly Beaux-Arts style of the masonry cladding that quite hid the underlying structural steel cage reflected the work of the New York architects of the day, many of whom they must have known in the Paris ateliers.[38] There is no sign in that of inspiration from the commercial architecture of Chicago, where Louis H. Sullivan had just completed the previous year his last major business building, the Carson Pirie Scott Store, and even the Burnham firm, in adding onto it at just this point, retained his direct expression of the steel construction.

In the 1870's, 1880's, and 1890's, however, the professional magazines of Europe were already providing evidence of foreign interest in the work of H. H. Richardson, his contemporaries who developed the Shingle Style, and the tall buildings of Sullivan and his Chicago contemporaries. Moreover, this interest was, for the first time, stylistic and not merely technical, especially after current developments in architecture in Europe, beginning in the 1880's, became divided more and more sharply between a conservative, or academic, direction and a freer one that eventually crystallized for a decade or more in the international Art Nouveau.

Interest in the work of Richardson actually began very early when *The Architect* of London published in its number for October 5, 1872, his project for a church in Columbus, Ohio, before anything of his had yet appeared in an American periodical (*Fig. 1-26*).[39] Yet this proj-

1-26. Project for church and parsonage, Columbus, Ohio. 1872. Henry Hobson Richardson.

1-27

1-27. Library. North Easton, Massachusetts. 1877–79. Henry Hobson Richardson. Elevation.—Town Hall. North Easton, Massachusetts. 1879–81. Henry Hobson Richardson. Elevation.—Library. Quincy, Massachusetts. 1880–83. Henry Hobson Richardson. Elevation and plan.

1-28. "Shingleside." Swampscott, Massachusetts. 1882. Arthur Little. Plans, elevation, and interiors.

1-29. Fred White House. London, Queen's Gate. 1887. R. Norman Shaw.

ect will, at that time, hardly have appeared very novel in England, for it was close to the Round-arched High Victorian Gothic much favored then by English Nonconformists for their churches. Upon its completion in 1877, Richardson's Trinity Church in Boston was also described in the English professional press.[40] A curious lack of precise information about Richardson's status is evident as late as 1883 when two of his North Easton buildings and his Quincy Library were attributed to Peabody & Stearns in *The British Architect* (*Fig. 1-27*).[41]

The greater novelty of the Shingle Style, to which Richardson himself had turned with his Bryant house in Cohasset of 1880, was recognized very early when Arthur Little's house called "Shingleside" (*Fig. 1-28*) at Swampscott, Massachusetts, was published in the English *Building News and Engineering Journal* for April 28, 1882, in a double spread prepared by Norman Shaw's associate Maurice B. Adams. Like other initiatory works in the Shingle Style, this owed a good deal to Shaw, and the Colonial Revival elements that were present from the first in Little's work could be seen by foreigners as parallel to the modulation of that leading English domestic architect's work, beginning in the mid-1870's, from "Queen Anne" to a sort of "Georgian Revival." Indeed it is perhaps significant that Shaw's first formal eighteenth-century house (*Fig. 1-29*), built in Queen's Gate in Kensington in 1887, was for an American diplomat, Fred White, since White may well have known the equally formal H. A. C. Taylor house that McKim, Mead & White had erected in Newport in 1885–86 (*see Fig. 4-25*).

In general, however, it was the freer aspects of the Shingle Style that appealed abroad. The agglutinative planning was a

26

1-28

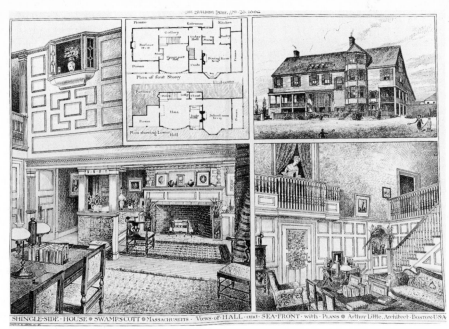

SHINGLE·SIDE·HOUSE ❦ SWAMPSCOTT ❦ MASSACHUSETTS · Views·of·HALL··and··SEA·FRONT··with··PLANS ❦ Arthur·Little, Architect·Boston·USA

1-29

1-30. "Thirlstane" (Mrs. R. B. Scott House). Bar Harbor, Maine. 1881. William Ralph Emerson. Elevation.—Casino. Elberon, New Jersey. Ca. 1885. Peabody & Stearns. Elevation.—General J. Van Alen House. Newport, Rhode Island. Date uncertain. Clarence S. Luce. Elevation.

revelation to the French,[42] but they showed little discrimination in the American houses they picked to publish. The English, with their greater sympathy for the tradition of the Picturesque, delighted rather in the ingenious variety of the massing. When a double spread (*Fig. 1-30*), with a design for a house at Bar Harbor, Maine, by W. R. Emerson, together with Peabody & Stearns's casino at Elberon, New Jersey—misattributed, curiously enough, like Richardson's work earlier, in this case to McKim, Mead & White—and a "cottage" by Clarence Luce at Newport, appeared in the Christmas number of *The Builder* in 1886, the accompanying editorial comment stressed the peculiarly American quality of the Emerson and the "McKim, Mead & White" items. Thus, their judgment, even if partly based on a false premise, was premonitory of Vincent Scully's recognition of these men as the real initiators, round 1879, of the Shingle Style.

When Richardson died in 1886 the fact that America had lost her greatest architect was widely recognized in published obituaries abroad.[43] It was at least hinted in England that, had he lived, he would before long have received the Royal Gold Medallion, an honor that has gone in this century to Wright, Gropius, and Mies, among Americans. He was, in any case, already an Honorary Corresponding Member. It would seem, ironically, that these obituaries led to very considerable posthumous interest in his work; certainly it was then for the first time that it was extensively published abroad, particularly in England—where his only permanent work on foreign soil was rising, "Lululund" (*Fig. 1-31*), the house of Sir Hubert von Herkomer at Bushey near Harrow—during the decade following his death when his influence in America was rapidly declining. The two most signifi-

1-31. "Lululund" (Sir Hubert von Herkomer House). Bushey (Hertfordshire), England. Remodeled by Henry Hobson Richardson, 1886–94.

1-32. Electric Works. Stockholm. 1892. Ferdinand Boberg.

cant articles, following years after the obituaries, were published in Germany and England, respectively, in 1892 and 1894.[44]

It is in the Scandinavian countries, however, that American influence in the 1890's has been most carefully and rewardingly studied so far.[45] In an article, "Richardson and Sullivan in Scandinavia," published in *Progressive Architecture* for March, 1966, the American architectural historian Leonard Eaton noted the particular interest that J. H. Pahne, a member of the Stockholm City Council, took in American garden suburbs when traveling in 1888 in the United States. In the new suburbs of Djursholm and Saltsjöbaden, not only the layout but the actual design of the houses offer reflections of American ideas, more especially the do-

1-33. Fire Station. Gävle, Sweden. 1894. Ferdinand Boberg.

mestic Richardsonian and the Shingle Style, even though both were in decline in America by the time these Swedish developments were under way in the mid-1890's.

In more monumental work, Ferdinand Boberg's electric works (*Fig. 1-32*) for Stockholm, built in 1892 before he visited America, were already distinctly Richardsonian. In 1893, the World's Fair brought him to Chicago, where two of Richardson's greatest late works could be seen and studied. As Eaton notes—and I myself had already realized when in Gävle a decade or so ago before I knew the building was by Boberg—what is perhaps the most successful Richardsonian work abroad is the fire station (*Fig. 1-33*) in the provincial Swedish town that Boberg

built in 1894 after he returned from America. Boberg also contributed at that time to the professional journal *Teknisk Tidskrift* two articles on the development of the public library in the United States —once more, the foreign critic's interest was in these articles, technical and organizational rather than stylistic—illustrating it with an excellent view of Richardson's first library, that at Woburn, Massachusetts,[46] begun in 1877 (*Fig. 1-34*). The Richardson phase of Boberg's work continued down to the turn of the century.

In an article in Number 9 of *Arkkitehti Arkitekten*[47] in 1967, the French architectural historian Marika Hausen has lately provided comparable visual evidence of Richardson's influence in Finland, especially on the early work of Eliel

1-34. Library. Woburn, Massachusetts. 1877–78. Henry Hobson Richardson.

1-35

Saarinen and his then partners, Herman Gesellius and A. E. Lindgren, an influence that extended even beyond 1900. Actually, to American eyes, such things as their National Museum in Helsinki[48] of 1901 or the Suur-Merijoki house of 1903 (*Fig. 1-35*), not to speak of the architects' own house Hvittrask[49] of 1902, appear not so much specifically Richardsonian as generically Shingle Style. But that these influences played an important part in the early formation of a man of great talent, who would much later in life come to America and die an American architect, is undeniable. He was, moreover, the father of another, even abler, American architect who, though born at Hvittrask in Finland, was educated at Yale.

Not surprisingly, most European visitors to the World's Fair in Chicago in 1893 observed and were impressed by such of Sullivan's principal works as were already in existence in that city, from the Auditorium to the Garrick Theater and the newly completed Stock Exchange Building. Probably it was not before 1904 that many foreigners saw the Wainwright Building of 1890–91 in St. Louis. In that year, another World's Fair took place there, to which, among other foreigners, both the Austrian J. M. Olbrich and the German Peter Behrens made contributions that were significant in their own development and that of early modern architecture in Europe. How much they may have been affected by the American *locus* of these modest exposition entries, it is not easy to say. At least their American biographers, Robert J. Clark[50] of Princeton and Stanford Anderson[51] of the Massachusetts Institute of Technology, make no claims that they were influenced by American architecture to the degree their contemporary Adolf Loos, who was also in the United States in the 1890's, may have been.[52]

It was mostly after 1900, when the

32

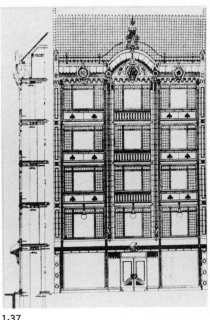

1-36   1-37

modest tide of influence from Richardson
and the Shingle Style was receding in
Europe, as it had done considerably
earlier in America, that emulation of
Sullivan began abroad, first and most
particularly in Scandinavia.[53] Already in
1898, however, Alfred Ravad, a Danish
architect who had come to Chicago in
1890 and who remained there until 1914,
published an article on American architecture emphasizing the interest of Sullivan's
work in the *Tidskrift for Kunstindustrie.*
Another Dane, Anton Rosen, who stayed
at home to be the leader of the freer
forces in architecture against Martin
Nyrop, the architect of the Copenhagen
Town Hall, had introduced even earlier,
in 1895, in a workers' clubhouse in Silkeborg (*Fig. 1-36*) certain unmistakably
Sullivanian features. His most conspicuous work, the Palace Hotel of 1907–10
near Nyrop's Town Hall, is less derivative
from American work, though notably un-
academic. But his Savoy Hotel (*Fig.*

1-35. House at Suur-Merijoki, near
Viborg, Finland. 1903. Eliel Saarinen. Elevation.

1-36. Workers' Clubhouse. Silkeborg, Denmark. 1895. Anton
Rosen.

1-37. Savoy Hotel. Copenhagen.
1906. Anton Rosen. Elevation.

33

1-38. Number 9 Regeringsgaten, Stockholm. 1912. G. A. Nilsson.

1-37) of 1906 followed Chicago models in its steel skeleton as well as in its generous fenestration, using throughout the sort of triple windows specifically called "Chicago windows" that are more characteristic of Holabird & Roche than of Sullivan. An even more striking work in this vein is an articulated steel-and-glass building at 9 Regeringsgatan (*Fig. 1-38*) in Stockholm of 1912 by G. A. Nilsson. This is as fine an example of "Chicago School" work executed by a non-American as the Gävle fire station is of the Richardsonian.

By 1912, however, the best-known infiltration of American influence in Europe had begun. Interested as some Europeans were—most particularly, it would seem in the present state of our knowledge, the Scandinavians—in what was happening in the United States, and particularly in Chicago, the very early work of Frank Lloyd Wright at the turn of the century, as presented in Robert Spencer's article that appeared in the Boston (not the London) *Architectural Review,* if it was seen abroad would have seemed to represent merely a broadening of the Sullivan mode rather than a new stylistic current. It is unlikely that at this crucial point in Wright's development the *Ladies' Home Journal* for January, 1901, in which the first project for a "Prairie House" was published, reached European architects— or many American ones either, for that matter.

In 1909, however, at the instigation of Kuno Franke, an influential professor of German at Harvard, the Berlin architectural publishing house of Wasmuth commissioned the major collection of plates, sumptuous even in the later near-facsimile edition,[54] which is usually known as the "Wasmuth Portfolio." Its sheets, lithographed after drawings prepared under Wright's detailed supervision and printed in pale inks on tinted paper with, in some cases, overprinting in gold as well, presented in fascinating form most of the executed work and many of the projects of Wright down to the end of the "Prairie Period." Wasmuth also issued a much more modest book illustrated with photographic half-tones of a considerable proportion of the executed work. This book, also brought out recently in a new edition,[55] had an introduction by the English architect C. R. Ashbee, a leader of the Arts and Crafts movement, though English interest in Wright was otherwise—and for long after this date—all but nonexistent.

Testimony to the influence of these major monographs arriving at a time when architecture was in a new ferment that had begun after the somewhat hysterical excitement of the Art Nouveau was over —the founding of the German Werkbund in 1907 provides a convenient date for the start of the new phase—has been offered by many European architects who were young at the time. None was more elo-

quent than Mies van der Rohe, who later became the great mid-century exponent of modern architecture in Chicago in succession to Sullivan, whom, curiously enough, he did not especially admire, and to Wright, whom he did. It was, moreover, in 1911 that the leading Dutch modern architect of Wright's generation, H. P. Berlage, visited America.[56]

Like any truly profound architectural influence—the earlier instances cited here were hardly of such an order—the effect of the study of the Wasmuth Portfolio was broad, so much so that there are architectural historians[57] who would date the twentieth-century architectural revolution, at least as regards houses, from Wright's "invention" of the Prairie House in the first year of the century and the transmission of his ideas abroad a decade later by the Wasmuth publications. The influence of his ideas about domestic architecture began to supersede that of the men of the English Arts and Crafts movement as transmitted by the *Studio*. If one compares the material presented in such a significant book from England as Baillie Scott's *Houses and Gardens*[58] of this period with Wright's houses as shown in the Wasmuth Portfolio, it becomes evident how crucial the years around the opening of the second decade of this century were for the international development of modern architecture, years in which leadership in Europe passed from the English and the Belgians to the Aus-

1-39. House at Huis ter Heide, near Utrecht, Holland. 1915. Robert van t'Hoff.

1-40. De dubbele Sleutel. Woerden, Holland. 1917. Jan Wils.

1-41. Administration Building. Cologne, Germany. Werkbund Exposition of 1914. Walter Gropius.

trians, the Germans, and the Dutch. It was the Dutch, moreover, introduced to Wright's work by their own leader, Berlage, who long remained the most fervent of Wright's admirers until the Italian Bruno Zevi belatedly took up the cause of Wrightian "architectura organica" after the last war.[59]

But it seems to have been Walter Gropius and Adolf Meyer who first gave specific evidence of their familiarity with the Wasmuth publications, not in a house but in the administration building associated with the Deutz exhibits at the Werkbund Exposition of 1914 in Cologne (*Fig. 1-41*). At least historians are generally agreed on this, and Gropius never denied it. Much closer, however, was the dependence of the Dutch architect Robert van t'Hoff in houses he built at Huis ter Heide, east of Utrecht, in neutral Holland (*Fig. 1-39*) during the years of

World War I when production had ceased in the combatant countries. These follow Wright's Sutton house of 1907 in McCook, Nebraska, in their formal organization, while in their construction of poured concrete they reflect Wright's employment of that material in the Unity Church at Oak Park, Illinois, in 1906. But van t'Hoff's Wrightian work was only the most extreme in a considerable flood that followed from many of the younger Dutch architects (*Fig. 1-40*).[60] With J. J. P. Oud, particularly, the Wrightian influence in the late 'teens seems to have been catalytic.[61] H. Th. Wijdeveld, the editor of the architectural magazine *Wendingen*, remained fascinated by the work of Wright well into the latter's fallow period in the mid- and late 1920's. Happily, as with the two Wasmuth publications, a reprint[62] of the numbers of *Wendingen* devoted to Wright has made this visual

37

documentation once more available, calling attention to the continuing significance of Wrightian influence in the years when leadership in modern architecture seemed generally to have passed from America to Europe. Not to be forgotten among the relevant events of these years is the fact that a former assistant of Wright, Walter Burley Griffin, won the international competition for Canberra, the Australian capital city, in 1913 (*Fig. 1-42*).[63]

Quite unrelated to the Wrightian influence was the prestige that American academic architecture had in England in the 1920's, in considerable part because of the enthusiasm of C. R. Reilly, who was later to be an effective champion of advanced Continental architecture. The firm of Carrère & Hastings was called on to design Devonshire House in Piccadilly across from the Ritz; in London also, Harvey Wiley Corbett built Bush House at the Strand end of Kingsway, and, finally, in a much fresher vein, there was Raymond Hood's National Radiator Building off Oxford Street (*Fig. 1-43*). Sullivan's work had never made the same impression in England that it had in Denmark

1-42

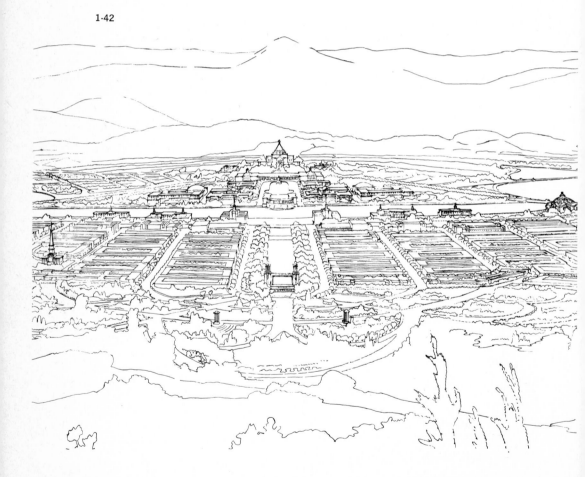

and Sweden, but when skyscrapers began to be erected on the Continent—the London buildings were not very tall—some belated influence from Sullivan was evident.

Fritz Höger's Chile House in Hamburg (*Fig. 1-44*), the most famous of the German near-skyscrapers of the 1920's that were actually erected—Mies's remarkable projects for all-glass towers of 1919–21 even he may have considered at that date unrealizable[64]—is over-all more horizontal than vertical, and the shape of the site encouraged his Expressionist treatment of

1-42. Preliminary project for the plan of Canberra. 1911. Walter Burley Griffin.

1-43. National Radiator Building. London. 1928. Raymond Hood.

1-44. Chile House. Hamburg, West Germany. 1923. Fritz Höger.

1-45. Stumm Konzern (Stahlhaus). Düsseldorf, West Germany. 1922–24. Bonatz & Scholer.

the southern end as a sharp prow. However, the windows throughout were organized in vertical bands between piers of decorative brickwork and, under the slab-cornices, the bays are capped with decorative lunettes in a fashion that recalls Sullivan's masterpiece, the Guaranty Building in Buffalo of 1894–95. The Chile House was built in 1923.

In a smaller office building, also of the early 1920's, for the Stumm Konzern in Düsseldorf (*Fig. 1-45*), now known as the Stahlhaus, Bonatz & Scholer reflected the verticalism of the early Chicago skyscrapers more successfully. On this, the alternation of relatively heavy vertical members, cladding the structural piers of the metal skeleton, with lighter members between, equally continuous vertically, that serve as mullions, suggests that the architects had some knowledge of Sullivan's Condict Building of 1897–98 in New York. The abrupt termination used first in America by Hood on his Daily News Building in New York in 1930, was at this point distinctly advanced, while the triangular section of the vertical elements can be seen as premonitory of those on Eero Saarinen's posthumous CBS Building in New York. The most famous work of Bonatz & Scholer, the Stuttgart railroad station, designed in 1911 and finally completed in the 1920's after the hiatus of the war years, has always seemed to American critics rather Richardsonian, thanks to its great arches and its boldly rock-faced masonry.[65]

But foreign attention in the boom years of the 1920's was more focused on contemporary New York than on the Chicago of the 1890's. In the tallest and the largest of these early European skyscrapers, the Krediet Bank (*Fig. 1-46*) in Antwerp of 1928–33, the architect J. Van Hoenacker followed in the main the later and less traditional work of the leading

New York commercial architects; but the vertical rows of oriels recall such early Chicago skyscrapers as Sullivan's Stock Exchange Building of 1893 and even a little the Reliance Building of the following year by the Burnham firm. It is interesting evidence of continuing American influence in a country where the principal postwar bank building, the Banque Lambert in Brussels (*Fig. 1-47*), and the largest new hotel, the Hilton across the way, are by American architects, that— like several big American buildings of the 1920's along Park Avenue—the Krediet Bank is soon to be stripped of its masonry cladding and glazed all over.

As one approaches the actual present, illustrating with specific examples the influence of American architecture abroad becomes difficult just because that influence has become so ubiquitous. Today it extends well beyond western Europe and from South America to Africa and Asia —even to the Communist states, as was noted earlier. But one curious form of evidence is of a negative nature, that is, the resentment of American architects by the more articulate professionals who write criticism. Le Corbusier in the 1920's, admirer that he was of American engineering, warned his readers against American architects, and, in the autumn of 1969, the Italian annual *Lotus* published an article on the "Decline and Fall of the North American Architectural Profession." On the other hand, it is a critic known hitherto for his harshness in dealing with current American architecture, Reyner Banham, who has, in his latest book, *The Architecture of the Well-tempered Environment,*[66] especially stressed the technical and organizational achievements of American builders and such men as Thomas Edison and, particularly, Willis Carrier,[67] without whose contribution, not just the latest skyscrapers, but most

1-46. Krediet Bank. Antwerp, Belgium. 1928–33. J. Van Hoenacker.

1-47. Banque Lambert. Brussels. 1965. Skidmore, Owings & Merrill.

1-48. United States Consulate. Bremen, West Germany. 1956. Skidmore, Owings & Merrill.

modern building in underdeveloped countries would be impossible.

But the distrust of certain individuals has not diminished the general Americanization of large parts of the building industry abroad. In England, where one firm of architects made its reputation with a very Miesian school, for whose mode of design the name "neo-Brutalism" was coined,[68] the posthumous skyscraper by the Americanized Mies that will soon be built in the City of London should be as much of a landmark of American influence as his museum in Berlin. The skyscraper eventually reached postwar France only in late and very undistinguished examples; the Italians, using ferroconcrete rather than steel, moved away from the American tradition in theirs, in the case of the Sede Pirelli in Milan quite effectively, in that of the Torre Velasca, also in Milan, rather unhappily.[69] But it was the Germans, catching up after the architectural confusion of the mid- and later 1930's, who learned the most from America.

At the crucial moment when the stabilization of the mark encouraged the revival of large-scale building, the U.S. Consulates General at Bremen and Düsseldorf by Skidmore, Owings & Merrill (*Fig. 1-48*), designed actually before the firm's great reputation was made with the building of Lever House in New York,[70] though itself but a modest three-story structure in an open setting, pointed the way for German postwar skyscraper design. Soon the Düsseldorf firm of Hentrich & Petschnigg was erecting for the BASF chemical firm at Ludwigshafen on the Main, opposite Mannheim, the first structure in Europe since the Eiffel Tower over 100 meters (300 feet) tall (*Fig. 1-49*),[71] quite putting in the shade the vast prewar headquarters of the I. G. Farbenwerke by Hans Poelzig at Frankfurt that

1-49. BASF Building. Ludwigshafen on the Main, West Germany. Ca. early 1960's. Hentrich & Petschnigg.

the U.S. Army was using as sort of transatlantic Pentagon. Appropriately, Helmut Hentrich is a former pupil of Poelzig's, though his partner Petschnigg is from Vienna, while the German chemical industry had been one of Peter Behrens's most important clients thirty years before at Höchst, where he built for I. G. Farben and at Leverkusen for Bayer.

But the American way of building tall office buildings was modified structurally in the Düsseldorf skyscraper of the Mannesmann Werke beside the Rhine that Paul Schneider-Esleben built next to Behrens's headquarters, of 1911–12, for that steel company by the substitution of tubular for rectangular members and the inclusion of a ferroconcrete core. With less elegance than Schneider-Esleben and more apparent dependence on the external vocabulary of Lever House, Hentrich & Petschnigg followed up its BASF skyscraper—in at least one respect more South American than North American, thanks to its cladding of lavender mosaic —with the very original plan-scheme of three slabs sliding past one another in their Thyssen Haus.[72] This dominates the Düsseldorf skyline quite in the way the latest skyscrapers in Boston and Chicago[73]

—and soon, doubtless, the World Trade Center in New York—have broken through the existing plateau formed by skyscrapers built in the 1920's, and at least as successfully.

The impact is different, but the Americanization of twentieth-century painting and sculpture, so evident at the 1968 Documenta exposition in Kassel,[74] is in this centenary year of The Metropolitan Museum paralleled by much Americanization in architecture, whether it be in the motels along the Dutch *autowegen* and the Italian *autostrade* or the new museums in Berlin and Bielefeld. Sadly one must note, however, that, in the field of housing, the design both of individual dwellings and of large-scale public housing, American leadership—in the one case, once of crucial importance, thanks to Wright, in the other, never consequential—has failed. If we may be proud of what we have contributed to world architecture in the nineteenth and twentieth centuries, we should also recognize that in this field we still have much to learn, as also in the protection of our architectural heritage, of which so much that was of prime historical importance, like the Tribune Tower, has already gone.

Notes

1. But it is a story that has never been adequately told. Since Robert Koch's article, "American Influence Abroad," of 1959, in the *Journal of the Society of Architectural Historians,* XVIII, 66–69, there has been recurrent evidence of rising interest in the topic; and the influence of Frank Lloyd Wright in Europe was recognized by both European and American historians of architecture long before that. Arnold Lewis kindly permitted me to include a list of English and German articles concerning Richardson, dating from the last quarter of the nineteenth century, in the 1961 edition of *The Architecture of H. H. Richardson and his Times,* 2d ed., Hamden, Conn., 1961. Parallel information concerning the Scandinavian countries has appeared more recently (see pp. 32-34). As for Holland, the trip of H. P. Berlage to the United States in 1911 has long been well known (see Note 56, below).

In the main, however, the subject has not been specifically investigated. Those aspects of the total story touched on in this article are matters that have come to the attention of scholars incidentally—if not, indeed, accidentally—as they studied other problems. That further investigation would prove fruitful, as regards both the 100 years before Richardson's work was first published abroad and also the period since World War II, when American influence reached its peak, the outline of the story offered here should suggest.

2. Mies was awarded the Presidential Medal of Freedom by President Johnson in 1963.

3. And also the first to write at length about his work: Philip C. Johnson, *Mies van der Rohe,* 2d ed., rev., New York, 1953.

4. For Johnson's work, see John Jacobus, *Philip Johnson,* New York, 1962.

5. Le Corbusier & P. Jeanneret, *Ihr Gesamtes Werk von 1910–1929,* Zurich, 1930, pp. 28–35.

6. The Bielefeld museum is the Art Gallery of the city, of which the director is Dr. J. W. von Moltke. A prominent citizen of Bielefeld, Rudolf August Oetke, was, however, the donor of the building. Oetke and von Moltke may properly be considered jointly as the clients rather than the city authorities.

7. Albert Kahn's brother Moritz was primarily responsible for the work done abroad. See Moritz Kahn, *The Design and Construction of Technical Buildings,* London, 1917, most particularly. See also H. R. Hitchcock, *Architecture: Nineteenth and Twentieth Centuries,* 3d ed., [Harmondsworth] © 1968, p. 464, for further references.

8. "Galerie Maeght, Vence," *Deutsche Bauzeitung* (December, 1965), p. 478, and "Shrine of the Book, Israel," *Progressive Architecture* (September, 1965), p. 128.

9. This is a subject that demands detailed investigation, in the East as well as in England, the West Indies, and the United States. See Clay Lancaster, "The American Bungalow," *Art Bulletin,* XL (September, 1958), 239–53.

10. John Plaw, *Ferme Ornée, or Rural Improvements,* London, 1795, Plate 17.

11. See below, p. 26.

12. *Allgemeine Bauzeitung,* 1846, Plates 20, 23.

13. The editions and issues of Nicholson's carpentry books, including those pirated in America, are difficult to disentangle. Dates on individual plates are often not only different but later than that on the

title page. See H. R. Hitchcock, *Early Victorian Architecture in Britain,* New Haven, 1954, I, 424–25.

14. See H. R. Hitchcock, "American Drawings at the Royal Institute of British Architects," in *Opus Musivum,* Assen, 1964, pp. 407–14.

15. Founded in 1964.

16. See *Die Ruhruniversität,* Bochum 1965.

17. H. R. Hitchcock, *Early Victorian Architecture in Britain,* II, 340.

18. W. H. Eliot, *A Description of the Tremont House,* Boston, 1830, Frontispiece and Plate II.

19. Hitchcock, *Early Victorian Architecture in Britain,* II, Plates XV, XVIII, and XIX.

20. *Illustrated London News* (April 3, 1858), p. 350.

21. See Hitchcock, *Early Victorian Architecture in Britain,* I, chap. XV *passim.*

22. The English one is by William Crawford, *Report on the Penitentiaries of the United States,* London, 1834.

23. F. A. Demetz and G. A. Blouet, *Rapports à M. le comte de Montalivet . . . sur les penitenciers des Etats Unis,* Paris, 1837, pp. 55–64, Plates 23–30.

24. *Illustrated London News* (January 7, 1843).

25. Gilbert had been a pupil of J.-N.-L. Durand at the Ecole Polytechnique. On the Nouvelle Force commission he was assisted by J.-F.-J. Lecointe. Hitchcock, *Architecture: Nineteenth and Twentieth Centuries,* p. 50.

26. More properly, the Berkshire County Gaol.

27. Accounts of technical developments in the architecture of the last 200 years have lagged behind the writing on other aspects of architecture history. Sigfried Giedion began a generation ago to give serious attention to these matters. For America the late books of Carl Condit (*American Building Art: The Nineteenth Century,* New York, 1960, and *American Building Art: The Twentieth Century,* New York, 1961) and of J. M. Fitch (*American Building,* 2d ed., Boston, 1966), have done much to fill the gaps in our knowledge. Reyner Banham in *The Architecture of the Well-tempered Environment,* Chicago, 1969, has studied in detail certain aspects having to do with heating and ventilation.

28. There is a considerable literature devoted to bridges, which need not be listed here. For those mentioned below, see Hitchcock, *Architecture: Nineteenth and Twentieth Centuries,* pp. 118–19.

29. See Solomon Willard, *Plans and Sections of the Obelisk on Bunker's Hill,* Boston, 1843.

30. See Hitchcock, *Early Victorian Architecture in Britain, I,* 386–93.

31. See advertisement in *Hotels of Europe,* published annually by Henry Herbert, London, 1873, p. 42.

32. See Gustav Eiffel, *La Tour de trois cents mètres,* Paris, 1900, I, 127–45.

33. *The Builder,* V, No. 242 (September 25, 1847), 464.

34. *Illustrated London News* (April 12, 1851).

35. See Andor Gomme and David Walker, *Architecture of Glasgow,* London, 1968, p. 115.

36. John Jacobus's research on such buildings in France has not yet been published. For Belgium, see R. L. Delevoy, *Victor Horta,* Brussels, n.d.

37. *The Architect,* LXXVI (October 19, 1906), 260. "This large building was one of the first examples of the American system of construction which was produced in the Metropolis. In it are steel framing, fireproof flooring, a grillage foundation and other specialities. . . . the elevators by the Otis Elevator Company."

38. Both the English and the Americans who studied at the Ecole des Beaux Arts frequented particularly the atelier of J.-L. Pascal. See Hitchcock, *Architecture: Nineteenth and Twentieth Centuries,* p. 475.

39. Richardson's work was first presented in his own country in *The Architectural Sketch Book,* I, No. I (July, 1873)— a project for Trinity Church, Buffalo, that was never executed. More appeared in the *New York Sketch-Book of Architecture* over the years 1874–76. Richardson and

McKim edited the latter: Montgomery Schuyler, "Charles Follen McKim," *Architectural Record,* XXVI (November, 1909), 381.

40. "A Boston Basilica," *The Architect,* London (April 28, 1877), p. 274.

41. "Modern American Architecture," *The British Architect,* XIX (January 5, 1883). The attribution was corrected in the number for March 30, 1883.

42. As demonstrated by Arnold Lewis, "European Discovery of American Architecture, 1885–1895," unpublished paper read January 28, 1966, at the nineteenth annual meeting of the Society of Architectural Historians.

43. H. R. Hitchcock, *The Architecture of H. H. Richardson and his Times,* pp. 333–34.

44. Karl Hinckeldeyn, "H. H. Richardson und seine Bedeutung für die amerikanische Architektur," *Deutsche Bauzeitung,* XXVI (February 6, 1892), 64–66; and Horace Townsend, "H. H. Richardson, Architect," *Magazine of Art,* London (1894), 133–38. Horace Townsend is not the same as C. Harrison Townsend, whose Bishopsgate Institute of 1893–94 and White Chapel Art Gallery of 1897–99, both in London, are often thought to show Richardson's influence. See the above mentioned list by Arnold Lewis in Hitchcock, *The Architecture of H. H. Richardson and his Times,* pp 333–34.

45. Less purposive research in Dutch magazines had produced some results. An American house by James T. Kelley at Ipswich, Mass. was published in the *Bouwkundig Weekblad XVII* (1897), plate opposite 321. In an article, 'Nieuwkunst," in the same, XIX (1899), 383–84, A. W. Weismann described favorably American domestic work but provided no illustrations. The illustration of the Kelley house may be unique, but the Dutch certainly saw what appeared in German and English professional journals and probably some American ones as well. This information derives from an unpublished Columbia doctoral dissertation, *"Michel de Klerk,"* by Suzanne Shulof Frank.

46. The same photograph used as Fig. 1–34.

47. Marika Hausen, "Gesellius-Lindgren–Saarinen vid sekelskiftet," in *Arkkitehti Arkitekten,* No. 9 (February, 1967), 6–12.

48. *Ibid.,* Fig. 4.

49. *Ibid.,* Figs. 13–14.

50. Robert J. Clark, "J. M. Olbrich, 1867–1908," in *Architectural Design,* XXXVII (December, 1967), 565–72 and *Architektur von Professor Joseph M. Olbrich,* 3 vols., Berlin, 1901–14.

51. Unpublished Massachusetts Institute of Technology doctoral dissertation.

52. This is a subject that cries for careful investigation. See Ludwig Münz and Gustav Künstler, *Der Architekt Adolf Loos . . . ,* Wien, 1964, especially p. 41.

53. See Leonard Eaton, "Richardson and Sullivan in Scandinavia," *Progressive Architecture,* XLVII (March, 1966), especially 170–71.

54. Frank Lloyd Wright, *Buildings, Plans and Designs,* New York, 1963.

55. Frank Lloyd Wright, *The Early Work,* with an introduction by Edgar Kaufmann, Jr., New York, 1968.

56. He and other Dutch architects already knew something of Wright's work, presumably from the Wasmuth publications of 1910 and 1911. After his return from America, Berlage published an article and a book in 1912 and a further book in 1913 on what he had seen, especially in the Middle West. See: Hendrick Petrus Berlage, *Een drietal Lezingen in Amerika,* Rotterdam, 1912; *Amerikaansche Reisherinneringen,* Rotterdam, 1913; and an article with the same title in *De Beweging,* Amsterdam, 1912.

57. Most notably, Sir Nikolaus Pevsner.

58. M. H. Baillie Scott, *Houses and Gardens,* London, 1906.

59. Bruno Zevi, *Verso un'architettura organica,* Turin, 1945; English translation, *Towards an Organic Architecture,* London, 1950.

60. For a summary listing of books that illustrate, *passim,* the more or or less profuse Wrightian work of the Dutch over the

years 1915–30, see Hitchcock, *Architecture: Nineteenth and Twentieth Centuries,* pp. 482 and 492.

61. H. R. Hitchcock, *J. J. P. Oud,* Paris, 1931; and Giulia Veronesi, *J. J. Pieter Oud,* Milan, 1953; K. Wiekart, *J. J. P. Oud,* Amsterdam, 1965.

62. *The Work of Frank Lloyd Wright . . . with an Introduction by the Architect H. Th. Wijdeveld,* 2d ed. New York, 1965.

63. Mark Peisch, *The Chicago School of Architecture; Early Followers of Sullivan and Wright,* London, 1965, chap. VII; and James Birrell, *Walter Burley Griffin,* St. Lucia, 1964.

64. Even earlier—1914–15—were the skyscraper projects of Antonio Sant' Elia, who died in 1916; tall buildings were, indeed, of the essence of his urbanistic ideas. See particularly L. Caramel and R. Longati, *Antonio Sant' Elia,* Como, 1962; J. P. Schmidt-Thomsen, *Floreale und futuristische Architektur, Das Werk von Antonio Sant' Elia,* Berlin, 1967. Wijdeveld in Holland also produced an architectural fantasy in the form of a skyscraper for a competition that Architectura ed Amicitia, a Dutch architects' organization, held in 1915, and de Klerk's entry was also very tall.

65. See Hitchcock, *Architecture: Nineteenth and Twentieth Centuries,* Plate 153. Whether, in fact, Bonatz & Scholer were influenced by Richardson has never really been investigated. Such an influence might have reached them via the older Stuttgart architect Theodor Fischer or, possibly, Bruno Schmitz, who had been in America in the 1870's and early 1880's. Schmitz's Völkerschlachtsdenkmal in Leipzig, designed after his return to Germany in 1898,

has a somewhat Richardsonian air, thanks to its rock-faced masonry and low round arches, as his earlier Civil War Monument in the center of Indianapolis does not, any more than his later Jugendstil work in Germany after 1900. *Ibid.,* pp. 467–68.

66. Chicago, 1969.

67. Margaret Ingels, *Willis Carrier, Father of Air Conditioning, Garden City,* 1952.

68. Alison and Peter Smithson, Secondary School, Hunstanton, Norfolk, 1949–54. See Hitchcock, *Architecture: Nineteenth and Twentieth Centuries,* pp. 431–32; Reyner Banham, *The New Brutalism,* Stuttgart, 1966, p. 19.

69. See R. Aloi, *Nuove architetture a Milano,* Milano, 1959, pp. 1–6 and 27–36.

70. Ernest Danz, *Architecture of Skidmore, Owings & Merrill,* 1950–1962, with an introduction by H. R. Hitchcock, New York, 1963, pp. 38–41.

71. Hentrich, Petschnigg & Partner, *Bauten 1953–1969,* Düsseldorf, 1969.

72. *Ibid.*

73. In Chicago, three new buildings overtop all the earlier skyscrapers: Skidmore, Owings & Merrill's John Hancock Building; the First National Bank by C. F. Murphy Associates; and Lake Shore Tower by Schipporeit & Heinrich, two pupils of Mies van der Rohe. In Boston, the John Hancock Building by I. M. Pei, next to Richardson's Trinity Church, will soon eclipse the Prudential Tower by the late Welton Beckett and the State Street Trust by F. A. Stahl that now dominate, respectively, the newer and the older portions of the city.

74. *Documenta,* international exhibition, Kassel, June 27–October 6, 1968, Vols. 1 and 2.

The American City:
The Ideal and the Real

2　The American City: The Ideal and the Real

Albert Fein

A social and institutional ideal—the development of a superior public environment including parks, parkways, and institutions devoted to the study of history, science, and art—remains America's most significant contribution to nineteenth-century urban design. This concept was no less important to the United States as an expression of cultural identity than was the Acropolis to Athens, forums and baths to Rome, or the cathedral to medieval France. It was a highly self-conscious effort on the part of America's liberal Protestant leadership to discover a secular expression for its religious values of public harmony, health, happiness, and morality. They believed that, once realized, such an environment would dramatically alter the social values—and life-style —of the changing city. Liberal Protestant leaders, such as William Ellery Channing, Ralph Waldo Emerson, Horace Bushnell, and Henry Whitney Bellows, were determined to channel the religious energy of the New England church into this new urban form. They were also insistent that the values of an agrarian-based Jeffersonian democracy guide the growing American city in overcoming its serious social and economic problems.

The principal source of inspiration for America's Protestant leadership—and for the men they influenced—was the school of Utilitarian thought founded in England

by Jeremy Bentham. During the first third of the nineteenth century, Bentham's followers were reconstructing English society —particularly in its cities. For American urban reformers, London was a model of a Utilitarian-planned city, while New York City was their principal object of concern. In Frederick Law Olmsted, the urban reformers found a remarkable designer to translate their complex social goals into a clear and humane physical plan. In short, the park-complex—like city planning generally—was born out of the interaction of religious-social need, English model, and individual genius.

Despite their best efforts, however, this mid-century generation did not effect permanent changes in the nation's thinking. The Reconstruction era after the Civil War marked the end of the movement. American society was dominated by a commercial and industrial leadership more interested in profits than in social improvement. But blame for the failure of the ideal of the park-complex must rest in part with the urban intellectual elite itself—particularly the designers—which proved incapable of communicating its objectives to the public and to the economic leadership. The deplorable condition of most of these American parks today is directly traceable to this failure of understanding. The nation soon regressed to a pattern of land use and planning no better than that which originally had called forth the generation of reformers.

The Urban Problem

By the 1850's, the technological, economic, and social changes of the century revealed a constant trend toward urbanization. To demonstrate this trend, *Putnam's Monthly Magazine,* a crusading New York magazine, in 1855 commissioned a long article on the subject based upon demographic data obtained from census returns and from official reports of American and European governments. The study found that from about 1810 the Western world had been experiencing a rapidly accelerating process of urbanization. By comparison with the urban revolution, all the wars, revolutions, discoveries, and inventions of human history were insignificant. *"The great phenomenon of the Age,"* the article concluded, *"is the growth of great cities."* [1]

Even within this pattern of world-wide change, America's rate of urban growth was unusually rapid. Underlying it was a transportation revolution serving an expanding commercial and pre-industrial economy made possible by a large labor force of new immigrants. As a result of these factors, between 1820 and 1860, the number of cities with 8,000 or more persons increased from 11 to 24, and the total urban population from less than half a million to over 5 million. During this time, cities came to contain more than 16 per cent of the total population and to be a vital force in the nation.[2]

The country was ill prepared for such rapid urbanization. Lacking urban centers based on church, palace, and university, or the guild and market-place heritage of the medieval free city, America had to turn for solutions to its agrarian past and to new techniques in town-planning pioneered in nineteenth-century England. Compounding the problem was an intellectual inheritance of agrarian, Protestant, and Jeffersonian thought that tended to regard cities as antithetical to the American experience.[3]

The fact that the majority of new immigrants were Catholics—from Ireland and Germany—enforced the view that urbanization was a foreign process. The crowding of unplanned-for immigrants into the older quarters of established cities added new dimensions to such ancient problems as poverty, alcoholism, epidemic diseases, crime, and inadequate housing (*Fig. 2-1*). The general decline of urban facilities and amenities led to the conclusion that the city was the antithesis of all that the nation had valued and a threat to the future of democracy.[4]

Certainly, part of the extraordinary receptivity of American audiences to the writings of the English art and architectural critic John Ruskin can be attributed to his expressed hatred of commercialism and the cities that nurtured it. Urban life, Ruskin believed, was a violation of the laws of nature and incompatible with great civilizations. "Our cities," he wrote, "are a wilderness of spinning wheels instead of palaces; yet the people have not clothes. We have blackened every leaf of English greenwood with ashes, and the people die of cold; our harbors are a forest of merchant ships and the people die of hunger." And he looked upon London as an architectural symbol of a decadent nineteenth-century civilization in the same idealized way that he viewed the cathedral as the embodiment of the Middle Ages, which he loved.[5]

Ruskin represented a class of aristocratic Europeans—particularly English— who doubted the capacity of a young democracy to produce great works of art and architecture. "We hear from Europe,"

2-1. "Dens of Death," Mulberry Bend, New York City. Ca. 1872.

Frederick Law Olmsted noted, "much reflection upon the tendency of democratic institutions to produce corruption in office, injustice, and violence."[6] Given this widely held opinion of American institutions, Ruskin's view of the relationship of art and architecture to American society took on particular urgency. "The art of any country," he warned Americans, *is the exponent of its social and political virtues.* The art, or general productive and formative energy, of any country, is an exact exponent of its ethical life. You can have noble art only from noble persons, associated under laws fitting to their time and circumstance."[7]

Ruskin, however, also confirmed— although unwittingly—American hope for urban reform. He was responsible, wrote one commentator, for dividing "the eras of art into the classical, the medieval and the modern."[8] Explicit in this analysis was Ruskin's judgment that nations must discover a modern idiom of architecture and art based on imagery and materials drawn from nature. This was taken by Americans to mean, in general, that a city similarly planned could be both healthy and moral.

A Religious Perspective

In this sense, Ruskin's writings were viewed as a confirmation of seminal ideas set forth during the 1830's and 1840's by William Ellery Channing (*Fig. 2-2*), a founder of the Unitarian Church. Channing successfully prepared his religious followers to accept the concept of a natural city as being both Godly and consistent with an American democratic tradition. "What a monument is a city," he declared, "to the immortal energies of the human mind; and what a witness to man's spiritual destiny."[9] His disciples readily became apostles for an improved urban America. "Our nation," wrote the Reverend Henry W. Bellows (*Fig. 2-3*), "runs to cities, and particularly in its northern latitudes." And he went on:

As cities have been the nurse of democratic institutions and ideas, democratic nations, for very obvious reasons, tend to pursue them. They are the natural fruits of a democracy. And with no people are great cities so important, or likely to be so increasingly populous, as with a great agricultural and commercial nation like our own, covered with a free and equal population.[10]

A significant index to the cultural importance of this natural image of the city was the support that the concept attracted from noted Americans of varied philosophical persuasions. Transcendentalists like Ralph Waldo Emerson approved, as did such conflicting types as the poet laureate of the raw metropolis, Walt Whitman, and that advocate of an ordered city, the conservative New York Episcopalian layman George Templeton Strong. Even the "radical" Transcendentalist Henry David Thoreau urged that every American town set aside a park of 500 acres as "a common possession forever, for instruction and recreation."[11]

The operative words were "common," "instruction," and "recreation." Most of America's cultural leaders could agree that the nation's most urgent need was the development of institutions in which all social classes participated and from which intellectual-moral instruction and psychological satisfaction were derived. Such a consensus flowed from the realization that there had taken place in the American city a dramatic decline in the social influence of the Protestant Church. "It had been replaced as a means of molding popular values," wrote Bellows, "by

2-2. William Ellery **Channing** (1780–1842). Statue by Herbert Adams, erected 1903, in the Boston Public Garden.

2-3. Henry Whitney **Bellows** (1814–1882). Undated photograph.

Schools, Colleges and popular literature." Nor was the church any longer the center of social life, "for in the cities at least these functions [were] filled by the social parties, the festivals, the Lyceum, the concert and the skating-pond and the theatre."[12]

In and around major urban centers, religious orthodoxy had given way to the more rational and secular doctrines of Unitarianism and Transcendentalism. Radical Protestant clergy led by William Ellery Channing and Ralph Waldo Emerson had successfully attacked such conservative thoughts as infant damnation and personal sin, replacing them with a new ethic of social responsibility. In the cities, the place of the New England village church and its associated common was taken not so much by the new Gothic- or Romanesque-styled ecclesiastical structures as by the public parks and the museums surrounding them. It was logical that Bellows, for example, should become one of the most prominent supporters of public parks and museums. He recognized Central Park as a moral agent of greater importance than even his own All Souls Unitarian Church, designed according to Ruskinian principles of architecture (*Fig. 2-4*).[13]

A more authoritative leader in the transference of religious energy to urban matters was Horace Bushnell (*Fig. 2-5*). A Hartford-based Congregational minister, Bushnell in the mid-1800's attempted a complete synthesis of Protestant thought. Through sermons and books, he expounded a philosophic basis for the secular expression of religious activity. He authored one of the century's most comprehensive essays on the need for a new profession of city planning[14] and in the process influenced two members of his community who were to become famous as urban reformers—Charles Loring

2-4. All Souls Unitarian Church. New York City. 1853–55. John Wrey Mould. Photograph, 1905.

2-5. Horace Bushnell (1802–1876), *ca.* 1870.

Brace, founder of The Children's Aid Society, and Frederick Law Olmsted, planner of Central Park. Bushnell took particular pleasure in learning, just before his death, that the park in Hartford for which he had fought, selected the site, and cooperated as designer with Olmsted would be named for him. Bushnell Park remains today as a secular monument to his religious thought.

Bushnell—like Channing and Emerson—provided pre-Civil War America with a new vision of the potential of the social environment to create a more democratic nation. Through sermons, lectures, and publications these men compelled a re-examination of such basic institutions as the family, the school, and the community in terms of a democratic ideology based on freedom and equality. Nature and not the church was to be the foundation of this new society. Organized religion, which tended to emphasize differences between people, could only forestall the development of a truly national—moral and democratic—society. Nature, expressed through socially democratic institutions, had become for these men and their many devoted followers a substitute for the mysteries and revelations of formal religion.

The theme of nature was dominant, as well, in other sectors of the cultural life of the nation. Such literary figures as William Cullen Bryant exalted it in their poetry and in their work as members of the Unitarian Church. And, in 1844, Bryant used his considerable influence as chief owner and editor of the New York *Evening Post* to urge the creation of public parks in New York City.[15]

Bryant was also a central figure in making New York City the art capital of the nation. With friends, he established the American Art Union, an organization concerned with the popular distribution of works of art. National in influence and urban-based, the Art Union was extremely effective in the 1840's in creating a market for a growing number of artists. In addition, Bryant was a founding member of such art-oriented groups as the Sketch Club and the Century Association, and he encouraged the publication of an experimental journal—*The Crayon*—devoted to all aesthetic matters. The dominant theme of all these art groups and of the magazine was landscape. By the 1850's, largely through such activities and because of Bryant's personal friendships with the painters Thomas Cole and Asher B. Durand, landscape painting had been accepted as a principal means of national cultural expression.[16]

The idealized dialect of nature also made it possible for Bryant to communicate effectively with America's most advanced architectural theorist, Horatio Greenough. Greenough, a prominent American sculptor, in 1843 initiated a theory of American building that he developed during the remaining nine years of his life. He was particularly critical—as were Bryant and other cultural leaders—of the tendency to pattern American building on past styles. This was especially lamentable, he argued, since the nation had before it a splendid example of "natural" architecture in such structures as the clipper ship. Such a construction, Greenough wrote, was no stylistic abstraction, but, rather, "the result of the study of man upon the great deep, where Nature spake of the laws of building . . . in the winds and waves, and he bent all his mind to hear and to obey."[17]

Greenough compelled his audience to view architecture as something broader than any single building. He sought the design of environments embodying the highest aspirations of a democracy. To be democratic, he reasoned, architecture

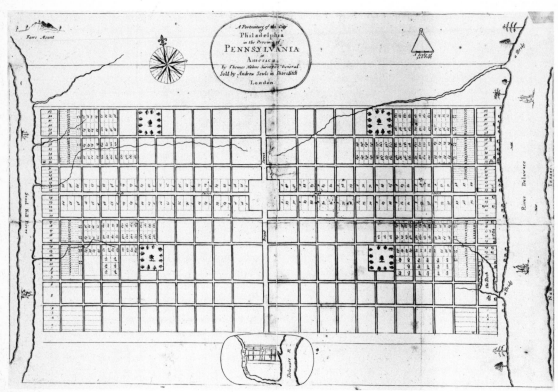

2-6. Plan for Philadelphia. 1682. William Penn.

must become more inspirational and scientific. He likened such design to the flowering of civilization, which, "like other plants, springs from God's ground, . . . has roots in the business and bosoms of men, throws into the sunshine and the air the stem and branches of its toil and its culture, blossoms in poetry and heroism, and bears at length the fruit of science."[18]

An Anti-urban Legacy

But where could Greenough—a New Yorker—look for such an environment in 1850? The record of the eighteenth and nineteenth centuries clearly showed the failure of America's Northern civic leadership to develop large-scale public environments that were both functional and attractive. This was most apparent in such metropolitan centers as Philadelphia, Boston, New York, and Washington. Some vestiges of older planning for the needs of the public survived, but they had had virtually no influence on the development of these cities. In fact, it was not until the first third of the nineteenth century had passed that any realistic attempts were made to insure that such earlier work would not be completely obliterated.

Philadelphia

The most notable failure to extend the wise planning of an earlier period was to be found in Philadelphia, designed as the "capital" of an English colony devoted to religious liberty. William Penn, the Quaker founder, had written elatedly in 1681 about the receipt of a charter: "My God that has given me it through many difficultys [sic], will, I believe, bless and make

it the seed of a nation. I shall have a tender care to the government, that it be well laid at first." And he sought a plan for the City of Brotherly Love that would embody his religious-social goals (Fig. 2-6).[19]

Penn authorized the surveyor Thomas Holme in 1682 to lay out the city using a rigid gridiron arrangement in a manner clearly influenced by the development of London in the seventeenth century. The planner divided the city into four equal parts. Two major streets crossing in the center of town formed an open space of ten acres to be surrounded by public buildings. And in the center of each quadrant there was an open space of eight acres designated as public parklands or walks.

Despite this rational and orderly beginning, the city grew without a plan, the squares remaining as symbols of the past rather than as examples for the future. It was not until 1825 that they were named. Washington Square was used as a potter's field and rented out as pastureland until 1775. Legislation protecting the spaces from usurpation was finally passed in 1821; but the law did not prevent the intersection of Centre Square at Market and Broad streets after 1826. Iron railings were erected in 1834 to protect Franklin and Washington squares. Finally, a year later, these open spaces were given protection by being placed under the supervision of the commissioner of city property.[20] At the root of the failure to extend Penn's plan lay the lack of an urban sensibility; indeed, until the middle of the nineteenth century, Philadelphia remained a town cast in an agrarian image. In such an atmosphere, squares were treated more as expendable rural land than as integral parts of a city's street pattern.

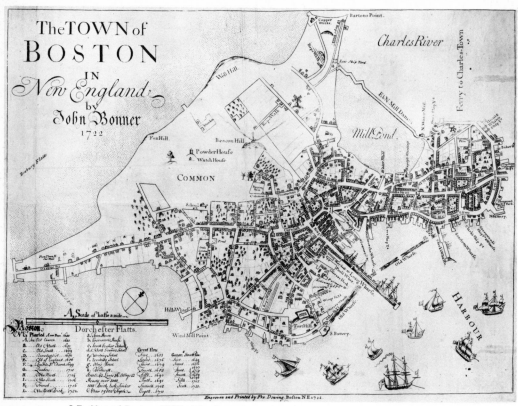

2-7. Map of Boston. 1722. John Bonner.

Boston

A similar attitude explained the neglect of what was probably the nation's most famous urban space—Boston Common. Designated a public ground in 1640, it was not until 1830 that the area was ordered closed to the pasturing of cows and landscaping was begun. For almost 200 years, the nation's most important intellectual center had as its principal open space a grazing ground—Boston Common (*Fig. 2-7*).[21]

In such a setting it was inevitable that —despite lack of civic interest—the space should take on a character and life of its own. It was often used for major public events (*Fig. 2-8*). The Reverend Edward Everett Hale recollected a childhood in which the Common served as a springtime romping ground and a winter sleighing arena. Such prominent Bostonians as Ralph Waldo Emerson, Oliver Wendell Holmes, and Nathaniel Hawthorne strolled there daily. This intensive recreational use led to the purchase of adjacent land in 1824 for a public garden (*Fig. 2-9*), but it did not bring about a re-examination of the needs of larger Boston. In fact, as late as 1850, the city fathers seriously considered dividing the Common into building lots for public sale.[22]

2-8. View of Boston Common, showing the National Lancers with the Reviewing Officers. 1837. C. Hubbard.

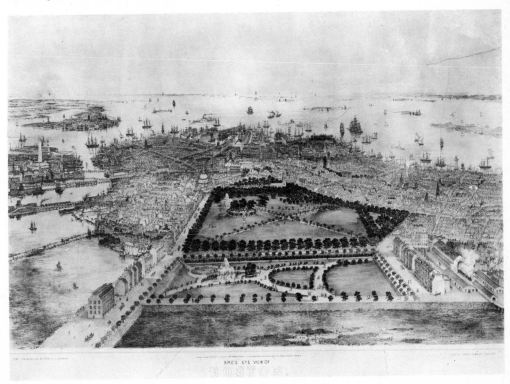

2-9. View of Boston, showing the Common and Public Garden. Ca. 1850. John Bachmann.

2-10. Public common, Worcester, Massachusetts. 1849.

2-11. Map of New Haven. 1748. (The outlines of the plan of 1641 can be detected in this map, which demonstrates the erosion of the original design.)

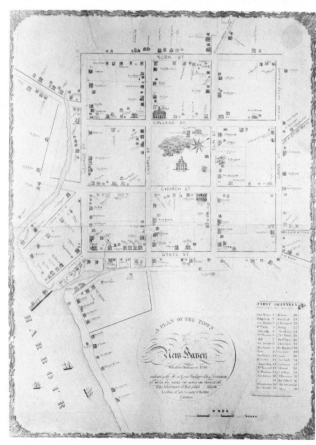

The New England Commons

In one aspect, at least, the history of Boston's Common differed from that of the other commons and greens which dotted the landscape of New England towns: Boston's open space originated for the express purpose of grazing cows. Most commons, however, were established to provide plots for the town ministers. In the great majority of cases, this land was transformed into the town commons. Varying religious and civic requirements gave each open space a unique character.[23]

Despite this difference in origin and function, most New England communities shared Boston's indifference to open spaces as urban amenities. Their commons and greens remained bare, ugly sights until well after the middle of the nineteenth century. Rural improvement societies did not achieve prominence until after the Civil War. As late as 1870, a commissioner of parks for the generally enlightened community of Worcester, Massachusetts, complained bitterly that "the condition of the Common does not challenge admiration. The Commissioners are helpless for its improvement. . . . Every old citizen has a separate pathway of his own across it" (*Fig. 2-10*).[24]

No more hopeful was the history of Connecticut's two largest cities—New Haven and Hartford. The decline of New Haven's public environment can be measured against an early plan of 1641 (*Fig. 2-11*). The town's central green had been designed to be surrounded by large residential blocks, each containing a generous allotment of open space. By the nineteenth century, however, this plan had been caught between the expansion of commerce and the growth of Yale University; little remained of the original concept but the central green (*Fig. 2-12*). A handsome public environment had been sacrificed to private and institutional needs. A similar attitude toward urban

2-12. Map of New Haven. 1837.

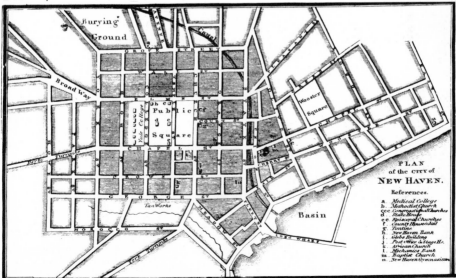

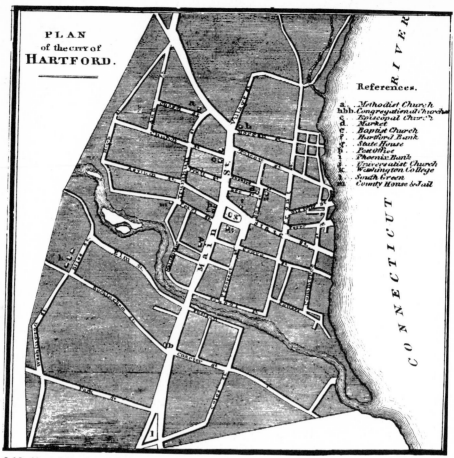

2-13. Map of Hartford. 1640.

amenities characterized the city of Hartford *(Fig. 2-13),* the southern metropolis of New England, before the construction of Bushnell Park in 1858 *(Fig. 2-14).*[25]

Such uniform failure to extend or to protect an original heritage must, in retrospect, be considered to have had at least one redeeming virtue. It created an image of urban ills that both angered and inspired a generation of New Englanders, born in the second and third decades of the nineteenth century and profoundly influenced by the writings of Channing, Emerson, and Bushnell. They were angry at the neglect and inspired, perhaps, by the vision contained in the original plan; they were eager to redeem the American city of their future.

The principal designers representative of this generation were Frederick Law Olmsted *(Fig. 2-15)* and Horace William Shaler Cleveland. Olmsted, born in Hartford, Connecticut, on April 26, 1822, was America's foremost environmental designer. His park work is in evidence in most of America's leading cities. In addition, he was a pioneer in the development of national parks, campus planning, environ-

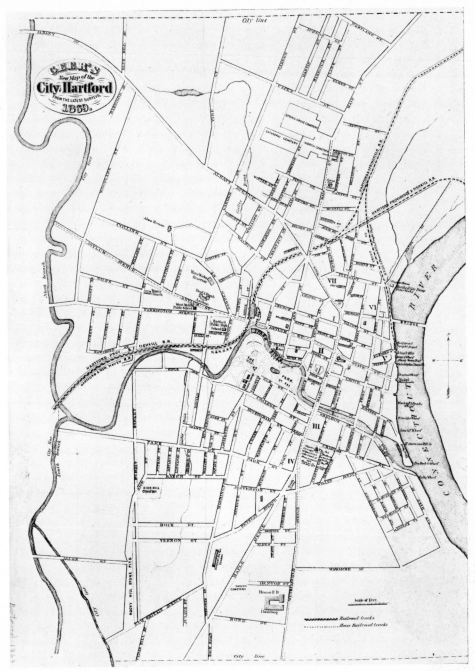

2-14. Map of Hartford. 1869. (The park, centrally located, was not to be named for Horace Bushnell for several years.)

ments for the mentally ill, and the United States Forest Service. Cleveland, born December 16, 1814, in Lancaster, Massachusetts, became a famed associate of Olmsted's. Cleveland completed some important commissions in the East—Sleepy Hollow Cemetery (Concord, Massachusetts) and Roger Williams Park (Providence, Rhode Island)—but his main contribution to the American environment was in Midwestern cities—Chicago, Milwaukee, and Omaha. In this work, undertaken in the 1870's and 1880's, Cleveland was extending and adapting principles of urban and regional design first developed by Olmsted—in collaboration with Calvert Vaux—in the 1850's and 1860's in Central Park (New York City) and Prospect Park (Brooklyn).[26]

Both men were bitter about the failure of their New England childhood environments. Cleveland recalled how fiercely Bostonians had resisted any improvement of the Common—even so small an expenditure as "replacing the old wooden fence . . . with . . . [an] iron enclosure." And he pointed to the fact that western Boston, before the marvelous design and con-

2-15. Frederick Law Olmsted (1822–1903). Photograph, *ca.* 1868.

2-16. Commissioner's plan for New York City. 1807–11.

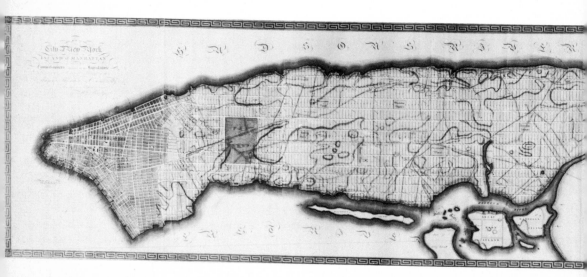

struction of the Back Bay, was nothing more than "[a] barren and forlorn . . . series of gravel banks and waste areas."[27] Olmsted was equally resentful of the failure to develop urban amenities for rural communities. He noted that roadsides were defaced by "raw banks of earth, mudpuddles, heaps of rubbish and slatternly fences," and that there was much that was "draggling, smirching, fouling." The deterioration of commons symbolized to him the failure of the countryside to function democratically. In a truly democratic community, he declared, such social facilities would no more go unattended "than house floors would fail to be systematically swept, or body-linen . . . systematically cleansed."[28]

New York City

Disregard of the public environment, however, seemed as likely to characterize the commercial city in the future as it had the agrarian community of the past. During the nineteenth century, commerce, rather than agriculture, increasingly occupied the attention of the legislatures of the Northern states. Nowhere was this trend more discernible than in New York, where, as early as 1805, a movement—led by DeWitt Clinton—was under way in Albany to construct the Erie Canal.

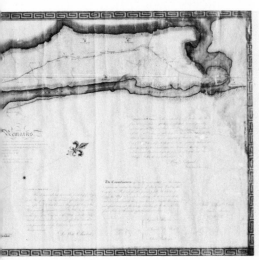

Completed in 1825, the canal had national significance, inaugurating a new era of commercial expansion. Its most immediate effect was to guarantee that New York City would be the nation's wealthiest and most influential city. The city profited enormously by being linked to the rich hinterlands of the Middle West through the Hudson River and the Great Lakes. It was therefore logical that, in 1807, Clinton should be the principal author of a plan for the city, which was ultimately adopted in 1811 (*Fig. 2-16*).

State and city were united in their expectations of continuing growth. "The city of New York," the planners wrote, "contains a population already sufficient to place it in the rank of cities of the second order, and is rapidly advancing towards a level with the first."[29]

The tragedy was that Clinton's vision was a patrician's, designing an environment for a low-level rural life. It was pioneer frontier mentality of the most primitive kind. In considering the plan for the city, the Commissioners of 1807 admitted that "they could not but bear in mind that a city is to be composed principally of the habitations of men, and that straight-sided and right-angled houses are the most cheap to build and the most convenient to live in. The effect of these plain and simple reflections was decisive."[30]

The plan was "plain and simple"—destructively so. It imposed on the city a grid system virtually compelling the destruction of much of Manhattan's naturally varied terrain. Only Broadway, already established as a major thoroughfare, was permitted to curve irregularly uptown. Particularly deplorable was the fact that the planners ignored the extreme lower portion of the city, settled by the Dutch who, in the seventeenth century, had developed an urban form resembling Amsterdam's, the most urbane city plan in the Western world (*Fig. 2-17*). In 1800, Joseph Mangin, the city surveyor and architect, had prepared a comprehensive design for New York that was both human in scale and social in function. Mangin's proposal, in addition to providing a generous allotment for squares and plazas, envisaged a broad promenade sweeping the island's perimeter, guaranteeing that the riverbanks—as in European cities—would be retained for pedestrian use.[31] But, seven years later, this, too, was set aside in favor of the universal grid.

68

The rural and anti-intellectual bias of the commissioners of 1807 was clear. They were perpetuating into the nineteenth century an anti-urban attitude already clearly apparent in most Northern cities. "New York," Olmsted wrote, "when the system was adopted, though vaguely anticipating something of the greatness that has since been thrust upon her, viewed all questions of her own civic equipment, very nearly from the position which a small, poor, remote provincial village would now be expected to take." Instead of looking outward toward the rivers that nourished their existence and across the ocean whence they had come, Gothamites now were forced to look inward. And to see what? "Some two thousand blocks . . . each theoretically two hundred feet wide, no more, no less; and ever since, if a building site is wanted, whether with a view to a church or a blast furnace, an opera house or a toy shop, there is, of intention, no better place in one of these blocks than in another."[32]

Full implementation of this plan would have made the island into a concrete desert. The allocation for open space was grossly inadequate. A military parade ground of 238.7 acres, 55 acres for a public market, and 5 small parks were the only open areas retained for an anticipated population of 400,000. None of the open spaces was ever provided as planned. The parade ground was supposed to extend from Twenty-third to Thirty-fourth streets and from Third to Seventh avenues. By a statute of April 15, 1814, it was sharply reduced to 89.1 acres, at about which time it received the name of Madison Square, in honor of James Madison. And, in 1847, when at last it was officially opened as a square, additional land had to be repurchased from private owners to constitute an area of 6.84 acres.[33] The sale of space to private developers in the generation that followed the adoption of

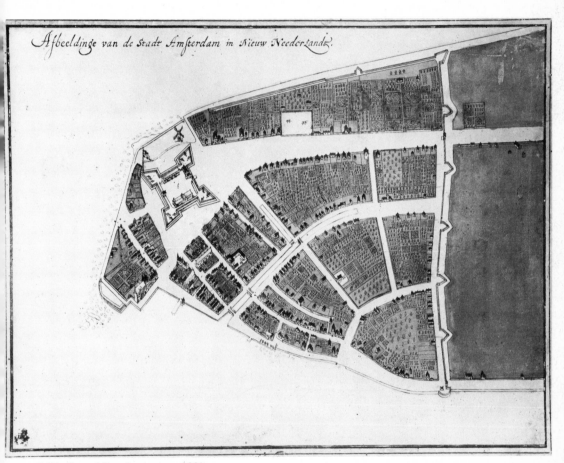

Afbeeldinge van de Stadt Amsterdam in Nieuw Neederlandt.

2-17. View of New Amsterdam. 1660.

2-18. The Battery promenade, New York City. 1851.

2-19. The Elgin Botanic Garden, New York City. *Ca*. 1859.

2-20. View of City Hall Park with fountain. New York City. *Ca*. 1850. John Bachmann.

the plan only mirrored the Commission's original concept of urban land use.

Fortunately, the history of New York City was not to be completely determined by the plan of 1807. The Battery promenade—framing the tip of lower Manhattan—was stripped of its military installations after the American Revolution and continued to be a place "where thousands walk[ed] every fine evening" (*Fig. 2-18*). Between 1807 and 1812, the Elgin Garden, a public botanical garden, came into being on the site of the present Rockefeller Center (*Fig. 2-19*). In 1832, the superintendent of buildings for the city was instructed to enclose City Hall Park with an iron fence and in 1834 to pave some of the streets fronting it. And,

in 1842, a handsome fountain was erected in the lower portion of the park to commemorate the introduction of the Croton water system—without which the city could not have continued to grow (*Fig. 2-20*).[34]

More important, symbolically, to the future environment of the city was the decision in 1831 of a prominent New Yorker, Samuel Ruggles, to assemble a parcel of land lying between Third and Fourth avenues and Twentieth and Twenty-first streets, for the purpose of building a "residential enclave." Gramercy Park was significant as an expression of a point of view rather than for the small impact it had on building practice in the city (*Fig. 2-21*).

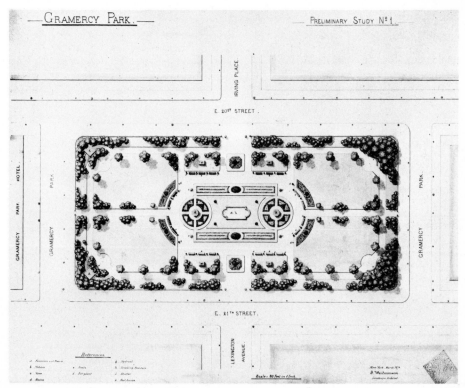

2-21. Plan for Gramercy Park, New York City. 1874. Jacob Weidenmann. (Weidenmann, landscape architect for this design, was Olmsted's frequent professional associate.)

A jurist and legislator, Ruggles occupied an important position as a theoretician of the Whig Party when that political conglomerate was emerging to seize control of New York State politics. Ruggles was also a brilliant statistician and economist. As such, he had an advanced view of the role of cities in the economic life of the nation. He argued against the dominant agrarian-minded view that urban centers were the parasites of society. They were, he reasoned, integral parts of the national economy. There must be a balanced relationship between the city and the services that it performed for the nation. New York City's "wealth and extent," he wrote, "must always be commensurate with the wealth and extent of the Country for which it distributes." Although Ruggles applauded the intent of the plan of 1807—to make New York City a commercial capital—he assumed a completely different attitude toward urban land use and design.[35]

Nor was Ruggles alone either in social outlook or in political strength. During the two decades following the design of Gramercy Park, the city developed a powerful and politically active land-owning group which saw the future in metropolitan terms. High-born, well-educated, and thoroughly urbane, their economic interest was conditioned by a deeply religious feeling more rooted in nature than in theology. In addition to Ruggles, the most prominent of this group were James W. Beekman and Luther Bradish; all three were Whig leaders in New York State in the 1850's.

The three men were among the archi-

2-22. View of Union Square, New York City. 1849. James Smillie.

tects of a grand design aimed at taking control of New York City from the Democratic Party. Through the establishment of commissions—appointed and empowered by the state—they sought to rationalize and professionalize the city's public services of education, public safety, and justice. One of their major efforts was the creation for Central Park of a board of commissioners with powers extending throughout the city. The Commission was, in effect, the first fully empowered city-planning agency in the nation. In 1859, it issued an imaginative design for the development of upper Manhattan Island. The intent was to alter the pattern established by the plan of 1807, but this hope was destined to remain essentially unfulfilled.[36]

Significantly, these men gave freely of their time and generously of their resources to those private institutions of history, science, and art which any great city requires to reform—or sustain—its social condition. Beekman took a deeply personal interest in public education, as did Bradish in scientific research. Without the direct political intervention of these two men, Central Park as we know it today would never have come into existence. Ruggles, in addition to promoting Gramercy Park, influenced the design of Union Square (*Fig. 2-22*) and the establishment of the Croton Aqueduct. He was also a trustee of Columbia College, in which capacity, in 1854, he defended the appointment of a Unitarian to the faculty of the college (at that time still a citadel of Episcopal doctrine) and authored a timeless document—"The Duty of Columbia College to the Community." Yet, he and that entire generation of urban-oriented men could not discover within the American experience a lastingly efficient and satisfactory design for Northern cities.[37]

Washington, D.C.

Until the 1830's, the record outside New York remains hauntingly barren. The same condition of neglect characterized Washington, D.C., which was a national capital in political terms only. As the distinguished historian James Bryce was to note critically, the United States was "the only great country in the world which has no capital." Bryce was referring, of course, not to a political capital alone but to one which, like London or Paris,

> is also by the size, wealth, and character of its population the head and centre of the country, a leading seat of commerce and industry, a reservoir of financial resources, the favored residence of the great and powerful, the spot in which the chiefs of the learned professions are to be found, where the most potent and widely read journals are published, whither men of literary and scientific capacity are drawn.[38]

Although Pierre Charles L'Enfant prepared a plan of the capital city for George Washington in 1791, all economic and social efforts before the Civil War to create a truly national capital on the banks of the Potomac and to complete L'Enfant's plan failed. The challenge, however, was recognized and faced by most presidents. John Quincy Adams, for example, urged the establishment in Washington of a national university and scientific center; but this, like other attempts to make Washington into a commercial and cultural metropolis, aborted. In fact, congressional reluctance to accept Washington as the most desirable location for the capital was rather widespread during the ante-bellum period, and even as late as 1870, there was a movement to shift it to the Middle West.[39]

In such an atmosphere, it was highly unlikely that anyone would have been permitted to complete the Mall, which was the heart of L'Enfant's plan. Nevertheless, Andrew Jackson Downing *(Fig. 2-23)* was invited late in 1850 by President Millard Fillmore to present a proposal for the Mall *(Fig. 2-24)*. This was indicative of the improvement that had taken place in national opinion regarding large-scale urban planning. Downing had become—in an incredibly short period of time—the nation's most influential figure in translating a natural image of religious and social significance into landscape theory and practice.[40]

Andrew Jackson Downing

Downing's influence was primarily a result of his enormous success as an au-

2-23. Andrew Jackson Downing (1815–1852). Undated drawing.

2-24. Plan for the Public Grounds, Washington, D.C. 1851. Andrew Jackson Downing.

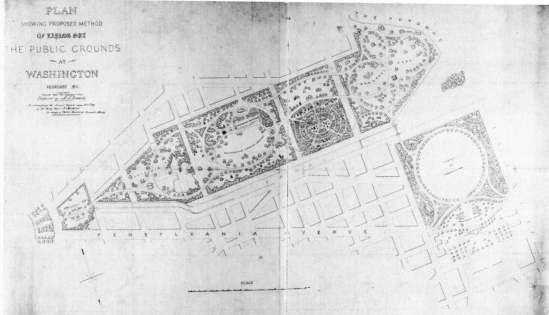

thor. Each of his books became best sellers and the magazine *Horticulturist,* which he owned and edited, received wide circulation. Downing's most famous architectural text, *Cottage Residences,* printed in 1842, was so much in demand twenty-five years later that a posthumous edition was seriously considered by his widow and editors. They asked Olmsted, who had succeeded to Downing's position nationally, to undertake the task. Downing was among the very first to have recognized Olmsted's talents and to have aided his early career.[41]

The most pronounced trend in Downing's career was a shift from rural and horticultural interests to urban and social concerns. Two factors best explain this. One was his involvement with the Unitarian and Transcendentalist movements. Downing had married into the wealthy and prominent De Windt family; his brother-in-law and friend was Christopher Cranch, a Unitarian minister turned Transcendentalist author and painter. The second was Downing's friendship in the 1840's with William Cullen Bryant. This was precisely the time when Bryant was urging the design of a new urban environment for New York City.

Assisting Downing in his professional practice was Calvert Vaux (*Fig. 2-25*), an English-born and London-educated architect whom Downing brought to this country in 1850. It was logical—if not inevitable—that when, in 1857, the City of New York announced a design competition for Central Park, Vaux and Olmsted should have collaborated. Their plan won the competition and began to revolutionize urban design throughout the Western world.

2-25. Calvert Vaux (1824–1895). Photograph, 1868.

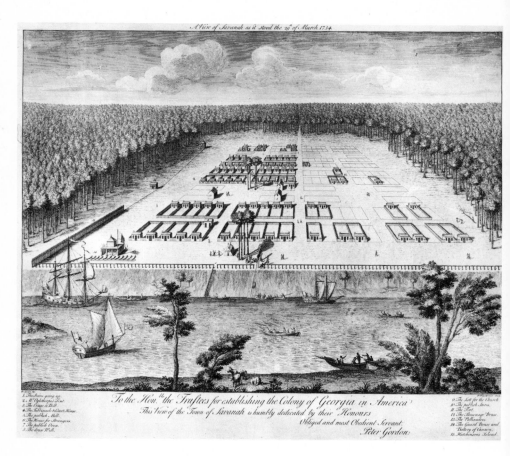

2-26. View of Savannah, Georgia. 1734.

Savannah, Georgia

The design of Central Park, as well as the plan of upper Manhattan Island in 1859, which Olmsted and Vaux directed, had no physical precedent either in Northern cities or in the nation's capital. The Southern record in terms of urban amenities was no worse than that of the rest of the nation, but one city, at least—Savannah, Georgia—was distinctly superior *(Fig. 2-26)*. And Georgia, like Pennsylvania, had been established as a humanitarian experiment.

James Edward Oglethorpe, founder of this colony for English debtors, in 1733 had requested that the city of Savannah be laid out in rectangular fashion. The plan resembled both Philadelphia and New Haven in the generous and orderly provision of open spaces. At the time of its founding, the city had six squares for a population of only 1,000. And surprisingly, for an American city, all but one of the original squares were retained, and the pattern was extended as new wards were added. By 1851, twenty-four squares served a population of 14,000. In that year, too, a new public space, Forsythe Park, was added.[42]

It was unfortunate that, just when Savannah completed its eighteenth-century plan, national opinion made it impossible for cities—Northern or Southern—to learn from its example or experience. Hatred based on the twin issues of slavery and race was unleashed by the passage of two laws: the Omnibus Bill, popularly known as the Compromise of 1850, and the Kansas-Nebraska Act of 1854.

America came to be viewed as two sections—one rural, agrarian, and aristocratic in origin, the other urban, commercial, and democratic. Southerners condemned urbanization as destructive of traditional civilization. Northerners defended urbanization as the only true basis for modern civilization and declared the South to be ignorant of such experience. No better example of the dramatic mid-century shift of opinion exists than the reactions to the city of Savannah by Northern intellectuals interested in city planning. In 1849, William Cullen Bryant, writing to his wife, described the city in glowing terms: "The grass is green here in the squares. The locust trees are in leaf, and the peach trees and almonds in blossom. I wish you could have seen what a beautiful aspect the groves on some of the slopes presented, as we came up to the city this morning."[43]

Thereafter, however, it became increasingly difficult to make this sort of judgment. Even as perceptive, well-informed, and good-willed a person as Frederick Law Olmsted could not disengage himself from the violent emotions that the nation was experiencing. In 1853, he was commissioned by Henry J. Raymond of the *New York Times* to undertake a series of tours through the South in order to describe Southern life and manners. Raymond, like Olmsted, was a member of the Whig Party and anxious to defuse national tensions. Olmsted seemed like the man for the task. In 1852, he had published an account of a trip taken through Great Britain and Western Europe that had been well received. Particularly noticeable was Olmsted's objective attitude toward the South. While condemning the institution of slavery, he urged that the South be given time to solve its own problem and that the North reject abolitionists, who, he believed, tended to confuse rather than to help the matter.[44]

By 1855, however, Olmsted had become directly involved in violence occasioned by the Kansas-Nebraska Act. He was an active member of the New England Emigrant Aid Society, which supplied arms and funds to Northerners settling in these territories. Olmsted was no longer an objective observer.

This changed attitude toward the South was reflected in his evaluation of Savannah. On his first trip in early 1854 Olmsted could appreciate the city's "rural and modest aspect, for a place of its population and commerce." He wrote: "A very large proportion of the buildings stand detached from each other, and are surrounded by gardens, or courts, shaded by trees, or occupied by shrubbery. There are a great number of small public squares, and some of the streets are double, with rows of trees in the centre."[45] But in a later book, he lumped Savannah together with other Southern towns as "simply overgrown villages in appearance, and in convenience."[46] Olmsted's Hartford neighbor, James W. Dixon, described Savannah to James W. Beekman as "an old decayed city whose houses cannot be filled by the population."[47]

The Utilitarian City

Where, then, could Americans turn to discover examples of successful city planning (successful, in so far as they served popular needs as permanent parts of the urban landscape)? Only to Europe, which had a 1,000-year history of urban development based on a feudal and aristocratic society. Moreover, European nations—particularly the German states and England—had been making some impressive advances in urban planning. The European experience became ever more important in the nineteenth century, as increasingly large numbers of affluent and educated Americans traveled abroad. The most influential of these travelers—those who published their accounts—were Northerners of liberal Protestant persuasion.

Americans were particularly attracted to the imaginative use of open space in German and English cities—although they reacted favorably to such planning in all European countries. "If you would observe the people of Munich more closely," William Cullen Bryant wrote to a friend, "you must walk in the English garden and its purlieus. . . . Nothing can exceed the beauty with which it is laid out."[48]

Charles Loring Brace, accompanying

Olmsted on his trip abroad, described the beauty of Dresden with its "parks and gardens and squares full of pleasant groups." And he also raised a question—already posed by Bryant, Downing, and other Americans—as to when "an American city [would] learn to provide for its free population, health, beauty, broad fields and cheerful landscapes, as these German princes have done for their subjects."[49]

The answer, of course, was: not until Americans could resolve the social tension of democratic potential versus aristocratic achievement. On the one hand, such Americans as Brace and Olmsted were self-conscious representatives of a new political democracy that had to be defended against criticisms of aristocratic nations. "The evidence of governmental corruption, injustice, and violence which we display," Olmsted wrote, "(and we take no care to conceal it) is trivial compared with that which escapes from the more distinctly aristocratically governed countries of Europe."[50]

On the other hand, it was evident that to many an American a European city was more attractive than the place of his birth. Indeed, by the 1840's and 1850's, there were comparatively large numbers of Americans living in London and Rome. "The great cities of Europe," admitted *Putnam's Monthly Magazine*, "charm the western traveller, and seduce him from his home affections. . . . He cannot help preferring a residence within easy reach of noble galleries of art, lovely public gardens, exquisite music, and rich libraries."[51]

A resolution of the problem—how to transform what were formerly aristocratic privileges into democratic rights—came from the Utilitarian philosophy of Jeremy Bentham and his devoted followers, who were restructuring English society—particularly cities—in the first third of the nineteenth century. Utilitarianism could be embraced by reform-minded Americans for its objects of scorn as well as for its social goals. As a group, Utilitarians were strongly anticlergy and antimonarchy. They viewed both institutions as the embodiment of irrationality and reaction. Bentham's goal of a just society was based on a belief in the scientific ordering of government through legislation and the need to measure all governmental actions by the standard of "the greatest good of the greatest number."[52]

The most valuable contribution of Utilitarianism to the American scene was the renewed intellectual strength which it provided for those seeking to recast an agrarian Jeffersonian tradition as an urban philosophy. Jefferson was the intellectual father of American reformers of this period. "He was a man of genius," declared William Ellery Channing, "given to bold, original, and somewhat visionary speculation, and at the same time a sagacious observer of men and events."[53] The South's problem, Northern reformers reasoned, was its rejection of a Jeffersonian tradition. Implicit in any defense of slavery, Olmsted wrote, was a denial of Jefferson's democratic principle that "all men are born free and equal."[54]

But Southerners also could quote Jefferson. They could point to his fear that cities were unnecessary and undesirable in a democratic, agrarian society. Jefferson had warned about the social ills inherent in eighteenth-century European urban life.[55] By the late 1820's and 1830's, identical problems of poverty, illiteracy, crime, alcoholism, prostitution, and insanity were visible in the small but growing slum areas of Northern cities inhabited by immigrants. It was hopeful for Americans interested in the alleviation of these conditions to discover the physical and institutional means by which Benthamites were attacking social problems. In this way they could counter the anti-urban arguments of Southern critics.

American reformers also were receptive to Utilitarianism because Benthamites were the most influential European group to admire the political traditions of Jeffersonian America. Bentham often described himself as an Anglo-American man, believing that Utilitarianism would find its most complete fulfillment in the United States. He was a strong influence on such important American statesmen as Edward Livingston and John Quincy Adams during his tenure as Ambassador to the Court of St. James's, before he was elected President.[56]

But more important to the American city in the late 1820's and 1830's was the relationship of Benthamites to the Quaker meetings and, through them, to other liberal Protestant movements. The New York Quaker philanthropist John Griscom was a link between the disciples of Bentham and Americans.[57] Griscom was particularly impressed with the social and environmental solutions of the problems of the urban poor. His son, the noted physician John H. Griscom, in 1845 authored a pioneering work on the effects of the environment on physical and social well-being—*The Sanitary Condition of the Laboring Population of New-York.*

Before the publication of this book, many Americans—particularly New Englanders of liberal Protestant persuasion, such as the educator Horace Mann—had visited England and discovered the work of such Benthamites as Edwin Chadwick, pioneering in the sanitary reform of English cities. In 1840, the American historian Richard Hildreth had translated Bentham's *Theory of Legislation* and later attempted an American version of Benthamite thought in *Theory of Morals*

(1844) and *Theory of Politics* (1853); also, in 1851, the journalist Edward L. Godkin—a confirmed student of Bentham—immigrated to America from Northern Ireland.[58] Both Hildreth and Godkin were close to the designer Frederick Law Olmsted. As part-owner and editor of *Putnam's Monthly Magazine* in 1855–56, Olmsted employed Hildreth, and in 1865 he invited Godkin to become the first editor of *The Nation,* a liberal magazine that Olmsted had helped to found.

To socially minded designers, such as Olmsted, Utilitarian planning of cities revealed advanced techniques and institutions that had been developed first on English country estates. For example, Chadwick's emphasis on drainage systems and open space as means of preventing disease was an extension of successful agricultural experiences made on Sir Robert Peel's farmland, and elsewhere, by Josiah Parkes. The introduction of agrarian techniques to the urban scene was particularly appreciated by American designers raised in a Jeffersonian age and seeking solutions to city problems.[59]

Many of the advantages proposed for cities were aristocratic in origin. Bentham, like Jefferson, emphasized the role of education as an environmental force. But, unlike the "Sage of Monticello," he trained a group of disciples who interpreted education to mean all those advantages formerly held by an aristocratic class living in rural isolation. An urban society needed to make available to all its citizens those means of education and leisure formerly enjoyed by the landed aristocracy—the park, the college, the library, and the museum.[60]

Underlying these uses was Bentham's pioneering approach to the importance of recreation for all classes living in the new urban habitat as shaped by technology. "Jeremy Bentham," Olmsted wrote, "in treating of 'the Means of Preventing Crimes,' remarks that any innocent amusement that the heart can invent is useful under a double point of view; first, for the pleasure itself which results from it; second, from its tendency to weaken the dangerous inclinations which man derives from his nature."[61] New methods and facilities of education and recreation were democracy's chief tools for alleviating social ills. Olmsted was particularly impressed on his visit to England with the social and architectural penal reforms pioneered by John Howard, one of Bentham's disciples.[62]

Utilitarian thought demanded a new approach to the design of environments. This was first expressed in the work and writings of Sir Humphrey Repton, deservedly considered by Olmsted to have been the originator of modern land planning. By 1795, Repton had broken with an earlier, more picturesque tradition of English landscape design; like the Utilitarians, he assumed a rational and scientific approach to environmental matters. In addition to aesthetic training, Repton wrote, "the [landscape] artist must possess a competent knowledge of *surveying, mechanics, hydraulics, agriculture, botany,* and the general principles of *architecture.*"[63]

The most influential demonstration of Repton's theory was the plan and development of Regent's Park and Regent Street in London's West End. Repton had collaborated with the architect John Nash on the 1811 plan for the park and its environs. The completion of this design had a dramatic effect on London's social landscape and it became a prototype for all urban designers. The full impact of Repton's ideas in the United States came after the wide circulation given his theories by John Claudius Loudon. As a result of the writings of Andrew Jackson Downing,

Loudon's friend and constant correspondent, Reptonian theory was popularly discussed in the United States.[64]

The American Cemetery

The most influential application of Repton's theory was the public park movement—it transformed most English cities in the second third of the nineteenth century. However, about a decade before this movement reached its height, Utilitarian planning appears to have been applied to the construction of cemeteries in major American cities.[65] In England, it was not until 1843 that Bentham's disciple, Sir Edwin Chadwick, published an official report on interments in towns and that Loudon published in his *Gardener's Magazine* a series of articles on the "Principles of Landscape Gardening Applied to Public Cemeteries."

The cemetery movement was initiated in the United States by the internationally prominent Boston physician and botanist Dr. Jacob Bigelow, who believed that health was dependent primarily on environmental factors. As Rumford Professor of Physics at Harvard (1816–27), he would have been one of the first scientists to know of the European interest in urban cemetery planning. Furthermore, Bigelow, as a liberal Congregationalist, must have shared the new view toward death which was being shaped by Transcendentalists and Unitarians. Mt. Auburn Cemetery in Boston was planned for the beauty of life, not the grimness of death —"a tribute of remembrance beyond the standard of the Egyptian pyramids or Roman Catholic crypts." Although it reminded some visitors of the Père-Lachaise cemetery in Paris, in design it was Reptonian—scientifically planned according to use and the natural potential of the site. As such, it was handsomely planted.

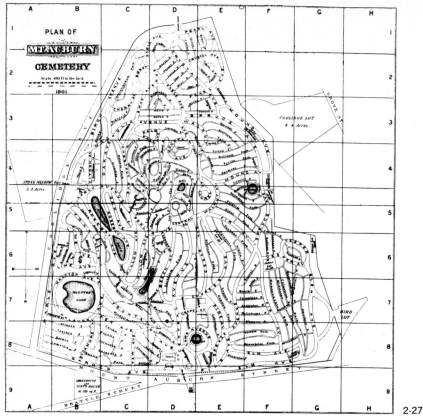

2-27

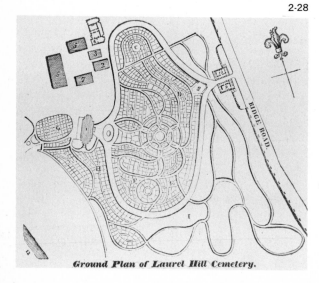

2-28

Ground Plan of Laurel Hill Cemetery.

2-27. Plan of Mt. Auburn Cemetery, Cambridge, Massachusetts.

2-28. Plan of Laurel Hill Cemetery, Philadelphia.

2-29. Plan and views of Greenwood Cemetery, Brooklyn, New York.

82

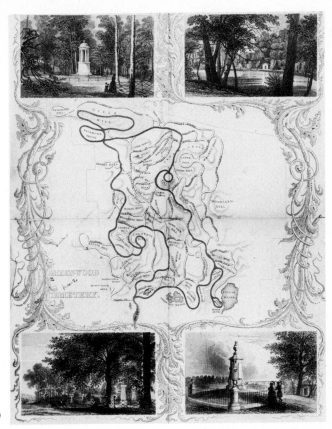

2-29

"There is nothing of the kind on this earth," wrote the Unitarian minister Samuel Osgood, "that equals the great rural cemeteries of our chief cities."[66]

Indeed, Mt. Auburn (1831)—like Laurel Hill in Philadelphia (1836) and Greenwood in Brooklyn (1838)—attracted thousands of city dwellers seeking planned open spaces (*Figs. 2-27, 2-28, and 2-29*). Cemeteries had become recreational places for the living.[67] Sensitive Americans like Downing recognized the value of such open spaces and noted that American cities in the 1840's remained deficient in planned urban amenities by comparison with cities of Europe—particularly London.

London: A Utilitarian Model

London had become the cynosure of Americans interested in urban development. It was the most important commercial center of the Western world and the largest in population. It was, wrote *Putnam's Monthly Magazine,* "the greatest city that has existed in the whole world since the final ruin of Egyptian Thebes."[68] It was the capital not only of an empire but of a nation that—after all criticisms were made of its aristocratic structure—was still loved by most American reformers. "Land of our poets! Home of our fathers! Dear old mother England!" declared Olmsted. "It would be strange if I were not affected at meeting thee at last face to face."[69]

Moreover, London contained the most complete examples of Utilitarian planning. Following the completion of Regent's Park and Regent Street by John Nash, his disciple, James Pennethorne, using these improvements in London's West End as prototypes, designed for that city's deprived East End Victoria Park and its approaches. In addition, he supplied plans for Battersea Park, Kennington Common, and a giant park for northern London.[70] At the same time, Sir Joseph Paxton was attempting to redesign London's main traffic arteries.[71] These plans were presented with the assistance of such political figures as Joseph Hume, a Utilitarian. Although only some of these designs were executed, London was better provided with planned spaces than was any other modern city. It could not help but become a standard for Americans—especially New Yorkers. "Not including the numerous Commons," wrote James W. Beekman, "more than 7,000 acres of park and garden are open to the London public. . . . New York, with over 600,000 inhabitants, has now hardly 100 acres . . . 16 acres to the 100,000 of population."[72]

The Park-Complex: An Environmental Ideal

The fact that New York was so deficient in urban amenities made the movement for Central Park something of a national crusade in the 1850's. Viewed in national terms, the city had become America's true economic and social capital. "Manhattan Island," wrote the noted scientist Alexander Dallas Bache (grandson of Benjamin Franklin), "was intended by nature as the site of a great commercial city."[73] The geologist-engineer Egbert L. Vielé was certain that the city's businessmen would continue to grow wealthy. "New palaces of trade and industry," he wrote, "are rising up on every hand, and so it will go on."[74] And the historian John Lothrop Motley later predicted that "not Byzantium, nor hundred-gated Thebes; nor London, nor Liverpool, nor Paris, nor Moscow can surpass the future certainties of this thirteen-mile-long Manhattan."[75]

In this context, New York was to be

2-30. Outline map of Central Park, New York City, showing transverse roads and differentiated circulation system. Ca. 1868. Frederick Law Olmsted and Calvert Vaux.

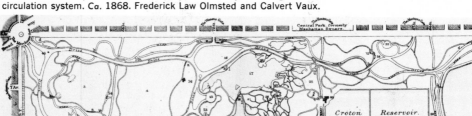

planned not in isolation but as a model for the world and the nation. The ultimate goal of such a capital was to establish standards of behavior and pride that would be emulated at home and abroad. New York City, wrote *Putnam's Monthly Magazine,* must contain "the *national, liberal* and *cosmopolitan spirit* that is generated only by *one acknowledged central city* of a great country; that shall frown down all local animosities, and sectarian bigotries, and give its stamp of approval to the political will of the majority . . . teaching the world 'to live like brothers and . . . embellish life.' "[76] To symbolize these universal qualities, the art critic James Jackson Jarves urged that a huge nondenominational cathedral be constructed in Central Park.[77] And Frederick Law Olmsted described the park to his Utopian-Socialist friend Parke Godwin as "a democratic development of the highest significance and on the success of which, in my opinion, much of the progress of art and esthetic culture in this country is dependent."[78]

This is not to detract in any way from the revolutionary nature of the design for Central Park, which remains unparalleled in the history of modern urban planning. Olmsted and Vaux succeeded in introducing a large section of new urban tissue into an old body without impeding the commercial circulation of the city. By the lowering of four transverse roads below the surface of the park, it became possible for traffic to cross Manhattan without either interrupting the flow of commerce or interfering with the recreational uses of the park—actually, visually, or aurally. In time, this set the pattern for modern highway design. In addition, the designers made separate provisions for three forms of movement within the park itself—in vehicles, on horseback, and on foot. Such attention to safety was revolutionary; for the first time in any city, a child keeping to the pedestrian walk "might toddle from one end of the Park to the other, and run no danger whatever" (*Fig. 2-30*).[79]

But the symbolic significance of the ideas motivating the design was more important. The park-complex—parks and parkways—was meant to establish national standards, demonstrating what a democracy required in its chief public environment, its open spaces. This was precisely the aspect of urban life in which failure had been most conspicuous throughout the history of the Republic. Open spaces—such as Penn, Oglethorpe, L'Enfant, and others had planned—were recognized as the chief "educators" of Jeffersonian values—liberty and equality—in an urban environment, surpassing the schools. "At present," Olmsted and Vaux wrote, "book learning and education are generally considered correlative terms," but to the designers these were less important than the training of the "perceptive faculties"—the multiple ways in which the average citizen perceived his daily environment.[80] And if this environment were dehumanized with respect to

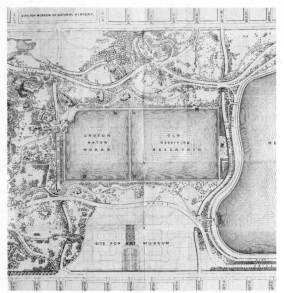

2-31. Map of Central Park, illustrating sites for museums of art and natural history. 1873. Detail.

crowding, noise, filth, or pollution, then the average citizen could not be expected to relate democratically to his society.

This ideal of public environment was incomplete without three interrelated concepts of history, science, and art, represented by the museums, which were planned to be associated with the park *(Fig. 2-31)*. The park-complex was conceived of by its designers as a social totality. An understanding of history was the principal factor motivating their efforts *(Fig. 2-32)*. Each of the museums had a primary duty to preserve and explain the record of the past, mirroring the historic imperatives outlined by Charles Fourier, the French Utopian-Socialist who was as influential as Bentham in American intellectual circles during the late 1840's and early 1850's.

2-32. Design for a proposed historical museum on the site of the Central Park Arsenal, New York City. 1866. Richard Morris Hunt.

According to Fourier's theory, an ultimate and harmonious society would evolve in the course of seven historic periods. The nineteenth century was in transition between the fourth period, barbarism, and the fifth, civilization. The latter period was characterized by uncontrolled individual ownership, while the sixth period, guaranteeism, would establish strict limitations on private property. In this way, the chaos, ugliness, and violence of urban life would gradually be replaced by order, beauty, and harmony. In a park report, in an essay entitled "Historical Development of Existing Street Arrangements," Olmsted and Vaux argued that the introduction of parkways as extensions of the parks and as new containers for urban transportation would be a significant step toward the realization

of Fourier's sixth stage of history. In the planners' judgment, the parkway (*Fig. 2-33*) was an improvement upon the boulevards of Paris constructed under the supervision of Baron Haussmann. New York's parkways would constitute a new community of urban landowners —similar to Jefferson's rural gentry— promoting a spirit of democratic responsibility.

Basic to such an ordered environment were a scientific understanding of and a system of dealing with the ecological problems posed by the city. Public-health needs were an important consideration to the designers as well as to the founders of The American Museum of Natural History, for there was widespread concern with such epidemic diseases as cholera and malaria during the nineteenth

2-33. Design for Eastern Parkway, Brooklyn, New York. 1868.

CITY OF BROOKLYN.

PLAN OF A PORTION OF PARK WAY AS PROPOSED TO BE LAID OUT

FROM THE EASTERN PART OF THE CITY

TO

THE PLAZA.

PROPOSED PLAN.

PRESENT PLAN.

2-34. First section of The American Museum of Natural History. New York City. 1877. J. C. Cady & Co. Photograph, 1879–81.

century. The archival purpose of the museum was to gather and exhibit "the scientific treasures of all the countries of the world." Its intellectual function was "the development of important truths"[82] as to the way nature and man interacted. And the museum was placed on Manhattan Square, eighteen acres of Central Park land (*Figs. 2-34 and 2-35*).

Albert S. Bickmore, the principal founder of the Museum of Natural History, had been trained as a geologist and zoologist by one of America's most eminent scientists—the Swiss-born Louis Agassiz.[83] Owing to the efforts of Agassiz —and others—environmental planners such as Olmsted and Vaux could hope to master the ecological problems inherent in designing such a large area of urban land as Central Park. Geologists and meteorologists had developed fairly sophisticated techniques for mapping the substrata of urban land as well as its climate. The very selection of the site on which Central Park was located was dictated in part by the belief—expressed in reports to governmental and private organizations—that it was particularly unhealthy. This condi-

2-35. The American Museum of Natural History. Photograph, 1890.

tion, explained the geologist Egbert L. Vielé, was due to the concentration of polluted streams in the rock formation lying beneath that part of the island out of which the park was formed.[84]

To neutralize this factor, Olmsted employed George S. Waring, Jr., a pioneer figure in American sanitary engineering. Under his direction the park became a model of urban land-drainage. The extension of the park from Ninety-sixth to One hundred and tenth streets in 1859 was principally due to the efforts of Luther Bradish, who felt strongly that

a great metropolis needed to have an astronomical and meteorological laboratory in that section of the park to keep accurate records of the city's climate. Weather could be measured best in such an environment. Olmsted's early parks—as evidenced in park reports—were designed as examples of optimum urban environments from which the city could best monitor and study its own ecology (*Fig. 2-36*).[85]

The third integral ideal of the park-complex was the importance of beauty and art in the life of the city dweller. This

89

was particularly compelling, since New York City, during the 1840's, had become the art capital of the nation. And there was a very close relationship between the designers and the artists, whose dominant mode of expression was landscape painting (*Fig. 2-37*). Calvert Vaux, an amateur landscapist, shared a home with his brother-in-law, Jervis McEntee, an active painter of scenic views. Two of the nation's most prominent artists, John F. Kensett and Frederic E. Church, were involved in the formation of The Metropolitan Museum of Art (*Fig. 2-38*). Church also served with Olmsted as a member of the Department of Parks from 1871 to 1873.

Olmsted, in turn, was a member of the provisional committee for the establishment of the museum and an author of a formidable report guiding the museum's collections and functions. The collection of art, the report stressed, particularly in a capital city, should serve to improve popular taste. The museum, it was hoped, would eventually become a "University of Art" and lead to the establishment of citywide schools of design. The function of such centers would be to apply design principles to all activities involving skilled labor—and to counteract a growing trend toward interpreting art as "ornamental accomplishment."[86] Each of the architectural structures of Central Park—bridges, terrace, buildings, fountains—were objects of strong, clearly defined principles of land design linking them to their environment—not isolated items of decoration.

The basic principles of land design

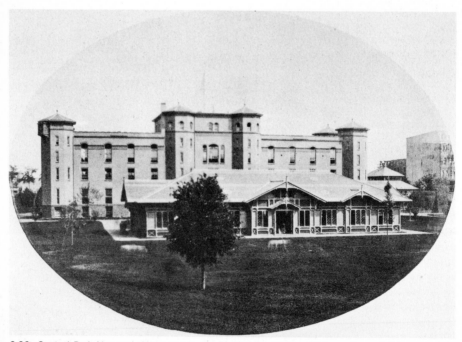

2-36. Central Park Museum, Observatory, and Menagerie. 1848. Photograph, ca. 1870.

2-37. View of Central Park, New York City, from the Belvedere looking southeast. 1869. (This view was drawn by the landscape painter Albert Fitch Bellows.)

2-38. The Metropolitan Museum of Art. New York City. 1874—80. Calvert Vaux with John Wrey Mould. Photograph, 1894.

were drawn from those of painting. On earth, as on canvas, Olmsted quoted a leading authority on landscape gardening, the first law of a good design is "that it shall be a whole."[87] The interior roads and walks and the wide exterior streets were the technical means by which varied sections of the park were brought together. But it was the views planned from the interior of the park that provided unity for the user. All objects were subordinate to this aesthetic function. It was vital that each piece of parkland enhance "general landscape effects, so that every part, whatever its special value, will be associated in such manner with other parts."[88]

A National Movement for Parks

The adoption in 1858 of Olmsted and Vaux's plan for Central Park sparked a national movement. It enabled Horace Bushnell to realize his plans for a park in Hartford, Connecticut. In 1860, Baltimore acquired slightly more than 518 acres, which became the core of Druid Hill Park. This park, however, had not been designed for recreational purposes; it began as a private estate that was converted to public purposes gradually. In the same year, Baltimore added Patterson Park (106 acres) to serve the eastern section of the city, and, in the 1870's, it added Riverside Park (17.21 acres) and Federal Hill Park (8.21 acres). The next large acquisition for the growing metropolis was Clifton Park (252.09 acres) in 1895.[89]

Interrupted by the Civil War, the park movement resumed after Appomattox with renewed vigor. At least five factors served to accelerate its growth: first, the spirit of reconstruction that swept the nation—a desire for a more rational, efficient, centralized, and uniform democracy; second, the dramatic expansion of cities —particularly in the Middle West—occasioned by the war itself; third, the vast increase in urban land values and speculation. The completion of Central Park brought increased personal profits to citizens and large revenue gains to the city, resulting in a new social landscape.[90]

A fourth factor underscoring the importance of rational urban planning with ample open spaces was the catastrophic fire of 1871, which leveled most of central and northern Chicago. Olmsted, who inspected the effects of the fire, concurred with the views of Horace W. S. Cleveland, who wrote:

> Our experience in Chicago has taught us that it is hopeless to try to contend with fire when it sweeps on from block to block in great billows of flame, before which all human defences must go down in utter helplessness. But when it comes to an avenue two or three hundred feet wide and lined with trees, the attack is reduced to a skirmish with cinders, and the firemen have an opportunity to hold their ground against it.[91]

Finally, there was the prominence of Olmsted himself. During the war he served as executive secretary of the United States Sanitary Commission and became a national figure. The Commission, following upon the experiences of Florence Nightingale during the Crimean War, was a comprehensive effort to organize a team of experts concerned with the research and planning of physical and social environments. As a result of heroic efforts and wide travels, Olmsted subsequently developed a small but influential and articulate following. In each of the major cities where he became active, he could rely on at least one prominent citizen to assist him in recommending improvements of the city plan.

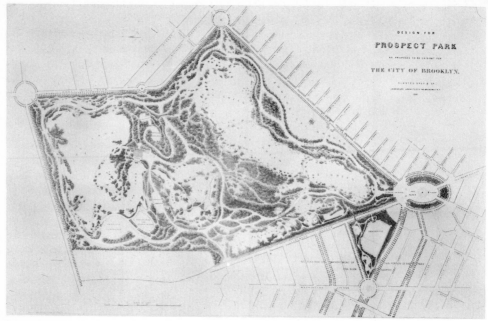

2-39. Design for Prospect Park, Brooklyn, New York. 1868. Olmsted, Vaux & Co. (A variation of the earlier design.)

The evidence of these personal relationships was to be found in Brooklyn, Chicago, Buffalo, and Boston. In Brooklyn, where Olmsted—with Vaux—designed Prospect Park (1866) *(Fig. 2-39)* and laid the theoretical foundation for a parkway system (1868), he had the support of James Stranahan, the city's wealthiest businessman. Stranahan's wife, Marianne Fitch Stranahan, had been chairman of the Woman's Relief Association of Brooklyn and Long Island, a branch of the Sanitary Commission.[92] In 1870-71, the designers proposed a park and parkway system for Chicago's South Park District and the model community of Riverside, nine miles from the center of the city. In these activities they had the assistance of Ezra B. McCagg, a learned and thoughtful philanthropist.[93]

In Buffalo, as in New York State generally, the planners could depend on the considerable influence of William Dorsheimer, an important Democratic politician whose social and aesthetic objectives coincided with those of Olmsted. The plan for the city of Buffalo was displayed at the Philadelphia Centennial Exhibition of 1876 *(Fig. 2-40)*. In 1880, Olmsted moved his home and office near Boston. In that city, he could call upon the assistance not only of Charles E. Norton, Professor of Fine Arts and Architecture at Harvard University, and of the noted architect Henry H. Richardson, but also of a large group of influential citizens with whom he had worked closely during the Civil War and Reconstruction period. Although New York City was no longer Olmsted's base of operations, many friends there actively assisted him in implementing plans for Riverside Park and Morningside Park.[94]

As the issues and memories of the Civil

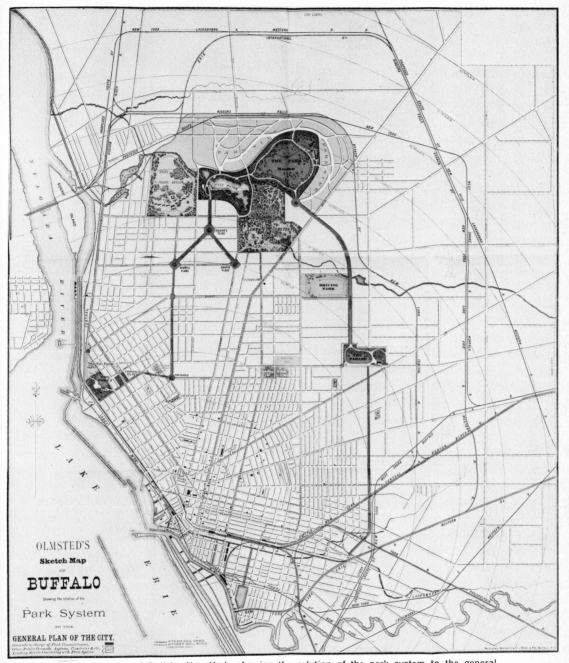

2-40. Sketch map of Buffalo, New York, showing the relation of the park system to the general plan of the city. 1876. (A smaller version of the original map by Frederick Law Olmsted.)

War dimmed, Olmsted's reputation as a professional landscape architect grew. In 1877, Montreal commissioned a park for the center of the city and in 1881, Detroit invited a plan for Belle Isle. In both cases Olmsted's interior designs essentially were adopted. In other instances, of course, plans were requested by cities and then either not adopted or adopted only in part. For example, Olmsted and Vaux prepared preliminary plans for a park in San Francisco and for one in Newark, neither of which were adopted. And of a park-parkway complex for Albany, only the broad concept of the park was eventually implemented.[95]

In Albany, as in other cities, Olmsted's concepts were adopted by a group of self-trained professionals who carried on his work. Jacob Weidenmann, who in the 1870's became Olmsted's partner, had served as Superintendent of Parks in Hartford, Connecticut, in the 1860's. In 1871–72, William Hammond Hall, the designer of Golden Gate Park in San Francisco, invited Olmsted's advice and comments. Olmsted and Vaux's plan in 1866 for that city had not been implemented. But much of the philosophy and some technical suggestions based on climatic conditions contained therein were now repeated in Olmsted's advice and adopted by Hall.[96]

Olmsted's most influential collaborator was H. W. S. Cleveland, the only other landscape architect to achieve a national renown. Although Cleveland was in practice as a land designer before Olmsted, he was not recognized until Olmsted had demonstrated the importance and practicality of the profession. It was under Cleveland's supervision in the 1870's that Olmsted's and Vaux's plans for Chicago were implemented (*Fig. 2-41*). Cleveland's most enduring contribution was a plan for the city of Minneapolis (*Fig. 2-42*).[97]

Responding to the impulse of the park

96

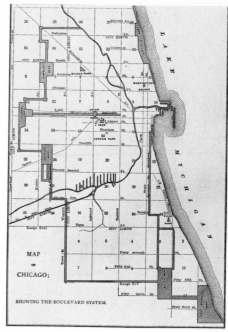

2-41. Map of Chicago, showing the boulevard system. Ca. 1886.

2-42. Map of Minneapolis, showing the park system as recommended by Horace W. S. Cleveland in 1883.

2-43. Plan of Tower Grove Park, St. Louis. 1867.

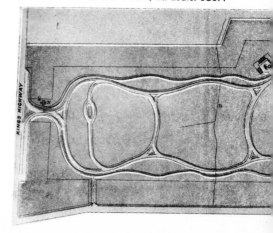

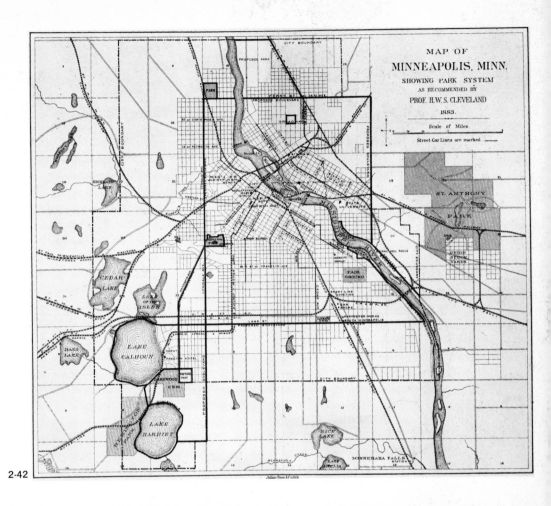

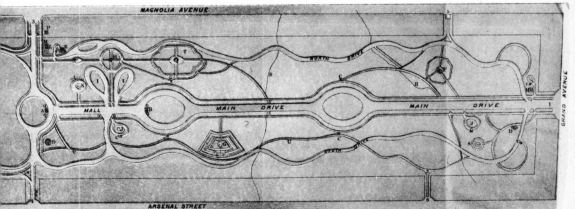

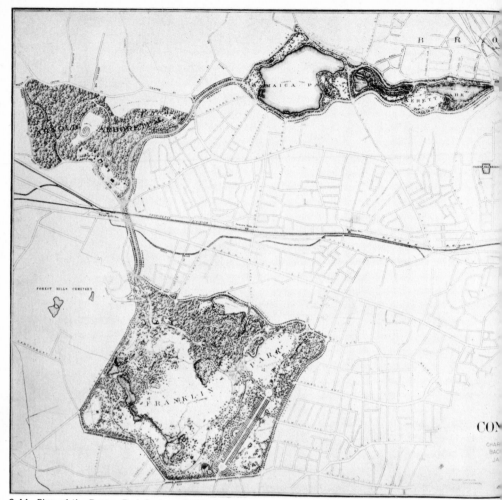

2-44. Plan of the Boston Park System. 1887. Detail.

movement, most cities soon adopted plans. St. Louis was aided by the philanthropist Henry Shaw, founder of the Missouri Botanical Gardens, which today is an internationally prominent center of ecology. Shaw made a careful study of Olmsted's work before donating land for—and supervising the design of—Tower Grove Park (1867) in St. Louis (*Fig. 2-43*).[98]

Cincinnati was fortunate to have the talented German-born gardener Adolph Strauch, who prepared plans for Burnet Woods, Eden Park, and Lincoln Park; sadly, the city did not implement them. Strauch's enduring contribution to Cincinnati remains Spring Grove Cemetery, an outstanding example of picturesque composition in plant materials.[99]

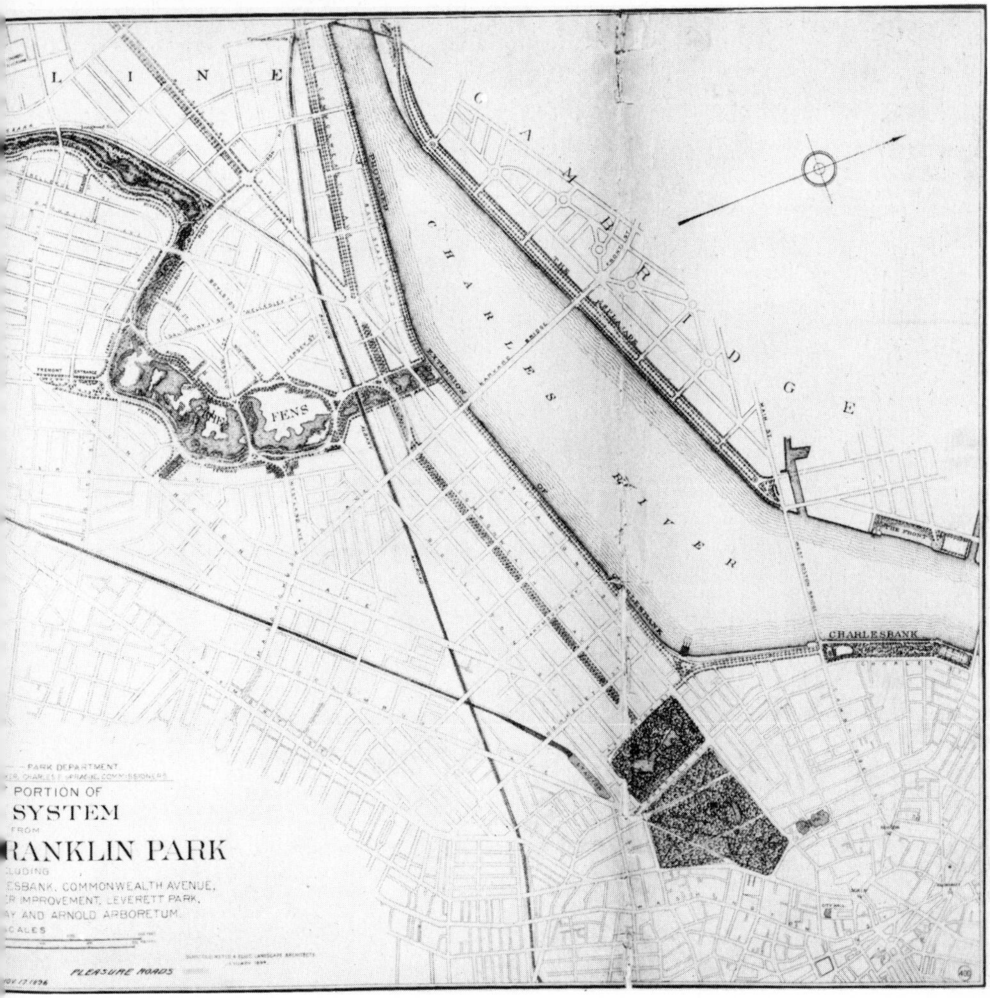

L I N E
CAMBRIDGE
CHARLES RIVER
FENS
CHARLESBANK
PORTION OF
SYSTEM
RANKLIN PARK
ESBANK, COMMONWEALTH AVENUE,
IMPROVEMENT, LEVERETT PARK,
AY AND ARNOLD ARBORETUM.
CALES
PLEASURE ROADS

A Park System

The park-parkway movement entered a new phase in the last decade of the nineteenth century with Olmsted's effort to categorize and formalize the open-space needs of cities. He pointed to the absence of any centralized source for a systematic gathering of data and for analysis of the regional needs of the relentlessly spreading metropolises. The important theme emphasized by both Olmsted and a gifted younger colleague whom he had trained, Charles Eliot (son of Harvard University's president), was the variety of urban amenities required to serve a large but coherent region (*Fig. 2-44*).[100] The Boston Metro-

2-45

2-46

politan Park Commission was organized in 1892 with powers granted to it by some thirty-seven different local governments. Through the activity of this commission, Boston's park system came to contain 10,000 acres of parks and public reservations, 30 miles of river banks, 8 miles of seashore, and 27 miles of boulevards and parkways.[101] Kansas City soon established a similar planning body on a smaller scale. George E. Kessler, a local landscape architect who directed the enterprise, called upon Olmsted and Eliot for advice.[102]

There was one aspect of this systematic treatment of urban amenities that deserves special mention—"vest-pocket" parks in the inner city. This idea was new, since the public park movement had at first assumed that open spaces were not vital to parts of the city dominated by commerce and industry. It was a belated admission on the part of Olmsted and others that the commercial heart of the city had been gaining—not losing—population owing to increased immigration

from eastern and southern Europe during the 1880's.

Inspiration for this new idea came from two men, not designers, working in the inner city. These were Jacob A. Riis (*Fig. 2-45*), a Boston-based Danish-born journalist and political reformer, and Joseph Lee (*Fig. 2-46*), a social worker interested in recreation. Riis, who discovered New York City's Lower East Side through his activities as a police reporter, came to believe in the health and social values of small parks for "new" Americans living in dense, impoverished, and ill-housed communities. It was principally through his efforts that Mulberry Bend Park (*Fig. 2-47*) and Corlears Hook Park (*Fig. 2-48*) were designed for the Lower East Side. Riis joined with Lee in a successful campaign to provide playgrounds (*Fig. 2-49*) connected with public schools in all American cities. These open spaces, planned with facilities for all age groups, soon came to characterize American cities more than the European metropolises where the concept originated.[103]

2-47

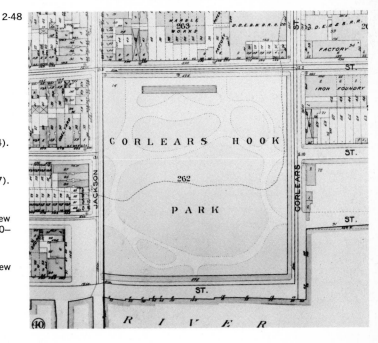

2-48

2-45. Jacob A. Riis (1849–1914). Photograph, *ca.* 1910.

2-46. Joseph Lee (1862–1937). Photograph, published 1937.

2-47. Mulberry Bend Park, New York City. Photograph, *ca.* 1890–99.

2-48. Corlears Hook Park, New York City. 1899.

101

2-49. School playground in the Bronx. New York City. Photograph, *ca.* 1890–99.

A Historical Perspective

In concluding a discussion of the history of American urban amenities of the nineteenth century, some mention must be made of certain failures as well as of the many accomplishments. The present is a product of the past; hence we are compelled to ask why the basic intellectual and social idealism of that mid-century did not have greater impact on our own. In retrospect, it is clear that although the principal failure of urban planning stems from post-Civil War America, the designers and the professions to which they gave rise also must share some of the responsibility. During much of the second half of the nineteenth century, America was dominated by industrial and commercial preoccupations, weak and often corrupt local governments, and a social interpretation of Darwin's theory of evolution that was hostile to comprehensive urban and regional planning.[104] Increasingly, public planning during this period arose from the new technological and commercial demands—not social, ecological, or aesthetic needs. The City Beautiful Movement, which dominated city and regional planning during most of the first two decades of the twentieth century, reflected this thinking. Both the Chicago world's fair (World's Columbian Exposition) of 1893 (*Fig. 2-50*), for which Olmsted provided the site plan, and the Burnham Plan for Washington, D.C., of 1901, to

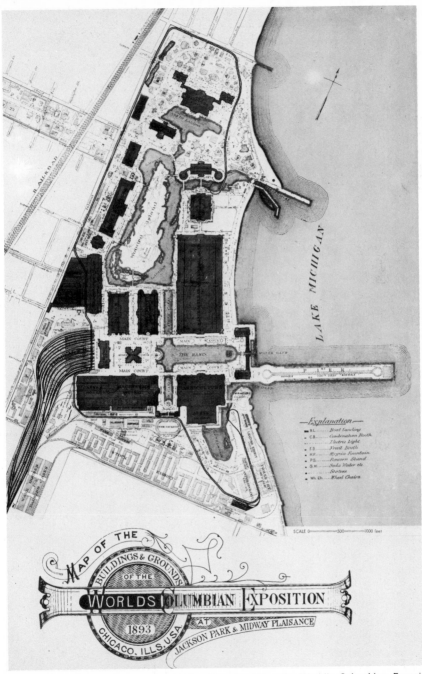

2-50. Map of the buildings and grounds of the World's Fair (World's Columbian Exposition). Chicago. 1893.   Site plan by Frederick Law Olmsted.

which Frederick Law Olmsted, Jr., contributed, used design as the handmaiden of monumental architecture. Urban amenities had become more decorative than functional—in scale more monumental than human.

Indeed, it often seemed as though a previous generation's contributions had been obliterated through some process of rejection. The social principles of the elder Olmsted were no longer utilized or cited even by his own son, a noted landscape architect. It was not really until the late 1920's and the national catastrophe of the Great Depression that a new generation of designers came to re-examine America's earlier environmental record and to rediscover Olmsted's work. The principal figure in this reawakening was Lewis Mumford, who first pointed the way to an understanding of a prophetic and rich environmental past. [105]

But if this continuing re-examination of the past, of which the Metropolitan's exhibition "The Rise of an American Architecture 1815–1915" must be considered an important step forward, is to have enduring significance, the limitations of the designers and of the professions they founded must also be noted:

1. Too much was taken for granted. Very few of the reports that Olmsted, Vaux, and Cleveland authored were meant for popular distribution. Olmsted, for example, never wrote a work on planning even remotely comparable to his classic works on Southern society. He failed even to complete an autobiography. But the scraps that remain demonstrate how valuable such a document would have been in defining for a later generation their goals and techniques.

2. The designers failed to create a single profession that might have unified the practitioners of architecture, engineering, and landscape architecture, who possessed a common concern for the environment. Instead, there developed separate professional schools and mutually conflicting objectives.

3. The scholarly disciplines interested in the environment similarly neglected to develop adequate materials for the study of the environmental past or to organize an integrated academic discipline that young scholars might pursue. Historians in particular until very recently have regarded the evolution of the social environment—rivers, streets, squares, parks, museums, hospitals—as a topic of antiquarian rather than scholarly study and as peripheral rather than central aspects of our social, economic, and political history.

4. The profession failed to carry its crusade for improved urban amenities into the legislative chambers and surround their new social, ecological, and aesthetic principles with the sanction of law. To this day, for example, there does not exist a New York State or New York City law that adequately defines urban park use and design.

5. Finally, there was a failure to create the political apparatus required for functional planning—even at the most primitive level—in a sophisticated, urbane society. Environmental issues were not elevated to the nonpolitical sphere of governmental action nor was environmental expertise given adequate decision-making power.

Retrospect

In sum, it is not sufficient today merely to memorialize the distinctive physical contributions of the past. The current decay and almost willful destruction of some of the most important monuments mentioned in this essay—the Buffalo and Boston park systems are only two examples —stems directly from ignorance of their original purpose and function. To do justice to those responsible for these monuments, we must seek to promote and apply those social, ecological, and aesthetic values that they expounded and which are applicable to the last third of the twentieth century. Thus, the preservation of the physical past is only part of the larger task of educating this generation and its successors to appreciate its environmental heritage. Americans also must be taught within their tradition what are their current social, ecological, and aesthetic rights as citizens of the world's most urbanized democracy. The nation must plan its environmental future with at least the same care and concern that it devotes to its political, diplomatic, and economic existence. Otherwise, the decline of its parks will merely mirror a large and more tragic failure—that of an entire civilization. We may not have another chance.

Notes

1. [?] Bacon, M. D., "Great Cities," *Putnam's Monthly Magazine,* V (March, 1855), 254–55. Italics in original.

2. Adna F. Weber, *The Growth of Cities in the Nineteenth Century* (Ithaca, 1963 [first published 1890]), p. 22.

3. For an interesting discussion of anti-urban attitudes in this period, see Morton and Lucia White, *The Intellectual Versus the City* (Cambridge, Mass., 1962), chaps. iii and iv.

4. This attitude crystallized politically in the formation in 1852 of the American Party —popularly known as "Know-Nothings."

5. Frederick William Roe, *The Social Philosophy of Carlyle and Ruskin* (New York, 1921), pp. 166–68.

6. Frederick Law Olmsted, *A Journey in the Back Country in the Winter of 1853–54* (New York, 1907 [first published 1860]), II, 253–54.

7. John Ruskin, "Lectures of Art," quoted in Raymond Williams, *Culture and Society, 1780–1950* (Edinburgh, 1961), p. 142.

8. "The Late Horace Binney Wallace," *Putnam's Monthly Magazine,* VI (September, 1855), 275.

9. William E. Channing, "The True End of Life," in *The Works of William E. Channing, D.D.* (Boston, 1897), p. 978.

10. Henry W. Bellows, "Cities and Parks," *Atlantic Monthly* (April, 1861), p. 418.

11. *The Writings of Henry David Thoreau,* ed. Bradford Torrey (Boston, 1906), XII, 387.

12. Henry W. Bellows to R. N. Bellows, March 1, 1865, Bellows Papers, Massachusetts Historical Society.

13. Henry W. Bellows, "Cities and Parks," p. 416.

14. See Horace Bushnell, "City Plans," in *Work and Play; or Literary Varieties* (New York, 1864), pp. 308–36.

15. William C. Bryant, "New York Evening Post," July 3, 1844, quoted in Allan Nevins, *The Evening Post* (New York, 1922), p. 123.

16. James T. Callow, *Kindred Spirits: Knickerbocker Writers and American Artists, 1807–1855* (Chapel Hill, N.C., 1967), *passim.*

17. Horatio Greenough, "American Architecture," reprinted in *The Crayon,* II (October 10, 1855), 225. For a perceptive interpretation of Greenough, see James M. Fitch, *Architecture and the Esthetics of Plenty* (New York, 1961), chap. IV.

18. Horatio Greenough, "Fourier Et Hoc Genus Omni," reprinted in *The Crayon,* I (June 13, 1855), 371.

19. Quoted in William Wister Comfort, "William Penn's Religious Background," *The Pennsylvania Magazine of History and Biography,* LXVIII (1944), 346.

20. For a discussion of Penn's original plan, see William E. Lingelbach, "William Penn and City Planning," *The Pennsylvania Magazine of History and Biography,* LXVIII (1944), 398–418; for a historical development of the squares until the 1830's, see Edward P. Allinson and Boies Penrose, *Philadelphia, 1681–1887* (Baltimore, 1887), pp. 79–80. It should also be noted that usurpation of these pitiful remains did not cease in 1835. The central square was given over to Philadelphia's mammoth city hall in the 1870's; another now is overshadowed by the bridge to Camden; and a third was cut through in the 1920's by the Fairmount Parkway; see Turpin C. Bannister, "Ogle-

thorpe's Sources for the Savannah Plan," *Journal of the Society of Architectural Historians,* XX (May, 1961), 62.

21. Hans Huth, *Nature and the American: Three Centuries of Changing Attitudes* (Berkeley, 1957), pp. 60–65. For an informal history of Boston Common, see M. A. De Wolfe Howe, *Boston Common* (Boston, 1921).

22. *Report of the Joint Committee on Public Lands in Relation to the Public Garden,* City Document No. 18 (Boston, 1850).

23. This is the thesis of John D. Cushing, "Town Commons of New England, 1640–1840," *Old-Time New England,* LI (Winter, 1961), 86–94.

24. *Annual Report of the Commissioners of Shade Trees and Public Grounds of the City of Worcester, 1870* (Worcester, Mass., 1871), p. 9; this judgment is documented also by Cushing, "Town Commons of New England," p. 92, and reluctantly implied in Louise A. Kent's *Village Greens of New England* (New York, 1948), p. 198.

25. Arthur B. Gallion, *The Urban Pattern: City Planning and Design* (New York, 1950), p. 74; John W. Reps, *The Making of Urban America: A History of City Planning in the United States* (Princeton, 1965), pp. 128–31. It was the almost total absence of urban amenities in Hartford that led Horace Bushnell in 1837 to urge the city fathers to "erect monuments and fountains, adorn public walks and squares, arrange ornamental and scientific gardens" for its citizens. Horace Bushnell, *The Principles of National Greatness* (New Haven, 1837), p. 17.

26. For an overview of Frederick Law Olmsted—his life and work—see Albert Fein, ed., *Landscape into Cityscape: Frederick Law Olmsted's Plans for a Greater New York City* (Ithaca, N.Y., 1968), Introduction; for an overview of Cleveland—his life and work—see the introduction to H. W. S. Cleveland, *Landscape Architecture as Applied to the Wants of the West* (Pittsburgh, 1965), edited by Roy Lubove.

27. H. W. S. Cleveland, *Terminal Facilities: The Cove Park and the Woonasquatucket Valley* (Providence, R. I., 1883), p. 11.

28. Frederick L. Olmsted, *A Few Things to Be Thought of Before Proceeding to Plan Buildings for the National Agricultural Colleges* (New York, 1866), p. 13; and Olmsted, *Public Parks and the Enlargement of Towns* (Cambridge, Mass., 1870), p. 6.

29. "Remarks of the Commissioners for Laying Out Streets and Roads in the City of New York, Under the Act of April 3, 1807," in *Manual of the Corporation of the City of New York,* D. T. Valentine, ed. (New York, 1866), p. 758.

30. *Ibid.,* p. 756.

31. Gallion, *The Urban Pattern,* pp. 54–59.

32. Frederick L. Olmsted and J. James R. Croes, *Document No. 72 of the Board of the Department of Public Parks: I. Preliminary Report of the Landscape Architect and the Civil and Topographical Engineer, upon the Laying Out of the Twenty-third and Twenty-fourth Wards,* reprinted in Fein, ed., *Landscape into Cityscape,* pp. 351–52.

33. For a history of Madison Square, see Meriden Monographs, No. 1, *A Historical Sketch of Madison Square* (New York, 1894), *passim;* for the process by which land was repurchased, see Document No. 25, Board of Aldermen of New York City, December 15, 1845.

34. James Willis Dixon to James Dixon, Esq., August 28, 1835, Dixon Papers (microfilm), Sheffield Public Library, Sheffield, England. The American Scenic and Historic Preservation Society, *An Appeal for the Preservation of City Hall Park* (New York, 1910), pp. 26–27.

35. Samuel B. Ruggles to N. P. Tallmadge, January 23, 1832, Samuel B. Ruggles Papers, Manuscript Division, New York Public Library; this long letter—really a report in urban economics—is a good summary of Ruggles' economic and social view of New York City. John B. Pine, *The Story of Gramercy Park, 1831–1921* (New York, 1921), *passim.*

36. Frederick L. Olmsted to Henry Elliott, *ca.* June, 1860, Frederick Law Olmsted Papers, Library of Congress—cited hereafter as Olmsted Papers.

37. For biographies of these men, see

D. G. Brinton Thompson, *Ruggles of New York: A Life of Samuel B. Ruggles* (New York, 1946); Philip L. White, *The Beekmans of New York in Politics and Commerce, 1647–1877* (New York, 1956), chap. 17; Walter L. Wright, Jr., "Luther Bradish," *Dictionary of American Biography* (New York, 1943), VII, 567–68.

38. James Bryce, *The American Commonwealth,* II (London, 1889), 644.

39. Constance M. Green, *Washington, Capital City, 1879–1950* (Princeton, 1963), p. 7.

40. For the most perceptive analysis of Downing's personality and career see George W. Curtis, ed., *Rural Essays by A. J. Downing* (New York, 1857), preface.

41. Downing first published an article by Olmsted in *Horticulturist,* II (August, 1847). In 1851 and 1852, two selections from Olmsted's first book, *Walks and Talks of an American Farmer in England* (New York, 1852), appeared there with editorial endorsement from Downing. The endorsement was part of a long review article (February 1, 1852, p. 141).

42. Bannister, "Savannah Plan," 47–48, 62.

43. William C. Bryant to Frances Bryant, March 25, 1849, Goddard-Roslyn Collection (microfilm), New York Public Library—cited hereafter as Goddard-Roslyn.

44. Olmsted, *Walks and Talks,* Part I, p. 221.

45. Frederick L. Olmsted, *A Journey in the Seaboard Slave States, with Remarks on Their Economy* (New York, 1856), p. 405.

46. Olmsted, *Back Country,* II, 34–35.

47. James Dixon to James W. Beekman, March 2, 1854, James W. Beekman Papers, The New-York Historical Society.

48. William C. Bryant to William Leggett, September 30, 1835, Goddard-Roslyn.

49. Charles L. Brace, *Home-Life in Germany* (New York, 1853), p. 352.

50. Olmsted, *Back Country,* II, 254.

51. *Putnam's Monthly Magazine,* IX (March, 1857), 331.

52. For a concise statement as to the Utilitarian point of view, see William L. Davidson, *Political Thought in England* (London, 1947), pp. 1–16; regarding Bentham's attitudes to monarchy and religion, see Charles M. Atkinson, *Jeremy Bentham, His Life and Work* (London, 1905), pp. 35–36, 210–11; the quote, significantly, is from Olmsted, *Walks and Talks,* Part II, p. 82.

53. William E. Channing, "Emancipation," *op. cit.,* p. 850.

54. Olmsted, *Seaboard Slave States,* p. 492.

55. See, for example, Jefferson's oft-referred-to, essentially anti-urban, section in *Notes on the State of Virginia* on "manufactures, commerce, interior and exterior trade" (New York, 1964 [from an 1861 edition, published as part of Volume VIII of *The Writings of Thomas Jefferson,* edited by H. A. Washington]), pp. 156–58.

56. Elmer L. Kayser, *The Grand Social Enterprise: A Study of Jeremy Bentham in His Relation to Liberal Nationalism* (New York, 1932), pp. 28–31, 87–88.

57. See, for example, correspondence between Joseph Hume, one of Bentham's chief political disciples, and Griscom, January 23, 1832, John Griscom Papers, Manuscript Division, New York Public Library.

58. Paul A. Palmer, "Benthamism in England and America," *The American Political Science Review,* XXXV (October, 1941), 863–64.

59. For a good discussion of Chadwick as an urban planner, see Richard A. Lewis, *Edwin Chadwick and the Public Health Movement 1832–1854* (London, 1952). Utilitarian thought had a great impact on English agriculturists; see Leslie Stephen, *The English Utilitarians* (New York, 1900), I, 69–86. Before Olmsted went to England, he had read Henry Colman, *European Agriculture and Rural Economy* (2 vols.; Boston, 1849), most of which is given over to England; Colman's work, like Olmsted's *Walks and Talks of an American Farmer in England,* is written from a Utilitarian point of view.

60. This is the logic of Bentham's aide, Francis Place; see Francis Place, "National Association of the United Kingdom for Promoting the Political and Social Improvement

of the People," British Museum. See also Albert Fein, "The Origins and History of Victoria Park," *East London Papers* (October, 1962), pp. 73–80.

61. Olmsted, *Public Parks,* p. 34.

62. Olmsted, *Walks and Talks,* Part II, p. 58.

63. John C. Loudon, *The Landscape Gardening and Landscape Architecture of the Late Humphrey Repton* (London, 1840), p. 30.

64. In 1852, for example, Downing edited, for an American audience, Mrs. Jane Loudon's *Gardening for Ladies*; see Curtis, ed., *Rural Essays,* preface, p. li.

65. The thesis being presented here is that Utilitarian planning in the United States was first widely applied in the 1830's in urban cemeteries—based on European models. This took place a full decade before the flowering of the English park movement in the 1840's, which had a profound effect on Bryant, Downing, Vaux, and Olmsted. As designers, Olmsted and Vaux brought Utilitarian planning to a new conceptual level in the 1850's and 1860's. Their achievements, as evidenced in plans for the Chicago Park System and Riverside, Illinois (1868–71), in turn influenced the thought and work of Ebenezer Howard, founder of the Garden City movement in England, who lived and worked in Chicago from 1872 to 1876.

This thesis is, of course, only being offered tentatively, for we still know far too little about Anglo-American social and cultural interchange in the nineteenth century. However, it is posited on the record of the very close and dynamic relationship between England and America during that period. It may even prove true that the most enduring and significant evidence of this Anglo-American partnership was in the realm of environmental planning. For a good discussion of Anglo-American relations during this period, see H. C. Allen, *Great Britain and the United States* (New York, 1955), chap. IV; Frank J. Klingberg, "Harriet Beecher Stowe and Social Reform in England," *The American Historical Review,* XLIII (April, 1838), 542–52; and Frank Thistlethwaite, "America and Two Nations of Englishmen,"

The Virginia Quarterly Review, XXXI (Autumn, 1955), 505–25. For an excellent evaluation of Olmsted and Vaux's influence on Ebenezer Howard see Walter L. Creese, *The Search for Environment* (New Haven, Conn., 1966), pp. 144–57.

66. Rev. Samuel Osgood to *The Crayon,* II (July 25, 1855), 54; Huth, *Nature and the American,* pp. 66–69.

67. For a good discussion of the social significance of cemeteries, see Neil Harris, *The Artist in American Society: The Formative Years, 1790–1860* (New York, 1966), pp. 200–208, 377–80.

68. Bacon, "Growth of Great Cities," p. 259.

69. Olmsted, *Walks and Talks,* Part I, p. 99.

70. George F. Chadwick, *The Park and the Town* (New York, 1966), pp. 112–33.

71. George F. Chadwick, *The Works of Sir Joseph Paxton, 1803–1865* (London, 1961), chap. VIII.

72. *Report of the Select Committee on the Bill Relative to a Public Park in New-York,* James W. Beekman and Henry E. Bartlett (New York State: Senate Doc. No. 82, June 21, 1853), p. 9.

73. Alexander D. Bache, *Anniversary Address Before the American Institute of the City of New-York* (New York, 1857), p. 37.

74. Egbert L. Vielé, *Topography and Hydrology of New York* (New York, 1859), p. 26.

75. John Lothrop Motley, *Historic Progress and American Democracy: An Address Delivered Before The New-York Historical Society* (New York, 1869), p. 4.

76. *Putnam's Monthly Magazine,* III (March, 1854), 243.

77. James Jackson Jarves, *The Art-Idea: Part Second of Confessions of an Inquirer* (New York, 1864), pp. 316–19.

78. Frederick L. Olmsted to Parke Godwin, August 1, 1858, Bryant-Godwin Papers, Manuscript Division, New York Public Library.

79. [Clarence Cook], *A Description of the New York Central Park* (New York, 1869), p. 83.

80. Olmsted, Vaux & Company, *Preliminary Report to the Commissioners for Laying Out a Park in Brooklyn: Being a Consideration of Circumstances of Site and Other Conditions Affecting the Design of Public Pleasure Grounds* (Brooklyn, 1866); reprinted in Fein, ed., *Landscape into Cityscape,* p. 124.

81. For a brief but perceptive discussion of the relationship of Fourierism to city planning theory and its influence in the United States, see Leonardo Benevolo, *The Origins of Modern Town Planning* (Cambridge, Mass., 1967), pp. 56–63. Olmsted and Vaux's essay is included in "Report of the Landscape Architects," in the *Eighth Annual Report of the Board of Commissioners of Prospect Park* (Brooklyn, 1868), reprinted in Fein, ed., *Landscape into Cityscape,* pp. 135–59. For the influence of London on Paris, see David H. Pinkney, *Napoleon III and the Rebuilding of Paris* (Princeton, N.J., 1958), pp. 30–31.

82. J. Berrande to Albert S. Bickmore, July 4, 1875, American Museum of Natural History Archives; James T. Gardiner to Calvert Vaux, March 7, 1878, James T. Gardiner Papers, New York State Library, Albany.

83. Autobiography of Albert S. Bickmore (manuscript), I, 18, American Museum of Natural History Archives.

84. Egbert L. Viélé in *Report of the Select Committee Appointed to Investigate the Health Department of the City of New York* (New York State: Senate Doc. No. 49, 1859), p. 209.

85. For a discussion of Waring's early career see James Cassidy, "The Flamboyant Colonel Waring," *Bulletin of the History of Medicine,* XXXVI (March-April, 1962), 163–76. Luther Bradish to Chamber of Commerce of the City of New York, February 22, 1859, Luther Bradish Papers, The New-York Historical Society; see, for example, "Appendix C: Reports of the New York Meteorological Observatory in the Central Park," in *Third General Report of the Board of Commissioners of the Department of Public Parks* (New York, 1875), pp. 69–150.

86. Frederick L. Olmsted *et al.,* "Report to the Executive Committee" (manuscript), Minutes of the Board of Trustees, The Metropolitan Museum of Art, I (January 14, 1870), 70, The Metropolitan Museum of Art Archives.

87. Quoted in Frederick L. Olmsted, *Mount Royal, Montreal* (New York, 1881), p. 43n.

88. Olmsted, Vaux & Company to the Commissioners of Prospect Park, *Ninth Annual Report of the Commissioners of Prospect Park* (Brooklyn, 1869), p. 40.

89. Ferdinand C. Latrobe, "History of the Public Parks of Baltimore," in *Report of the Public Park Commission of the City of Baltimore, Md.* (Baltimore, Md., 1896), pp. 1-14.

90. One estimate as to the net worth of Central Park to New York City was "seventeen millions of dollars over cost and all expenses for thirty years, and . . . two hundred millions of dollars' worth of real estate." See *Re-hearing of the New York Park Bill Before the Committee of the Assembly, April 24, 1884: Luther R. Marsh's Argument in Favor of the Bill* (New York, 1884), p. 20.

91. H. W. S. Cleveland, *Suggestions for a System of Parks and Parkways for the City of Minneapolis* (Minneapolis, Minn., 1883), p. 6.

92. L. P. Brockett and Mary C. Vaughan, *Woman's Work in the Civil War* (Philadelphia, 1867), pp. 651–58.

93. G. P. Upton, "Institutions of Art, Science, Literature," *The Lakeside Monthly,* VII (January, 1872), 72, 79.

94. It was Dorsheimer, for example, who saw to it that Olmsted was invited to participate in the planning of the New York State Capital building; and in the 1870's, when Olmsted was under attack from New York City politicians for "moonlighting," Dorsheimer protected him. Olmsted was involved with the planning of the city of Buffalo over a period of twenty years—1868–88. For a summary statement as to his plans for that city, see Olmsted to the Common Council of Buffalo, April 11, 1887, "Proposed Extension of the Park Sys-

tem," *Eighteenth Annual Report of the Buffalo Park Commissioners* (Buffalo, 1888), pp. 32–39; for the best single description of Olmsted's plans for a park system in Boston, see "Report of the Landscape Architect Advisory," *Thirteenth Annual Report of the Board of Commissioners for the Department of Public Parks, Boston* (Boston, 1888), pp. 51–71; for Olmsted's work in New York City in the 1880's see Fein, ed., *Landscape into Cityscape,* pp. 385–457.

95. Olmsted, *Mount Royal*; Olmsted, *The Park for Detroit: . . . Belle Isle Scheme* (Boston, 1882); Olmsted, Vaux & Company, *Preliminary Report in Regard to a Plan of Public Pleasure Grounds for the City of San Francisco* (New York, 1866); Olmsted, Vaux & Company, *Report of the Park Commissioners . . . for a Public Park for the City of Newark* (Trenton, N.J., 1868); Olmsted, Vaux & Company, *Report on the Proposed City Park* (Albany, 1868).

96. The two designers of Albany's Washington Park in the 1870's were John Bogart and John Y. Cuyler, two engineers who were trained under Olmsted and Vaux. For Weidenmann's service in Hartford, see *The Picturesque Parks of Hartford* (Hartford, Conn., 1900), p. 29; for Olmsted's advice to Hall, see letter from Olmsted to Hall, February 20, 1872, Olmsted Papers.

97. Cleveland, *City of Minneapolis, passim*; William W. Folwell, in "postscript" to Charles M. Loring, "History of the Parks and Public Grounds of Minneapolis," *Minnesota Historical Society Collection,* XV (1915), 608.

98. David H. Macadam, *Tower Grove Park of the City of St. Louis* (St. Louis, Mo., 1883), pp. 9–11.

99. Latham Anderson in *Annual Report of the Board of Park Trustees* (Cincinnati, Ohio, 1892), pp. 14, 21.

100. Frederick L. Olmsted, "Parks, Parkways and Pleasure-Grounds," *Engineering Magazine,* IX (May, 1895), 253–60.

101. John Nolen, *The Parks and Recreation Facilities in the United States* (Philadelphia, 1910), pp. 7–8.

102. *Springfield Republican,* November 22, 1903; Andrew W. Crawford, *The Development of Park Systems in American Cities* (Philadelphia, 1905), p. 21.

103. Louise Ware, *Jacob A. Riis: Police Reporter, Reformer, Useful Citizen* (New York, 1938), pp. 160–65; Joseph Lee, *Constructive and Preventive Philanthropy, with an Introduction by Jacob A. Riis* (New York, 1902), pp. vii, 124–27, 164–67.

104. For a seminal interpretation of this aspect of American intellectual life, see Richard Hofstadter, *Social Darwinism in American Thought* (rev. ed.; Boston, 1955).

105. See, for example, Lewis Mumford, *The Brown Decades: A Study of the Arts in America, 1865–1895* (2d ed.; New York, 1955).

Selected Bibliography

BENEVOLO, LEONARDO. *The Origins of Modern Town Planning.* Cambridge, Mass.: M.I.T. Press, 1967.

CALLOW, JAMES T. *Kindred Spirits: Knickerbocker Writers and American Artists, 1807–1855.* Chapel Hill: University of North Carolina Press, 1967.

CHADWICK, GEORGE F. *The Park and the Town.* New York: Praeger, 1966.

CLEVELAND, H. W. S. *Landscape Architecture As Applied to the Wants of the West.* Roy Lubove, ed. Pittsburgh, Pa.: University of Pittsburgh Press, 1965.

CREESE, WALTER L. *The Search for Environment: The Garden City, Before and After.* New Haven, Conn.: Yale University Press, 1966.

FEIN, ALBERT, ed. *Landscape into Cityscape: Frederick Law Olmsted's Plans for a Greater New York City.* Ithaca, N. Y.: Cornell University Press, 1968.

FITCH, JAMES M. *Architecture and the Esthetics of Plenty.* New York: Columbia University Press, 1961.

HARRIS, NEIL. *The Artist in American Society: The Formative Years, 1790–1860.* New York: Braziller, 1966.

HOFSTADTER, RICHARD. *Social Darwinism in American Thought.* Rev. ed. Boston: Beacon Press, 1955.

HUTH, HANS. *Nature and the American: Three Centuries of Changing Attitudes.* Berkeley: University of California Press, 1957.

MUMFORD, LEWIS. *The Brown Decades; A Study of the Arts in America, 1865–1895.* 2d ed. New York: Dover, 1955.

REPS, JOHN W. *The Making of Urban America: A History of City Planning in the United States.* Princeton, N.J.: Princeton University Press, 1965.

A New View of
Skyscraper History

3 A New View of Skyscraper History

Winston Weisman

In 1899, Montgomery Schuyler, the eminent critic of the *Architectural Record,* wrote an article called "The Skyscraper Up-to-Date," in which he lamented that the element of experiment seemed to have disappeared from the design of the skyscraper. He recalled the early days, especially in the first half of the 1880's, when much "wild work" was done. But now, he said, architects seemed to have settled down to a tripartite formula involving a base, shaft, and capital composed of certain groupings of stories. This formula, he went on to say, may be clothed in a variety of historic styles. Schuyler claimed the first example for George B. Post, in his Union Trust Building,* of 1889–90, which he described as Richardsonian Romanesque (*Fig. 3-1*). He said this was soon followed by others in classical garb, such as Bruce Price's American Surety Building, of 1894–95 (*Fig. 3-2*).

Ten years later, in *Scribner's Magazine,* Schuyler reported again on "The Evolution of the Skyscraper." There, he commented on the towers that had recently been, and were then being, built. In the article, Schuyler explained the advances in technology that made possible the rapid rise of building heights. These included the elevator, cage and skeleton construc-

*The date, architect, location, and condition of the buildings discussed by Professor Weisman are to be found either in the list of illustrations or in the table that follows this essay.

3-1. Union Trust Building. New York City. 1889–90. George B. Post.

115

3-2. American Surety Building. New York City. 1894–95. Bruce Price.

tion, fireproof protection for columns and beams, isolated footings and caisson foundations, and the rest.

Without quite realizing the significance of his insight, Schuyler was actually laying the groundwork for an approach to the history of the skyscraper that has been neglected until now. For one thing, he suggested by what he said that the evolution of the skyscraper seemed to be divided into a series of periods marked by fairly distinct architectural forms and methods of designs.

He further suggested that these changes of shape resulted from the increasing size and height of the skyscraper and were made possible by technological advances under the pressure of a strong surge for profits. He made it clear that change in form was not basically a matter of style. Once the frame was formulated, the exterior details could be borrowed from the Romanesque, classical, or any one of a number of other historical styles. In his 1913 article for the *Architectural Record* on "The Towers of Manhattan," he had high praise for Cass Gilbert's Gothicized Woolworth Building, and kind words for Ernest Flagg's Beaux-Arts Singer Building, and for Napoleon Le Brun & Sons' Metropolitan Tower, which was inspired by the medieval campanile on the Piazza San Marco in Venice (*Figs. 3-3, 3-4, and 3-5*).

In other words, while recognizing the impact of technology and the presence of revival styles, Schuyler was aware of an underlying set of conditions that produced a sequence of solutions. The first he identified with the "wild work" being done in the 1880's. The second was a tripartite pattern beginning about 1890. The third, in the form of a tower, evolved largely in the pre-World War I period.

In 1908, he wrote another article for the *Architectural Record,* called "To Curb the Skyscraper," aimed at finding

3-3. Woolworth Building. New York City. 1911–13.
Cass Gilbert.

3-4. Singer Building. New York City. 1906–8.
Ernest Flagg.

3-5. Metropolitan Tower. New York City. 1909.
Napoleon Le Brun & Sons.

some way to stop the malpractice of over-exploitation that was turning the down-town city streets into dark canyons. In this crusade, he was joined by architects George B. Post and Ernest Flagg, who agreed that there was a real danger to the city in unregulated practices. He quoted a scheme of D. Knickerbocher Boyd, President of the Philadelphia Chapter of the American Institute of Architects, that suggested controlling the over-all height of a building by the width of the street. Boyd's system would give the architect the choice of stepping back the plane of a building in the form of "terraces," or setting back from the property line a given distance that would allow for a straight plane of rise.

What we have here, of course, in 1908, is a prediction of things to come in 1916, when the New York building code was revised, resulting in the creation of the "set-back" or "ziggurat" skyscraper as well as the seed idea for the "slab." Once again, Schuyler seemed aware that the size and height of buildings and their relationship to urban requirements would of necessity produce a new form or forms that could be viewed historically as distinct phases.

But Schuyler was primarily an architectural critic and not a historian, and, therefore, he apparently missed the signs of where his thoughts and remarks were leading. He saw the changes taking place but, perhaps because he was too close to the scene, he seems to have not been able to see it in historical perspective. That is the purpose of this essay: to see whether a new view of skyscraper history can be conceived which would take into account both the influence of technology and the role of revival and more modern modes. The approach used here is based primarily on architectural form as dictated by the ever-growing size and height of sky-

3-6. Equitable Life Assurance Company Building. New York City. 1868–70. Gilman & Kendall and George B. Post.

scrapers responding to broad cultural forces operating in the nineteenth and twentieth centuries.

Such a view of skyscraper history might be divided into seven chapters or phases.

Phase I, a preskyscraper phase, dated roughly between 1849 and 1870, composed of buildings containing the essential elements of the skyscraper but not as yet assembled into a single structure.

Phase II, starting with the Equitable Life Assurance Building, of 1868–70, which contains the necessary ingredients for the early skyscraper but where the compositional features of Phase I still persist (*Fig. 3-6*).

Phase III, beginning about 1878, when the French mansardic mode gives way to a flat-roofed formula involving a free and varied grouping of stories producing, in Schuyler's words, much "wild work."

Phase IV, starting in the late 1880's and characterized by a tripartite system of composition corresponding to the parts of a classic column with its base, shaft, and capital.

Phase V, dealing with the skyscraper in tower form. In this category three variants are recognized: the "isolated" tower, conceived as early as 1888 but not realized until 1894–95; a "mounted" tower, dating about 1911, as exemplified by the Woolworth Building (*see Fig. 3-3*); and a "set-back" tower, resulting from the rights provided by the revision of the zoning codes from 1916 onward.

Phase VI, associated with the "set-back" form of skyscraper, dictated by the zoning-code revisions effective after 1916.

Phase VII, dating from 1930 and represented by Rockefeller Center, features a solution with limited space

3-7. Tribune Building. New York City. 1873–75. Richard Morris Hunt.

3-8. Western Union Building. New York City. 1873–75. George B. Post.

development, parklike setting, and often of multiblock dimensions (*see Fig. 3-48*).

The first four phases can be assigned terminal dates because the compositional formulas employed rarely appear in present-day solutions. However, the last three continue in use and promise to do so for some time in the future.

Having established the order of the phases and briefly described their natures,

dates, and contents, it might be best to begin a lengthier discussion with Phase II, because it is here where we find the greatest controversy as to what a skyscraper is. Obviously, the question of a skyscraper definition would determine when and where our history starts.

Schuyler believes the Tribune Building by Richard Morris Hunt and the Western Union Building by George B. Post were the first skyscrapers (*Figs. 3-7 and 3-8*).

3-9. St. Paul Building. New York City. 1898–99. George B. Post.

In his article "The Skyscraper Up-To-Date," he says they were the first business buildings in which the possibilities of the elevator were recognized ". . . they were much more conspicuous and comment-provoking than even the St. Paul and the Park Row now are because they were alone and because lower New York then had a skyline, from which they alone, excepting the church spires, were raised and detached" (*Figs. 3-9 and 3-10*).

3-10. Park Row Building. New York City. 1896–99. Robert H. Robertson.

I was of the same opinion when I re-introduced this material in an article for the *Journal of the Society of Architectural Historians,* called "New York and the Problem of the First Skyscraper" (JSAH, March, 1953). Henry-Russell Hitchcock takes a similar position in his monumental work *Architecture: Nineteenth and Twentieth Centuries.* The main guide line taken by these writers and myself was height, with the elevator as a means of attaining that height, both physically and financially.

Carson Webster, in his article "The Skyscraper: Logical and Historical Considerations" (JSAH, December, 1958), considers the Tribune and Western Union "elevator buildings" or "proto-skyscrapers." He believes the Masonic Temple Building was the first skyscraper because of its twenty usable stories, its height of 300 feet, and its skeleton construction (*Fig. 3-11*). So Webster adds, to the element of height, usable stories and skeleton structure.

Francisco Mujica, in his *History of the Skyscraper,* published in 1930, is of a different mind. Basing his definition of the skyscraper on the presence of an elevator and a skeleton frame, he identifies, in the captions of his illustrations, the Home Life Insurance Company Building as the "first skyscraper" (*Fig. 3-12*) and the Tacoma Building as the "second."

3-11

3-11. Masonic Temple Building. Chicago. 1891–92. Burnham & Root.

3-12. Home Life Insurance Company Building. Chicago. 1884–85. William Le Baron Jenney.

3-12

3-13

3-14

3-15

3-13. Chamber of Commerce Building. Chicago. 1888–89. Baumann & Huehl.

3-14. Mutual Life Insurance Company Building. New York City. 1863–65. John Kellum. (Photograph shows building after alteration of the roof.)

3-15. New York Life Insurance Company Building. New York City. 1868–70. Griffith Thomas. (Photograph shows building before alteration of the roof.)

Webster notes that Mujica at two points calls the Home Life Insurance Company Building an "embryo skyscraper" but prefers the term "proto-skyscraper" because he feels the ten-story building lacks sufficient height. The thirteen-story Chamber of Commerce Building is put in the same category by Webster (*Fig. 3-13*).

In other words, Schuyler would start the history of the skyscraper in 1873–75, with the Tribune and Western Union buildings of New York. Mujica would begin in 1883–85, with the Home Life in Chicago. Webster prefers 1891–92, in Chicago, with the Masonic Temple. Involved is not only the starting date but also the place and the name of the architectural firm that erected the first skyscraper.

After much contemplation, I would like to change my earlier position. My vote for the "first skyscraper" goes to the Equitable Life Assurance Company Building raised in New York during 1868–70 by Gilman & Kendall and George B. Post (*see Fig. 3-6*). The reasons: The Equitable was the first business building in which the possibilities of the elevator were realized. It rose to a height of 130 feet, which made it twice as tall as the average five-story commercial building. Admittedly, the Tribune at 260 feet and the Western Union at 230 feet were much more dramatic, being twice again as tall as the Equitable. But this jump may be viewed as proof that once the height barrier had been broken by the Equitable, others rose rapidly within a very few years.

With this opinion, Carl Condit appears to be in complete agreement. In his book *American Building Art,* he says, "If any one building may be said to mark the beginning of the New York skyscraper, it was the office building of the Equitable Life Assurance Company, at 120 Broadway (1868–70). Five stories high, it rose

to 130 feet at the top of its Mansard roof." If the Equitable marked the "beginning of the New York skyscraper," then it was the first of its type, because no other city can claim an earlier one.

Historically speaking, the Equitable was the first building to break with practice of the past. Its exceptional height was made possible by the introduction of the passenger elevator, which made the upper stories as rentable as the lower, and, in so doing, made the taller-than-average structure financially feasible. From it flowed all the others, such as the Tribune, the Western Union, the Home Life, and the Masonic Temple. The economic success of the Equitable even resulted in raising the height of older Italianate structures like the Mutual Life Insurance Company Building of 1863–65 and the New York Life Insurance Building of 1868–70 which added elevators and mansard roofs shortly after 1870, when the economic significance of the Equitable became clear (*Figs. 3-14 and 3-15*).

What the Equitable and the remodeled Mutual Life and the New York Life buildings had in common was their link with the immediate past. Their design was based on the French mansardic mode, which was first introduced to this country in the 1850's and flourished after the Civil War until the early years of the 1870's, when it was gradually replaced by the Queen Anne mode. Typical were the Herald Building, the National Park Bank, and Lord & Taylor (*Fig. 3-16*) in New York.

The last three structures were done in the same manner as the Equitable, the Western Union, and the Tribune buildings. The only difference between the two groups was that the latter were considerably taller than the former. In both the Tribune and the Western Union, it was becoming painfully clear that these

3-16

3-16. Lord & Taylor. New York City. 1869–70. James H. Giles.

3-17. Boreel Building. New York City. 1878–79. Stephen Hatch.

3-18. Morse Building. New York City. 1879. Silliman & Farnesworth.

edifices had outgrown their French costumes, even though they still wore them. Apparently, the architects involved did not realize that these tall buildings required a different design solution, one that was more like that of the Home Life Insurance Company Building and the Masonic Temple. The need for change was understood by the end of the depression of the late 1870's. It can be seen in the Boreel Building of 1878–79 by Stephen Hatch and the Morse Building of 1879 by Silliman & Farnesworth (*Figs. 3-17 and 3-18*).

As a matter of fact, the Western Union Building already heralded the change that was to take place. In the six floors below the mansard, the stories were grouped horizontally by moldings and other devices into a 2-1-3 arrangement and vertically into five bays containing windows in a 1-2-2-2-1 pattern. The façade in this area was strongly articulated to create the appearance of structure, with the piers designed so as to reflect their load-bearing function. Those supporting the pavilions on the Broadway and Dey Street fronts were wider than the others. This means the design was dictated by the demands of function and structure, not by abstract rules of regularity and symmetry.

Already, in 1874, the general formula appeared in the Evening Post Building by Charles F. Mengelson. In this case, the Broadway elevation was divided by piers into three bays and horizontally into a 2-1-3-2-2 scheme. Unlike the Western Union, the structure was topped off with a fairly flat roof interrupted by a low pavilion. What we seem to have, then, between the late 1860's and the mid–1870's is a phase in the evolution of the skyscraper wherein buildings are becoming tall enough to be considered sky-

3-17

3-18

3-19. Jayne Building. Philadelphia. 1849-52. William L. Johnston.

scrapers by some scholars but being designed in much the same way as other commercial buildings of average five-story height. At the same time, there are signs of a changing concept of composition pointing to the future. For these reasons, this period may be considered as a transition between the earlier preskyscraper phase, designated as Phase I, and Phase III, with the transitional phase containing the first and other early skyscrapers between 1868–78 as Phase II.

Before going on to Phase III, a discussion of Phase I is, therefore, necessary. In the material presented above, three features have been stressed by scholars, namely, height, the passenger elevator, and iron-framing. It we study the commercial building prior to 1868, we note that there were a number of structures that contained these features, but in no case were all three elements assembled in one building.

The Jayne Building was a ten-story structure composed of eight loft stories and a two-story tower (*Fig. 3-19*). To help support the floors, centrally placed iron columns ran the length of the building, carrying wooden beams that rested on the masonry side walls. It had a hoist to lift and lower raw materials and finished products, but there was no passenger elevator.

About the same time, Calvin Pollard designed an eight-story building for a Dr. Brandreth for 241 Broadway, judging from a rendering in The New-York Historical Society (*Fig. 3-20*). There is no evidence that it was actually built or whether Pollard was planning to use structural iron or a passenger elevator. What the rendering signifies is that a much-taller-than-average structure was conceived by the architect for a particular site.

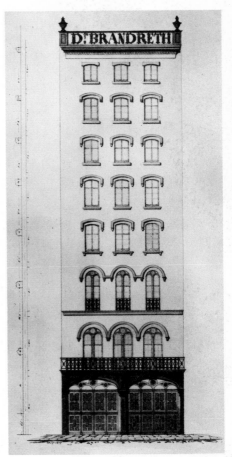

3-20. 241 Broadway scheme. New York City. Ca. 1849. Calvin Pollard.

ARCHITECTURAL IRON WORKS   NEW-YORK

3-21. Haughwout Store. New York City. 1857. John P. Gaynor.

130

3-23. Harper Brothers Building. New York City. 1854. James Bogardus. Section.

3-22. McCullough Shot Tower. New York City. 1856. James Bogardus.

On the other hand, there were two edifices, the Haughwout Store (*Fig. 3-21*) and the Fifth Avenue Hotel, which were about the same size as hundreds of other commercial buildings, that is to say, five stories and about sixty feet, but which had passenger elevators.

Into Phase I might also be put structures that had a construction system closely related to later skyscraper framing. An example that springs to mind is James Bogardus's Harper Brothers Building (*Fig. 3-23*). His McCullough Shot Tower of 1856 had a metal frame that supported a curtain wall of brick between iron columns and girders (*Fig. 3-22*). Thus, during the nine-year period just before the

Civil War, it is possible to find such features as well-above-average height, the passenger elevator, the employment of cage and curtain-wall construction, but— and this is the significant point—not in the same building. The ingredients were present, but up to that time no one had thought to put them together. This first occurred in the Equitable Life, which was more than twice the height of the average office building, thanks to the planned use of a passenger elevator and iron construction. One could, therefore, refer to a preskyscraper phase dating from 1849 to 1870, which paved the way for the first skyscraper period of 1870–78, with its transitional characteristics.

131

3-24. Mills Building. New York City. 1881–83.
George B. Post.

The third phase may be said to have begun about 1878 when the economic depression of 1873–79 lifted and a resumption of building activities ensued. Stephen Hatch's Boreel Building of that year reflected the change that had taken place in the design of tall commercial structures (*see Fig. 3-17*). The mansard roof is replaced by a flat one, because the latter provided better and more rental space at less cost. The ostentatious and expensive French "Empire" decorative system is dropped for a more austere astylar usage that subordinates ornament to structure and substitutes brick and terra cotta for marble and cast iron.

Most characteristic, however, is the method of grouping the stories as a means of achieving a sense of order in a façade involving so many windows, piers, spandrels, mullions, and so on. Two methods appear to prevail. The first grouped the stories in what appears a capricious fashion with each architect doing what seemed to him most attractive. This tendency resulted in what Schuyler referred to as the "wild work" of the period prior to 1890 and produced many solutions that were interesting and some that were bewildering. The second method was not quite so personal and subjective, being based on a mathematical progression that dictated the number of floors to be grouped and the size and number of the elements to be contained in each.

In the Boreel Building, of 1878–79, Stephen Hatch follows Mengelson's lead in dividing his elevation vertically and horizontally. The piers create a composition of five bays with the windows arranged in a 3-2-2-2-3 pattern, while broad-banded moldings and cornice group the stories in a 2-3-3-1 scheme. As in the Evening Post, decoration is minimized, with a central accent provided

3-25. Mills Building preliminary scheme. New York City. 1880. George B. Post.

by a two-story entrance and a Queen Anne pediment over the attic story.

The ten-story Morse Building is a variation on this theme (*see Fig. 3-18*). The roof-line is flat. The piers make for a three-bay, 4-2-4 solution. And the stories are grouped 2-1-2-1-2-1 by double-string courses running past the piers. The tenth story is in the form of a corbeled arcade topped off by a modest cornice.

The Mills Building is larger in size but follows the same principle of design (*Fig. 3-24*). Here, two wings flank a central entrance and light court. These are subdivided on the Broad Street façade into four bays each, two windows wide. The horizontal division is 1-1-2-3-2-1. Of interest is an earlier solution of 1880, which presented an unbroken façade of eight bays, each three windows wide, with the stories grouped in a 1-1-3-1-1-2 pattern (*Fig. 3-25*). The terminating stories are in the form of a mansard with colossal dormers. The formula shown in the rendering reflects the transition from Phase II to Phase III, with a flat-roofed scheme replacing the mansard.

The Produce Exchange introduces the

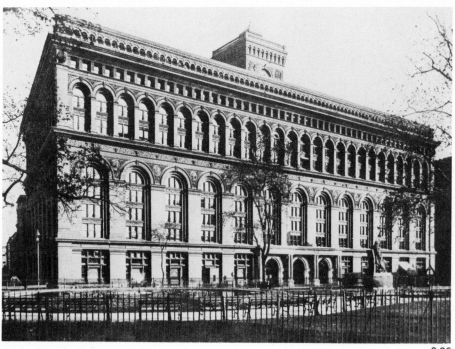

other way of achieving unity during this time (*Fig. 3-26*). In this instance, horizontal grouping is 1-4-2-1-1. But the four-story arcade, the two-story arcade above it, and a single floor below the cornice and the attic story are arranged in a vertical geometric progression of 1-2-4 windows. The architect must have felt the need of a solution of this sort to attain a sense of order in a structure of so many parts and of such massive size. By employing this progression, he managed to avoid monotony and to relate the elements in a most agreeable way.

This system also was used later by H. H. Richardson, when he was commissioned to do a building of similar size, the Marshall Field Warehouse. Richardson prefers the Romanesque vocabulary to the classic but his progression is of the same character. The openings are arranged in a 1-2-4 horizontal system that is accompanied by a three-story, two-story, and one-story grouping of the floors.

In the Auditorium, Sullivan again makes use of this solution in the upper seven floors but varies the vertical composition to a 4-2-1 and the horizontal into a 1-2-3 progression (*Fig. 3-27*).

The more typical design system, however, during this period was the one described earlier, namely, an arbitrary and seemingly capricious grouping of stories designed to produce the most attractive composition. The Rookery by Burnham & Root uses a 1-2-3-3-1 pattern (*Fig. 3-28*). Cobb & Frost in the Chicago Opera House prefer a 2-2-4-2. Baumann & Huehl employ a 2-3-3-4-1 formula in the Chamber of Commerce Building (*see Fig. 3-13*), and Shepley, Rutan & Coolidge favor a 1-2-5-3-1-1 for the Ames Building, of 1889–91, in Boston (*Fig. 3-29*).

3-26. Produce Exchange. New York City. 1881–84. George B. Post.

3-27. Auditorium. Chicago. 1887–89. Adler & Sullivan.

3-28. The Rookery. Chicago. 1885–86. Burnham & Root.

3-29. Ames Building. Boston. 1889–91. Shepley, Rutan & Coolidge.

3-27

3-28

3-29

3-30. Hammond Building. Detroit. 1889–90. George H. Edbrooke.

It should be noted at this point that the introduction of a new formula of design does not necessarily mean the end of the older one. Thus, the Park Row Building, for some years the tallest office structure in the world, followed the Phase III formula, even though the Phase IV system had been in practice for about eight years (*see Fig. 3-10*). Vertically, the façade of the Park Row Building was divided into three parts, the central section slightly recessed and composed of piers of a colossal order rising three and four stories. These did not always coincide with the flanking elements that were three windows wide and topped by four-story towers with cupola. Horizontally, the composition could be read two ways, depending on whether one was using the center or side sections as marking means. But whichever system was employed, the number of groupings produced an elevation that was confusing, monotonous, and awkward. Architect

Robertson did not seem to be aware that the height of his structure was such that he could no longer make use of the old formula, and that a new one was required.

Actually, a new system already had been worked out, namely, the tripartite division associated with the classic column, which Schuyler noted in 1899. This can be considered Phase IV. As stated earlier, Schuyler felt that an early example of this formula was George B. Post's Union Trust Building (*see Fig. 3-1*). The façade not only has the base, shaft, and capital but also a transitional story between the base and the shaft and a similar one between the shaft and the capital. An equally early instance is George H. Edbrooke's Hammond Building, Detroit's first skyscraper, which features the three-part system (*Fig. 3-30*).

A more successful solution, because of its height, can be seen in the Havemeyer Building, (*Fig. 3-31*). Here, the shaft is given greater emphasis by being seven

136

3-31. Havemeyer Building. New York City. 1891–92. George B. Post.

3-32. 715–727 Broadway. New York City. 1894. Robert Maynicke.

stories tall rather than five. The base is three stories, as is the capital, while the transitional stories are one each. To give the capital greater elegance, an elaborate balcony supported by caryatids is added at the start of the capital. This was considered highly desirable by Schuyler, who believed the capital needed to be more decorative than the base following the treatment generally accorded the Ionic and Corinthian orders.

Substantially the same method was employed in Robert Maynicke's building at 715–727 Broadway (*Fig. 3-32*). The two-story base carries the transitional story leading to a six-story shaft surmounted by another transitional story with heavy cornice and topped by a two-story capital. The difference between this solution and that of the Havemeyer Building is that in the former, the shaft is composed of a colonnade instead of an arcade.

A Chicago version of the Phase IV formula without the upper transitional story is to be seen in a building for the New York Life Insurance Company. A St. Louis variant is the Union Trust Company Building, where the arcade is used in the shaft and where there are no transitional stories, merely a base and capital elegantly articulated (*Fig. 3-33*).

Into this category I would also put Adler & Sullivan's Wainwright Building. In his book on Sullivan, Hugh Morrison says that Sullivan's composition was dictated by function and the desire to achieve a "soaring" effect in a building of such height. Apparently, the tripartite concept played little or no part in determining the design of the elevation. A rental plan of the Wainwright Building discovered recently in the St. Louis Free Library shows, however, that the second floor was identical with the floors above,

138

3-33. Union Trust Company Building. St. Louis. 1892–93. Adler & Sullivan.

3-34

3-35

excepting the top story, so that the heavy molding that appears to separate the second story from the third was introduced not for a functional but an aesthetic purpose. The ten-story façade obviously looked better with a two-story base, a seven-story shaft, and a taller-than-average capital housing various services.

The tripartite pattern is repeated in the Schiller Building, where there is little indication on the façade that the structure houses a theater. It occurs in the Marquette Building, which has a two-story base, a transitional story, an eleven-story

shaft, and a one-story transition and capital (*Fig. 3-34*). One building that is questionably tripartite in the same sense as the examples cited so far is the Guaranty Building of Buffalo, where the base and shaft are distinct entities but where the one-story terminating element is hardly big enough to be considered a capital or separate section.

A final aspect of the tripartite phase needs noting. This is well illustrated by the American Surety Building (*see Fig. 3-2*). Here we have a three-story base with Ionic order and a caryatid story, an

140

3-34. Marquette Building. Chicago. 1893–94. Holabird & Roche.

3-35. Washington Life Building. New York City. 1897. Cyrus L. W. Eidlitz.

3-36. Broadway-Chambers Building. New York City. 1899–1900. Cass Gilbert.

3-36

eleven-story shaft, and then an extremely elaborate and tall capital. The major difference between the American Surety Building and the others discussed is that the shaft is not formed by a vertical system of well-articulated piers but by a treatment that emphasizes wall and window. The wall plane is flat or textured to produce a rich ornamental effect, while the windows are primarily openings in the surface.

Just when this practice began it is difficult to say at the moment. More study is needed. But it appears to have been popular in the late 1890's and was used well into the twentieth century. A good example, with highly decorated base, capital, and transitional stories, is the Washington Life Building, where the simple eight-story shaft offers an effective foil for the ornament above and below (*Fig. 3-35*).

At the very end of the nineteenth century, Cass Gilbert designed the Broadway-Chambers Building, which offers one of the best examples of this shaft treatment of the tripartite formula (*Fig. 3-36*). Not only do we have a decorous capital with base and transitional stories but the three

3-37. Tower Building. New York City. 1888–89. Bradford Gilbert.

essential parts are distinguished by a difference in material and color. The shaft is dark-brown brick, the capital a warm marble, and the base a gray granite. When Daniel H. Burnham & Company was commissioned to do the Flatiron Building in New York between 1901–3, the firm's design proved that the tripartite arrangement was still fashionable. It was without question the most widely used solution for the design of a skyscraper in the United States at that time and was practiced in all regions of the country.

But it was not the only formula used. Ever since the early days of its history, the concept of a tower had been associated with the skyscraper. We have seen it used by Hunt in the Tribune Building. Earlier, in preskyscraper days, Johnston had used a two-story Gothic version in the Jayne Building. In both examples, the towers were mere appendages, essentially expressive symbols. Height had an economic value, and a tower atop a business building was the cheapest way to achieve it.

When Bradford Gilbert was commissioned to do an office structure in 1887 for a narrow site at 50 Broadway, he was successful in having the building code revised to permit the use of skeleton construction. The 21-foot-6-inch-wide façade was designed as a Romanesque tower, and it was thought appropriate to call it the Tower Building (*Fig. 3-37*). But, in fact, it was not a tower. The structure was about 108 feet deep and when seen from the side its form was actually slab-like.

Philadelphia had an earlier version of this form in the Tower Building by Samuel Sloan of 1855 (*Fig. 3-38*). Thus, it appears that a reference to towers had an appeal that was aesthetic and expressive. How widespread was its use may be realized by its employment in religious, civic, domestic, and exhibition architec-

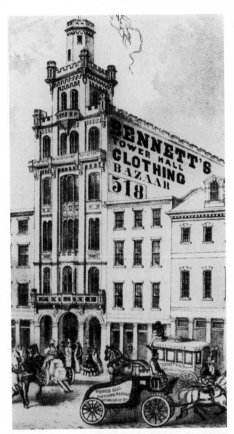

3-38. Tower Building. Philadelphia. 1855. Samuel Sloan.

3-39. Design for a twenty-eight-story office building. 1888. Leroy Buffington.

3-40. Odd Fellows' Temple scheme. 1891. Adler & Sullivan.

ture, railway stations, and the like. Its appearance, in commercial buildings, is, therefore, to be expected.

Nevertheless, toward the end of the nineteenth century, a more practical reason was added to the others. The ever-increasing height of buildings from five to ten and then to twenty and thirty stories forced the architects to search for an appropriate compositional solution. The tripartite system seemed ideal for a twenty-story structure, because a five-story base, a ten-story shaft, and a

five-story capital produced a well-proportioned scheme. Entrance details and a colossally ordered colonnade above contributed to a harmonious combination of elements. However, at thirty stories or beyond, this formula worked less well, and as building height increased, the problem of attractively relating the parts to the whole became more difficult.

It is no coincidence that one of the first of the projects for a free-standing tower office building, namely, Leroy Buffington's scheme of 1888, was for a

3-41. Sun Building scheme. 1890.
Bruce Price.

3-42. Prudential Life Insurance Building Tower project.
1899. George B. Post.

twenty-eight-story structure in the Richardsonian Romanesque manner (*Fig. 3-39*). Adler & Sullivan's Odd Fellows' Temple project of 1891 was planned with thirty-five stories (*Fig. 3-40*). In 1890, Bruce Price suggested a thirty-story isolated tower, inspired by the campanile of San Marco in Venice, for the Sun Building (*Fig. 3-41*). Sometime in the late 1890's, George B. Post designed an addition to the Prudential Life Insurance Building that was intended to be about forty stories high (*Fig. 3-42*). At approxi-

mately the same time, but surely before 1898, Post proposed a 500-foot tower as an addition to the Equitable Life Assurance Company. Glover and Carrel submitted a twenty-five-story polygonal tower to a competition for the New York Herald Building; their scheme appeared in the *American Architect & Building News* for August 6, 1898.

What all this proves is that towers were on the minds of many architects during the 1890's as possible solutions for the design of the new tall and ever-taller sky-

3-43. The Spreckles Building. San Francisco.
1897. J. W. & M. J. Reid.

3-44. Book Tower. Detroit. 1926. Louis Kamper,
Inc.

scrapers. The earliest tower designs meant to be more than symbols were associated with immense structures, such as the tower of the Produce Exchange (*see Fig. 3-26*), which was used for elevators and offices. The one at the Auditorium (*see Fig. 3-27*) served the same purpose, with the upper part of the tower housing the offices of the architects.

It is thought that the first free-standing tower to be erected was the American Surety Building by Bruce Price (*see Fig. 3–2*), because the architect expressed his preoccupation with the tower concept verbally. Whether this was, in fact, the first free-standing tower building actually built depends on an acceptable definition. Russell Sturgis, prominent as architect and critic in the period under discussion, defines the "tower" in his *Dictionary of Architecture and Building* (1905) as "A structure of any form in plan which is high in proportion to its lateral dimensions, or which is an isolated building with vertical sides and simple character . . . The general rule is that towers stand upon the ground and rise from it without serious break in their verticality." The twenty-two-story, 312-foot American Surety would, therefore, certainly qualify as a tower according to Sturgis's definition. But would this apply as well to the thirteen-story Guaranty Building and the ten-story Wainwright Building? Here, lateral dimensions come into play. While the Guaranty might be considered a possible entry, the Wainwright would not qualify, in my opinion.

This, of course, is really beside the main point, which is trying to estimate when the tower phase, or Phase V, of skyscraper development begins. Though the projected schemes start about 1888 and continue throughout the 1890's, it would seem that the first towers were erected about 1895. Within a few years, the use of the concept spread, and the buildings continued to grow even taller. The Spreckles Building (*Fig. 3-43*) was twenty stories high to the top of its cupola. The Bankers' Trust Building in New York was thirty-nine stories, 540 feet; the Singer Building fifty-three stories and 612 feet; and the Metropolitan Tower was fifty-two stories and 700 feet (*see Figs. 3-4 and 3-5*).

Of the towers mentioned, the Metropolitan had the finest appearance, not especially because of its style or proportions but because it had the best site. The Singer and Bankers' Trust towers were hardly visible in the congestion of construction on Wall Street and off Broadway. On the other hand, the Metropolitan Tower had before it the expanse of Madison Square, making it possible for observers to enjoy the sight of the building from bottom to top. It could be seen as an aesthetic entity, despite its considerable size. So successful was the composition and its location that, when it became known recently that plans were afoot for its demolition along with the older headquarters erected in 1890 along Twenty-third Street, public opposition was sufficiently strong to save the tower.

Isolated towers continued to be built after World War I. Examples are the Tribune Tower of 1923–25 by Howells & Hood in Chicago; Detroit's Book Tower of 1926 and Eaton Tower of 1927, both by Louis Kamper; and the thirty-two-story Foshay Tower of 1927–29 in Minneapolis (*Figs. 3-44 and 3-45*). But design problems created by the ever increasing height of business buildings and economic factors combined to introduce a variant, in the form of a tower mounted on a base. One of the earliest of these was the much admired Woolworth Building (*see Fig. 3-3*) of New York, erected by Cass Gilbert in 1911–13. This structure was

3-45. Foshay Tower. Minneapolis. 1927–29.
Magney & Tusler, Inc.

750 feet tall and consisted of a thirty-story tower on a twenty-five-story base. An isolated tower like the Foshay could serve as a prestige symbol, a memorial to an individual, but it was not economically sound. Relatively little rental space could be developed in such a slender shape. The Tribune Tower was essentially a monument to an important newspaper. But those by Kamper follow the pattern established by Bruce Price, having sufficient girth to be financially feasible.

The thirty-six-story Book Tower points up some of the design problems that such a tall structure poses. Like the American Surety (*see Fig. 3-2*), the Book Tower appears to be composed on a tripartite formula. The shaft is so long that the architect has sought to relieve its monotony by the addition of an ornament at its middle. The ten-story capital is made of two blocks, with a colonnade of piers below and an arcade of addorsed columns above. The ensemble is not a happy one, being awkward in proportion and confused in the relationship of its parts. In comparison, the Woolworth Building, though nineteen stories higher than the Book Tower, by having its tower set on a broad base provides for an abundance of first-rate office space and yields a most attractive design.

This solution was not entirely new. The fact is that both the Singer and Metropolitan towers, though conceived as separate units, were nevertheless attached to low, broad blocks of about ten stories, which were built earlier. These provided the requisite space.

Architects were well aware of the aesthetic problems created by the ever growing skyscraper, and there was much thought and discussion concerning a solution. On December 30, 1894, an article appeared in the *New York Tribune* in connection with the American Surety competition, which had been won by Bruce Price. The winner was quoted as saying that "when a skyscraper can be constructed on a square lot and it is possible to have four fronts it might be a fine addition to the city . . . construction of this sort of skyscraper should be encouraged."

In the same piece, the architect Thomas Hastings was less certain that a successful solution could be found. He said:

From the artistic point, it is admitted by almost everyone who has tried to solve the problem that the limitations are almost unsurmountable. The extreme height, tending to the treatment of every building as a tower, on the one hand; the exaggerated demand for light, which destroys all possibility of wall surfaces which are requisite to the design of a beautiful tower and the impossibility, owing to fire laws and other regulations, of using even the structural features of the building to accentuate the design have resolved the problem into vain attempts resulting in absolute monotony, expressive only by its size or absolute decoration of wall surfaces.

Before leaving this subject, it is necessary to note one other factor that played a part in producing the tower-with-base formula. This was the revision of the N.Y. building code in 1916. Brought on by the ill effects these gigantic buildings were having on the city and the public, the code introduced a zoning ordinance that necessitated a set-back system based on the width of the street. However, once 25 per cent of the site had been reached, it was then legally possible to go up indefinitely. A drawing by Harvey Wiley Corbett and Hugh Ferriss illustrated in Mujica's *History* shows how the following code would result in a tower with base. Most dramatic examples are the Chrysler Building by William Van Alen, of 1929–32, that rose sixty-seven stories and 808 feet, and the Empire State Building by Shreve, Lamb & Harmon, of 1930–31, which tops all others at 102 stories and 1,250 feet.

The introduction of zoning codes in New York and other cities produced a new form of skyscraper, constituting Phase VI. The period began in 1916 and continues to the present, though its heyday was in the 1920's, between the end of World War I and the depression of 1929.

149

The zoning code in New York resulted from the clamor and criticism, raised by civic leaders and architects alike, of the irresponsible exploitation of office-building space. Examples of this practice are illustrated by such gigantic schemes as the twin office building at 111–115 Broadway by Francis H. Kimball (*Fig. 3-46*): the Trinity Building and the U.S. Realty Building. Together, these 308-foot-high structures produced 552,873 square feet of floor area. The Hudson Terminal was another twin office building of 275 feet and twenty-two stories that developed 18,150,000 cubic feet of space. The Equitable Life Assurance Building by E. R. Graham, of 1913–15, is typical of the kind of scheme that had made the revision of the zoning code imperative (*Fig. 3-47*).

In the Fisk Rubber Company Building, one can see an early effort to comply with the code. A comparison between the Paramount Building and the Daily News Building shows the difference between an insensitive solution and an inspired one. More representative are the Indemnity Building and the Lincoln Building.

While the zoning code tended to restrain the size and height of skyscrapers, it was not always successful, as witness the Chrysler and the Empire State buildings. Developments of such magnitude present difficult economic and aesthetic problems. In prosperous times, when they were planned, it might well have been possible to operate both structures profitably. But in the event of a depression, the loss of tenants, the reduction in revenue,

3-46. 111–115 Broadway. New York City. 1906–7. Francis H. Kimball.

3-47. Equitable Life Assurance Building. New York City. 1913–15. E. R. Graham.

3-46

3-47

3-48. Rockefeller Center. New York City. 1930–40. Reinhard & Hofmeister; Hood, Godley & Fouilhoux; and Corbett, Harrison & MacMurray.

and the cost of maintenance could prove disastrous. This is precisely what did happen in the 1930's to the Empire State Building, which was ridiculed for some years as the "Empty" State Building.

Equally troublesome was the aesthetic problem. I was told by a member of the firm of Shreve, Lamb & Harmon that the architects first recommended to the syndicate a scheme that would not exceed thirty stories. Such a solution, it was believed, would be more attractive and far less hazardous. Despite the architects' objections, the syndicate voted in favor of the conception as we see it today. Aesthetically, the main fault with the present structure is that, because of its enormous height (1,250 feet) and its crowded site, the 102-story base and tower cannot be properly seen. What is needed is an open parklike area of sufficient size to provide a vista.

The objection to the Empire State and Chrysler schemes was overcome at Rockefeller Center, in what may be considered the beginning of Phase VII (*Fig. 3-48*). Its characteristic feature is a limited exploitation of space rights in a parklike setting often involving a multiblock site.

The conception of a skyscraper city probably grew out of the heated debates of the mid-1890's, when unregulated development began to be noticeable and when some visionaries, like George Post and Bruce Price, could see the need for some kind of ordered control.

In the first decade of this century, picture books by Moses King featured a New York of the future, coordinating in a fanciful way the architectural and transportation needs of the city. After World War I, Norman Bel Geddes, Hugh Ferriss, and Francisco Mujica became interested in the problem. The latter's thoughts were visualized in his book of 1930. Europeans like Tony Garnier, Mies van der Rohe, Ludwig Hilberseimer, and Le Corbusier, tried their hands at planning on a large scale, as did Frank Lloyd Wright.

As far as the skyscraper is concerned, the realization of such a scheme occurred at Rockefeller Center. There, an unexpected series of circumstances transformed what started out to be a cultural center into a commercial center (see my "The Genesis of the Rockefeller Center Plan," *The Architectural Review,* December, 1950).

The precedent set by Rockefeller Center was followed later by many groups of architects and planners, with not always happy results. The developments at Pittsburgh's Golden Triangle, Philadelphia's Civic Center, and Chicago's Civic Center indicate that the potentialities of multiblock planning can be negated by excessive exploitation of space rights. The windy canyons of Philadelphia's Civic Center are not a great improvement over those created in the Wall Street area of New York at the turn of the century.

Examples of the multiblock formula now in the works are the World Trade Center in New York by Yamasaki & Associates and Emery Roth & Sons, featuring two gigantic towers placed in an open plaza and surrounded by far smaller structures. Scheduled for 1970 is John Portman & Associates' Embarcadero Center in San Francisco, which is composed of a series of thin slab towers of various heights, set in an irregularly shaped green belt studded with low units.

For a prediction of things to come, one has but to look at Battery Park City being planned for a site of 118 acres in New York by Harrison & Abramovitz, Philip Johnson & John Burgee, and Conklin & Rossant. The present scheme, scheduled for completion about 1980, will include shops, office towers, and apartments in a unified design estimated to cost $1 billion.

The breakdown included $300 million for office and commercial structures, $500 million for housing, and $250 million for highway construction, land fill, civic facilities, planning, and administration.

Less spectacular, but a part of Phase VII, is the kind of solution, represented by Lever House, where a more limited site is involved, often of block size or less. What relates these projects to Rockefeller Center is the interest in creating an attractive environment by a limited development of space rights and the introduction of fountains, shrubs, trees and flowers in the resulting open areas. This category would include the Seagram Building, of 1956–57, by Mies van der Rohe and Philip Johnson, with plaza and reflecting pools. It would also include Pittsburgh's U.S. Steel Corporation Building, of 1967, by Harrison, Abramovitz & Abbe, which features a triangular tower on stilts set on a terrace flanked by shrubs and a pool, and Skidmore, Owings & Merrill's Hartford Plaza, completed in 1967 in San Francisco.

In summary then, what is being suggested here is a new approach to skyscraper history. Though still in a tentative stage and subject to revision and refinement by further study, it is worth consideration, because it offers an explanation to a number of controversial subjects. For example, it provides a view of skyscraper evolution from its conception to the present and even into the immediate future. This is not possible with a purely technological approach. Advances in technology can, in large part, explain the growing height of the skyscraper up to about 1900, when the skeleton frame was widely accepted, but it cannot account for the dramatic changes that took place afterwards. New construction methods, such as bolted, riveted, then welded frames had virtually no effect on sky-

scraper appearance. Faster, smoother, and, finally, automatic elevators improved service but did not influence form. The electric light, better plumbing, more dependable heating systems and the telephone made life more comfortable and business easier to conduct, but these had virtually no effect on the shape of the structure.

It is interesting to note that in the case of air-conditioning and fluorescent lighting, where one could have expected a change in building form, at least in the cladding of the structure, we do not find this to be the case to any great extent. Rather than encase the building in an opaque curtain to prevent the cool air from escaping to the outside and to control light, many architects and clients appear willing to suffer the resulting expense of leakage in favor of glass for the sake of appearance and the psychological effect upon employees. Even the substitution of reinforced concrete for steel in Cincinnati's Ingalls Building by Elzner & Anderson, of 1902–4, produced no appreciable change. The first major change brought on by a new material and structural system was in the Price Tower by Frank Lloyd Wright, where reinforced concrete and a core system of cantilevering made possible a more flexible ordering of the floor spaces and an exterior that broke away from the square or rectangular box. But this still leaves fifty years, or half of the skyscraper's history, unaccounted for.

Nor does the technological approach shed any light on why the Home Life Insurance Company Building (*see Fig. 3-12*), which had a skeleton frame, for all practical purposes, looked so much like E. L. Roberts's Standard Oil Building in New York, of the same date, which did not have skeleton construction. The resemblance springs from the fact that both structures were designed in the same man-

3-49. West Street Building. New York City.
1906–7. Cass Gilbert.

ner, despite the difference in their construction system.

A history of the skyscraper based on style is no more helpful and can be extremely confusing. Many scholars believe it incorrect to use the word "style" in connection with the use of historical architectural revivals. They prefer the term "mode" or "manner," because forms were borrowed from the past and had no deep organic associations with the modern era.

To talk about the Greek, Roman, or Egyptian revival as it relates to the skyscraper makes little sense, although one may see occasionally a temple or pyramid terminating such a structure. The "French Empire" mode was quickly dispensed with during the early days of the tall business building, as was the "Queen Anne." The "Richardsonian Romanesque" was practiced for only a few years during the last half of the nineteenth century, because it proved so burdensome, although it did seem suitable for the tower phase (V). The "Chinese" and "Saracenic" revivals apparently played no part in skyscraper evolution. The only historical formula to lend itself with some success as a solution to the design problems presented by the growing skyscraper was the Gothic.

By the 1920's a skyscraper style seemed to have evolved. It appears to have been an amalgam of the early efforts to create a vertical system contributed to by the Jayne Building (*see Fig. 3-19*), the Wainwright and Guaranty buildings, the Woolworth Building and such others by Cass Gilbert as the West Street Building (*Fig. 3-49*) and the New York Life Insurance Building, with a simple system that lined up the windows perpendicularly by means of a slight recession from the wall plane or by the use of a specific material or color. Good examples are the American Insurance Union Citadel, the Chanin Building, and Rockefeller Center (*see Fig. 3-48*).

The vast majority of these buildings in this period display no evidences of the revival modes and are an obvious prelude to the emphatic verticalism of many present-day skyscrapers, such as the CBS Building in New York and the First National Bank in Chicago.

From a stylistic point of view, then, the history of the skyscraper appears to consist thus far of two periods: one composed primarily of historically inspired structures erected prior to World War I; and a second group of buildings, largely of post-World War I vintage, that are characterized by their vertical articulation. The objection to such an approach is that, while the selection of a revival mode certainly reflects the taste of its time and the vertically accented trend was suggested by the fact that the building was essentially tall rather than long, in neither case are the deeper forces within American culture taken into account. The surface treatment of the later period mirrors neither the steel or reinforced-concrete frame nor the economic, sociological, or municipal factors involved in the project.

One other view to skyscraper history that suggests itself is a method based on "schools" or regional difference. This system has been used in connection with Romanesque architecture in Italy and France. There has been much written about a "Chicago School" and a "New York School." There has even been reference to three "Chicago" schools dating from the 1870's to the present. While there is good reason to argue in favor of a regional system based on differences that did exist between various geographical areas in the mid-nineteenth century, such as Boston, New York, and Philadelphia, these differences were no longer noticeable by 1890, when much the same formula was being used widely throughout the East and Middle West. By the turn of the century, Montgomery Schuyler was lamenting the uniformity, and Louis Sullivan was predicting that the classical style of the World's Fair of 1893 would dominate skyscraper design for the next half century.

The rejection of a historical concept founded primarily on technology, style, or school leaves little else to choose from, unless it be a chronological account dealing with the skyscraper's development year by year. While this probably would be desirable in the future, it is doubtful whether it could be done at present, when we are still unable to see the basic patterns, their variations, and the reasons and dates of their appearances. By 1900, so many kinds of skyscrapers were being erected that it was difficult to distinguish the trees, so dense was the forest. Often the lag between what was happening in the East and West made matters more confusing, chronologically considered.

The advantage of the system suggested here is that it not only takes into account the other approaches just discussed, but it also transforms the broad and deep cultural factors in American life into architectural terms. It establishes within each phase or category the criterion that would permit an understanding of the significant structures within each category. Thus, the Washington Building, though erected after Phase III got under way, is really a late example of Phase II, because of its colossal mansard, numerous dormers, oriels, and other features which belong to the French mansard mode (*Fig. 3-50*). This is to be expected when it is remembered that Kendall helped design the Equitable Life Assurance Building of 1868–70 (*see Fig. 3-6*).

It also helps us understand the historical and aesthetic significance of the Wainwright Building. This structure should not be evaluated in a general way as "one of

3-50. Washington Building. New York City. 1882–85. Edward Kendall.

the ten best skyscrapers in the world." It should not be made to compete with tower forms or multiblock solutions, because it is different in nature, having been created in different times and under different conditions. What makes the Wainwright important is that it is the finest solution to the problem facing architects during the 1880's, or during Phase III. Once Sullivan's statement was made, the "grouped-story" formula was outmoded.

It not only helped establish the solution for Phase IV but was one of its best examples. The Guaranty Building of 1894–95 was but a taller version of the Wainwright and led logically to the tower form of Phase V. In many ways, the Guaranty was superior to Bruce Price's American Surety Building, being less fussy and more sure and clear in its intentions.

Similarly, Sullivan's Odd Fellows' Temple project (*see Fig. 3-40*) takes on new meaning when seen in the historical context recommended here. Sullivan's scheme was not unusual from a stylistic or technological point of view. But as a concept suggesting a solution for architectural problems of the future, it was brilliant. It pointed a way around the economically hazardous isolated towers being considered in its day and proposed a viable design that took into account the financial, functional, expressive and aesthetic needs of the time. It was the forerunner of the Woolworth and other great towers. With its major tower and subordinate elements, its large site and limited development, it contained the seed for Rockefeller Center.

Finally, such a historical method will help determine the key monuments and architects. A tentative selective list, subject to revision, would include:

Phase I—the Jayne Building (Philadelphia), by William L. Johnston; the James Bogardus Harper Brothers Building (New York); and the Haughwout Store and elevator (New York), by John P. Gaynor and Elisha Otis.

Phase II—the Equitable Life Assurance Building (New York), by Gilman & Kendall and George B. Post; the Western Union Building (New York), by George B. Post; the Tribune Building (New York), by Richard Morris Hunt; and the Evening Post Building (New York), by Charles F. Mengelson.

Phase III—the Mills Building (New York), by George B. Post; the Produce Exchange (New York), by George B. Post; the Home Life Insurance Company Building (Chicago), by William Le Baron Jenney; The Rookery (Chicago), by Burnham & Root; the Tacoma Building (Chicago), by Holabird & Roche; the Marshall Field Ware-

house (Chicago), by H. H. Richardson; and the Chamber of Commerce Building (Chicago), by Baumann & Huehl.

Phase IV—the Union Trust Building (New York), by George B. Post; the Wainwright Building (St. Louis), by Adler & Sullivan; the Havemeyer Building (New York), by George B. Post; Washington Life Building (New York), by Cyrus L. W. Eidlitz; the Broadway-Chambers Building (New York), by Cass Gilbert; and the Flatiron Building (New York), by Daniel H. Burnham & Company.

Phase V—the Guaranty Building (Buffalo), by Adler & Sullivan; the American Surety Building (New York), by Bruce Price; the Singer Building (New York), by Ernest Flagg; the Metropolitan Tower (New York), by Napoleon Le Brun & Sons; the Woolworth Building (New York), by Cass Gilbert; the Empire State Building (New York), by Shreve, Lamb & Harmon; and the CBS Building (New York), by Eero Saarinen & Associates.

Phase VI—the Daily News Building (New York), by Howells & Hood; the Indemnity Building (New York), by Buchman & Kahn; the Chanin Building (New York), by Sloan & Robertson; and the Lincoln Building (New York), by J. E. Carpenter & Associates.

Phase VII—Rockefeller Center (New York), by Reinhard & Hofmeister, Hood, Godley & Fouilhoux, and Corbett, Harrison & MacMurray; the World Trade Center (New York), by Yamasaki & Associates and Emery Roth & Sons; the Embarcadero Center (San Francisco), by John Portman & Associates; Lever House (New York), by Skidmore, Owings & Merrill; and the Seagram Building (New York), by Mies van der Rohe and Philip Johnson.

Appendix to Chapter 3:
Supplementary List of Buildings[*]

American Insurance Union Citadel. Columbus, Ohio. 1926–27. Howard Crane.

Bankers' Trust Building. New York City. 1910–12. Trowbridge & Livingston.

CBS Building. New York City. 1962–64. Eero Saarinen & Associates.

Chanin Building. New York City. 1928–29. Sloan & Robertson.

Chicago Opera House. Chicago. 1884–85. Cobb & Frost. *Demolished.*

Chrysler Building. New York City. 1929–32. William Van Alen.

Daily News Building. New York City. 1929–30. Howells & Hood.

Eaton Tower. Detroit. 1927. Louis Kamper, Inc.

Empire State Building. New York City. 1930–31. Shreve, Lamb & Harmon.

Evening Post Building. New York City. 1874. Charles F. Mengelson. *Demolished.*

Fifth Avenue Hotel. New York City. 1856–59. Griffith Thomas and William Washburn. *Demolished.*

First National Bank. Chicago. 1967–69. C. F. Murphy Associates and Will & Perkins Partnership.

Fisk Rubber Company Building. New York City. 1918–19. Carrère & Hastings and Shreve & Lamb. *Demolished.*

Flatiron Building. New York City. 1901–3. Daniel H. Burnham & Company.

Guaranty Building. Buffalo, New York. 1894–95. Adler & Sullivan.

Hartford Plaza. San Francisco. 1967. Skidmore, Owings & Merrill.

Herald Building. New York City. 1866. John Kellum. *Demolished.*

Hudson Terminal Buildings. New York City. 1898–1909. Clinton & Russell. *Altered.*

Indemnity Building. New York City. 1927–28. Buchman & Kahn.

Ingalls Building. Cincinnati, Ohio. 1902–4. Elzner & Anderson.

Lever House. New York City. 1950–52. Skidmore, Owings & Merrill.

Lincoln Building. New York City. 1928–29. J. E. Carpenter & Associates.

Marshall Field Warehouse. Chicago. 1885–87. Henry Hobson Richardson. *Demolished.*

National Park Bank. New York City. 1866–68. Griffith Thomas. *Altered.*

New York Life Insurance Building. New York City. 1926–28. Cass Gilbert.

New York Life Insurance Company Building. Chicago. 1894. Jenney & Mundie. *Demolished.*

Paramount Building. New York City. 1924–26. C. W. & G. L. Rapp.

Price Tower. Bartlesville, Oklahoma. 1953–56. Frank Lloyd Wright.

Schiller Building. Chicago. 1891–92. Adler & Sullivan. *Demolished.*

Seagram Building. New York City. 1956–57. Mies van der Rohe and Philip Johnson.

Standard Oil Building. New York City. 1884–85. E. L. Roberts. *Enlarged.*

Tacoma Building. Chicago. 1888–89. Holabird & Roche. *Demolished.*

Tribune Tower. Chicago. 1923–25. Howells & Hood.

U. S. Steel Corporation Building. Pittsburgh. 1967. Harrison, Abramovitz & Abbe.

Wainwright Building. St. Louis. 1890. Adler & Sullivan.

[*]Data for other buildings discussed by Professor Weisman will be found in the list of illustrations.

Selected Bibliography

BIRKMIRE, WILLIAM H. *Skeleton Construction in Buildings.* New York: John Wils and Sons, 1894.

CONDIT, CARL W. *American Building Art: The Nineteenth Century.* New York: Oxford University Press, 1960.

————. *The Chicago School of Architecture: A History of Commercial and Public Building in the Chicago Area, 1875–1925.* Chicago: University of Chicago Press, 1964.

DAMRELL, CHARLES S. *A Half Century of Boston's Building.* Boston: Louis P. Hager, 1895.

FERRY, W. HAWKINS. *The Buildings of Detroit.* Detroit, Mich.: Wayne State University Press, 1968.

GIFFORD, DON. *The Literature of Architecture: The Evolution of Architectural Theory and Practice in Nineteenth Century America.* New York: E. P. Dutton, 1966.

A History of Real Estate, Building and Architecture in New York City. New York: Arno Press, 1967.

History of Architecture and the Building Trades of Greater New York. 2 vols. New York: The Union Historical Company, 1899.

HITCHCOCK, HENRY-RUSSELL. *Architecture: Nineteenth and Twentieth Centuries.* Harmondsworth and Baltimore: Penguin Books, 1958. 3d ed. [Harmondsworth] © 1968.

MORRISON, HUGH. *Louis Sullivan, Prophet of Modern Architecture.* New York: W. W. Norton, 1935.

MUJICA, FRANCISCO. *History of the Skyscraper.* New York: Archaeology and Architecture Press, 1930.

RANDALL, FRANK A. *History of the Development of Building Construction in Chicago.* Urbana: University of Illinois Press, 1949.

SCHUYLER, MONTGOMERY. *American Architecture and Other Writings.* William H. Jordy and Ralph Coe, eds. 2 vols. Cambridge, Mass.: Harvard University Press, 1961.

TALLMADGE, THOMAS E. *Architecture in Old Chicago.* Chicago: University of Chicago Press, 1941.

TORBERT, DONALD R. *Significant Architecture in the History of Minneapolis.* Minneapolis, Minn.: City Planning Department, 1969.

American Houses: Thomas Jefferson to Frank Lloyd Wright

4

American Houses: Thomas Jefferson to Frank Lloyd Wright[1]

Vincent Scully

Twenty years ago, the historian who wanted to write about nineteenth-century houses had to confront two prejudices. One of them regarded domestic architecture as too insignificant a topic for art-historical investigation; the other reflected a widespread aversion to the forms of nineteenth-century "Victorian" architecture as a whole. The scholar working in that field, therefore, tended toward various apologetics and polemics of a kind that is entirely unnecessary today. Prejudice against the nineteenth century has almost entirely disappeared among responsible critics—though shockingly ill-informed books (and ignorant reviews) still occasionally wander into sight like leftovers from the Mesozoic. Yet the apologetic instinct lingers, because the other prejudice, that against domestic architecture as a topic, I now find, at least in my own case, not so much to have disappeared as to have turned itself right around. The single-family houses that are most historically significant throughout the period, and upon which I worked more than twenty years ago, now seem not too common but somewhat too esoteric to be studied without apology at the present moment in history. One cannot help but see them today as in some measure the products of a blindly complacent and unduly favored minority able to live out a

suburban dream of permissive peace on the spoils of a ravaged continent and the subjugation of other peoples. Such would not necessarily vitiate their artistic quality, but it might cast doubt upon their historical relevance when studied by themselves. Should we not rather be studying the nineteenth-century city as a whole, in all its urbanistic complication, its tenements, social mixtures, gas houses, trolley lines, and colonial dependencies?

The answer, if there is one, has to be that we must study both at once, largely because architecture is at least two different related but separable things. It is at once the entire manmade environment in itself and in relation to the natural world, and also a special corpus of humanistic achievements embodied in physical form. In consequence, its study may be either social history or intellectual history, its method behavioral or aesthetic. But because architecture is both polarities together, no study of it can or ought to be methodologically pure (except in the purity of a commitment to experience), though it can and will lean one way or the other. I believe that the architectural research of this moment in time should especially strive toward the physical perception of the environment entire. We have in the past studied too few of the elements that go to make up our constructed world;

we must cast our nets wider in the future. But this should not preclude some concentration upon specific building types. Such is especially relevant here, because two of those types, the center-city office building and the suburban house, were the major vehicles of America's architectural invention during the nineteenth century. In this way, they most markedly changed large segments of the environment in which people lived and, at the same time, embodied some of the liveliest strains of American feeling in directly symbolic terms.

Both of them leaped toward freedom. There are no other words by which the case can be stated so clearly. The nineteenth-century office building leaped for height, "skyscraper," casting off the trammels of older programs, divesting itself of weight like an athlete in training. The house, conversely, stretched out to cover the ground, bursting through partitions inside, extending porches outside. The boxy, thin-skinned Colonial tradition was burst apart, to be returned to, in "modern" and "traditional" architecture alike, only when the more peculiarly inventive nineteenth-century movement had spent its force. It was a leap for freedom in every way, and its great years were those of the Republic from its inception until something went wrong with it about the time of World War I. Middle-class and fundamentally reasonable, with that kind of gentle romanticism which is one of the most sympathetic products of a protected life, the movement lasted until reason and gentleness began to go out of the world. When the freedom which the Republic had promised began to seem less attractive than security and conformism— or rather, when the middle class which had invented that freedom was willing to forget that it had done so—then the domestic program was in a sense divested of

its magical aspirations, and the true skimpiness of the environment as a whole showed threadbare through. Put another way, the child was born of Revolution and died of—what? Imperialism? Certainly, its life stretched from Thomas Jefferson, who imagined the first, to Frank Lloyd Wright, who despised the second. Or perhaps the whole movement only marked the necessarily temporary ferment which arose in the transition from a small-scale agrarian world to a choked urban one; it died just about the moment when the transition was largely complete.

Hence the proper century for this study is one which ends about 1915. In one sense, it may not wholly have gotten under way until about 1840, with Jefferson, in architecture at least, coming somewhat before his time, as prophets do. His early plans for Monticello, of about 1770, go perfectly together with house plans of 1885 by Bruce Price and those of 1902 by Frank Lloyd Wright (*Figs. 4-1 and 4-2*). I pointed this out long ago, but should say a fresh word here. Each architect set himself the same problem, which was: how to break out of the box. Freedom from ancient constraints is the common theme. Jefferson took the merest hint of such from English sources, and, where the relevant English plan shows only a slight projection of the center block, Jefferson's first scheme already proposes a crossing of two dynamic spatial directions, an intersection of two roads in space. The plans by Price are much the same. But in Jefferson's succeeding studies the axes are extended further. The confines of the box are denied and extended by the projection of polygons beyond the corners; the axes are trying to break free. In Wright, they finally do so. An archaeologist of some later age, with only these ghosts to go on, might be led to believe that they revealed a century which was wholly single-minded

4-1. Monticello. Charlottesville, Virginia. 1770–1809. Thomas Jefferson.

in its speculation upon a single theme. That was clearly not the case; the century was characterized, much more than ours, by its hectic diversity. All the more striking, therefore, that the theme was there at all: persistent from beginning to end, marking the beginning no less than celebrating the climax and heralding the close. Everything else happened in those 100 or so years: mass industrialism and democracy, creating slums, racism, genocide and war, a world won, a civilization lost. But the single theme of freedom, of leaping to freedom, lived through it; however compromised or abstracted, it never died.

Equally large, though less obvious, is the point of the completed Monticello as a whole. It is about a man owning the earth (*see Fig. 4-1*). The house caps the conical hill, controls it, like a hero's tomb. That again was what the century to come was to be about: how to control nature, how to own it. There was also the consistent Romantic convention of love for nature, perhaps real love for it, but the clearly directive instinct was toward ownership, embodied in the single-family house on its plot of land. That land is *owned;* there are few English complications of ninety-nine-year leases and so on, reflecting older systems of communal control and somehow respecting the eternal autonomy of the earth. The American land is possessed, and is soon worn out with possession. Across the continent, it

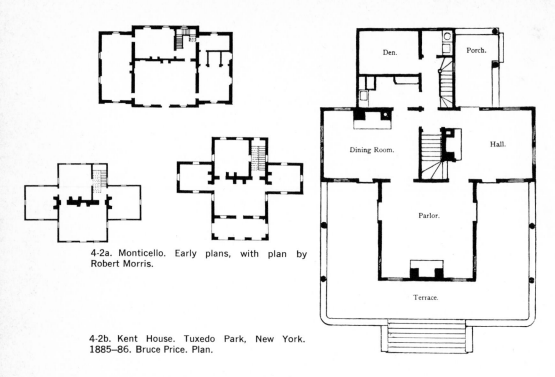

4-2a. Monticello. Early plans, with plan by Robert Morris.

Den.		Porch.

Dining Room.   Hall.

Parlor.

Terrace.

4-2b. Kent House. Tuxedo Park, New York. 1885–86. Bruce Price. Plan.

4-2c. Monticello. Plan with porches and bays.

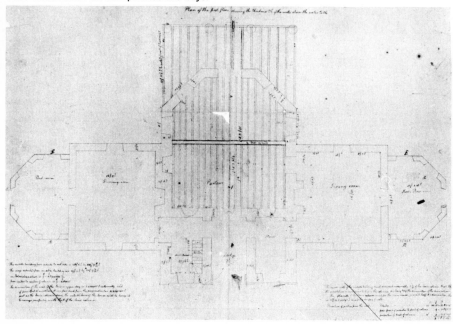

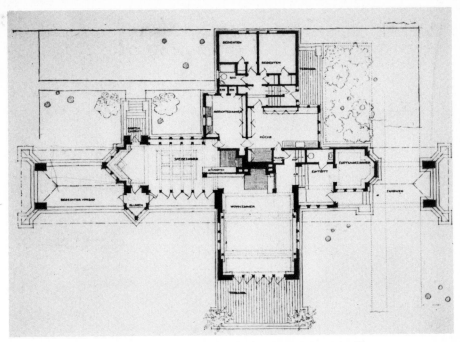

4-2d. Ward Willitts House. Highland Park, Illinois. 1902. Frank Lloyd Wright. Plan.

4-2e. Monticello. Final plan.

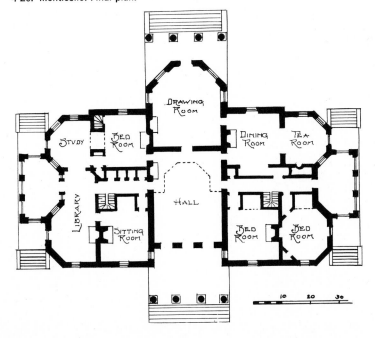

4-3. David Sears House (Somerset Club). Boston. Ca. 1816. Alexander Parris. As enlarged for Somerset Club.

was to be raped to death generation by generation. Monticello still woos it, but grasps it all.

The completed Monticello shows a contradiction: Its instinct toward diversity in plan is countered by a determination to achieve monumental scale by means of the columned portico and the dome (*see Figs. 4-1 and 4-2 e*). It would seem that Jefferson was perfectly aware of this. He was determined to create an architecture at once freer and more massively permanent than any the Colonial period had been able to bring about. And these two complementary drives were also to share the nineteenth century between them. So Jefferson's variety of room shapes, in part derived by him from English Palladian precedent, and in part suggestive of Robert Adams's contemporary work, found their successors quite soon in the Federal house architecture of Samuel

McIntire and others. The Sears House, in Boston, of about 1816, is already sterner and more dramatic than they (*Fig. 4-3*). It employs a great Regency bay to extend the interior space. In the original design, that single bay was a hugely scaled feature, dominating the exterior massing and seeming to override all sense of row-house civility in order to dominate the street. Indeed, the row houses around it may be taken as representative of the kind of urbane deference to other beings and to the city environment as a whole that was to become exceedingly rare in America, while the Sears House, though urban enough itself, is at least indicative of the kind of individual assertion that was to help break up the order of towns and to find its natural field for invention in the suburbs. Inside, too, during the Greek Revival of the next decades, the details tended to become larger; spaces

168

4-4. Hillhouse House. New Haven. 1835. Town & Davis.

opened up and were punctuated by screens of substantially scaled columns.

In the great Greek Revival country houses, that monumental determination found its outlet in the peripteral colonnade. Nicholas Biddle's "Andalusia," by Thomas U. Walter, makes the point. It was an old house. Biddle turned it into a temple by enclosing it on three sides within a massive Doric colonnade, which was more or less closely derived from that of the Hephaisteion in Athens. The Jeffersonian portico now engulfs the house. Though the forms tend toward the drynes of their model, still the pressure they exert on the land is greater than had been characteristic of American architecture before. The Colonial experience is transformed into a statement of permanent presence. One recalls the House of Augustus on the Palatine; it was voted a gable by the Senate, which intended by this gesture a delicate allusion to the semidivinity of its most distinguished colleague. At "Andalusia," a nineteenth-century banker gives himself the whole works, pediment, columns, and all. Streets of such houses do indeed take on a kind of divine radiance. The trees of the American East are everywhere, a sacred grove. The houses stand among them, gleaming white like Greek temples for the most part but by the 1830's often turning a soft brown (see Fig. 4-4). It was an idyllic world. Even the mills at Lowell were dignified rather than stupendous and their housing proper rather than sordid or nonexistent. The Industrial Revolution was only beginning, and the demographic explosion had not yet occurred.

Hillhouse Avenue in New Haven was one of the loveliest of such streets. It was a noble northward extension out of New Haven's original Colonial grid. The Hill-

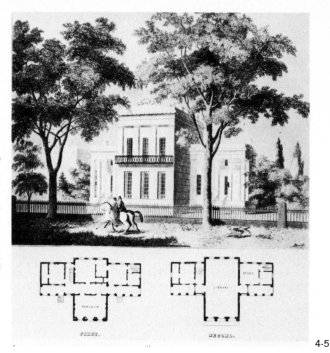

4-5. Ithiel Town House. New Haven. 1830. Town & Davis. Perspective drawing and plans.

4-6. Edward King House. Newport, Rhode Island. 1845–47. Richard Upjohn.

4-7. "Kingscote." Newport, Rhode Island. 1841. Richard Upjohn.

house mansion stood on its axis (*Fig. 4-4*). One of the houses that lined it, designed by Town & Davis for Ithiel Town himself, had a cross-axial plan, like some of Jefferson's early studies (*Fig. 4-5*). But the instinct for freedom was already taking a new turn, of which the Norton House on that avenue is an excellent example. It was directly modeled upon a design published by Andrew Jackson Downing in his book *Cottage Residences,* of 1842. Downing was the first and remained the most influential American descendant of the English picturesque landscape gardeners, who had been promoting the cult of natural beauty for almost a century by this time. Downing's books held the Greek Revival up to derision and proposed a domestic architecture that would be asymmetrical in plan, varied in massing, and subdued in tone. It was thus intended to blend with, rather than to stand out

against, nature's forms, and to provide an interior environment of maximum variety as well. The various types of houses that Downing proposed, whether "Gothic," "Italian villa," or whatever, all served these objectives and may reasonably be regarded as forming the vocabulary of a single "picturesque-eclectic" style. The Norton House is an Italian villa, as is the King House in Newport (*Fig. 4-6*), while "Kingscote" in that town is a Gothic cottage by the same architect. (*Fig. 4-7*). There are differences in proportion and in profile, but the asymmetrical composition is much the same in both. The Gothic cottage is gentler and opens out to porches; the Italian villa is more gruff. But the cubical blocks and the columned façades of the Greek Revival are breaking up into articulated masses in each of them. Downing and his successors, such as the great landscape architect Frederick

170

4-6

4-7

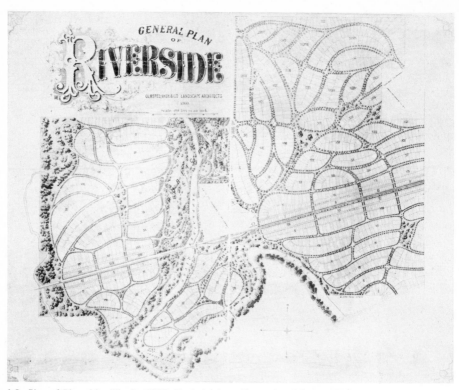

4-8. Plan of Riverside, Illinois. 1869. Frederick Law Olmsted and Calvert Vaux.

4-9. "Small Bracketted Cottage." Andrew Jackson Downing. Drawing, published 1850.

4-10. "Bracketted Veranda from the Inside." Andrew Jackson Downing. Drawing, published 1853.

Law Olmsted, soon proposed irregular and curvilinear plans for parks and suburbs (*Fig. 4-8*) which were intended as the appropriate larger environment for such houses and which remain to this day the major complement to the American grid plan for towns.

But Downing was interested in other qualities as well. He came to prefer houses built of wood, with light, open porches, as most appropriate to American materials and conditions; and, like the Gothic Revivalists who were redirecting the Picturesque movement in England toward more structural and ethical considerations, he was determined that the nature of the material should be expressed in the design (*Figs. 4-9 and 4-10*). So he renounced horizontal clapboards in favor of vertical board-and-batten sheathing, which he felt to be most properly expressive of the vertical studs of the wooden frame. That visual preference coincided with the structural development of the balloon frame in America, wherein the studs were vertically continuous from sill to rafters, with the plates of the intermediate floor levels nailed to their backs. This visual and structural coincidence produced that domestic architecture which I once named the "Stick Style." It proliferated all over the country, from the resorts of Rhode Island to the mining camps of California. A company town like Madrid, New Mexico, shows the persistence of the type to a much later date (*Fig. 4-11*). It produced not only cottages but also a real vernacular of one- two- and three-family houses in the cities as in the suburbs. It thus succeeded to the Colonial tradition but cast the old closed skin aside.

The Stick Style was a builder's architecture even more than an architect's. Its development was most dramatically carried by pattern books for house building, of which Downing's remained the most important. In them, such writers as Gervase Wheeler emphasized the English Gothic Revival view that an ethical recognition of

4-11. Boarding house. Madrid, New Mexico. Date uncertain.

4-12. J. N. A. Griswold House. Newport, Rhode Island. 1862. Richard Morris Hunt.

4-13. Sturtevant House. Middletown, Rhode Island. 1872. Dudley Newton.

4-14. "Olana" (Frederic Church House). Hudson, New York. 1870–72, 1888–89. Calvert Vaux.

"reality" demanded an expression of all the elements of the structural frame. Hence, in later phases of the Stick Style, horizontal and diagonal members also appeared and further skeletonized the exteriors of wooden houses into a complex basketry of interwoven sticks (*see Figs. 4-12 and 4-13*). Such coincided as well with French Gothic Revival structural determinism. This positivistic view was best enunciated by Viollet-le-Duc, who enormously influenced American architects and critics during the 1870's and 1880's, and who, Frank Lloyd Wright was to tell us, was almost the only theoretician he could read with approval. A house such as that for J. N. A. Griswold, by Richard Morris Hunt, who had studied at the Ecole des Beaux-Arts in Paris, well shows the syncretic character of the late Stick Style (*Fig. 4-12*). It is medieval half-timber recast in terms of nineteenth-cen-

tury framing techniques and inspired by an increasing desire for spatial freedom. The porches have gotten bigger and their framing is braced by multiple diagonals. The Sturtevant House near Newport is an even stronger example, with sharp, high, "masculine" profiles (*Fig. 4-13*). The interiors of such houses were highly articulated, too, with small halls, individualized room shapes, and a good deal of dark paneling, heavily compartmented and not lacking in diagonal members.

During the mid-century, an alternative to the articulation and skeletonization of the Stick Style was offered by mansarded, often symmetrical types, which were more or less based on contemporary French precedent and so were called "Second Empire." They are more compact and sculpturally plastic than the Stick Style houses, forming a kind of semiclassical counterpoint to the prevailing picturesque

175

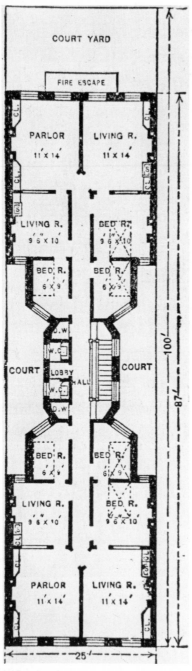

COURT YARD

FIRE ESCAPE

| CL. | | CL. |

PARLOR
11' x 14'

LIVING R.
11' x 14'

LIVING R.
9' 6" x 10'

BED R.
9' 6" x 10'

BED. R.
6' x 9'

BED. R.
6' x 9'

D.W.

W.C.

COURT   LOBBY   COURT
HALL

W.C.

D.W.

BED. R.
6' x 9'

BED. R.
6' x 9'

LIVING R.
9' 6" x 10'

BED. R.
9' 6" x 10'

PARLOR
11' x 14'

LIVING R.
11' x 14'

100'

87'

25'

4-15. "Dumbell" tenement. Design by James E. Ware, 1879. Plan.

mode. Combinations constantly occurred. Frederic Church's famous "Olana," high above the Hudson, is a picturesque "Moorish" villa, massed in actuality like the "Italian villa" type but also making use of high, mansarded roofs (*Fig. 4-14*). The decorative paneling of the exterior is typical of the period's tendency to skeletonize surfaces even when the material employed is brick or masonry. But "Olana" is more than a synthesis of several modes of design. It rises above the Hudson as an archetypal image of that desire for sovereignty over the earth, for command of space, which was the essence of the century's yearning. Church himself wanted to possess all creation, and did his best to do so by traveling all over the globe to paint vast landscape scenes on canvases of enormous size. He regarded his house as the center of the world—with the whole great sphere curving off below it.

That chance to enjoy the freedom of natural space was probably open to more people during the second half of the nineteenth century than had ever been the case throughout the history of mankind. At the same time, the opportunity to experience a moderate amount of freedom in nature was being withheld from more people than ever before. The famous "dumbbell" tenement plan of the 1870's should be seen as "Olana's" natural polarity (*Fig. 4-15*). Imprisoned in its airless darkness, the proletarianized inmate was also imbedded in a vast urban spread, bigger and thus harder to get out of than had been normal in previous centuries though the marvellous spread of urban and interurban trolley lines was to ameliorate that condition for a while. The world was getting bigger during the 1870's, perhaps bigger than one liked. Those free to choose especially thought so. They began to travel to old Colonial

4-16. Fairbanks House. Dedham, Massachusetts. 1636, with eighteenth-century additions.

4-17. "Redwood" (C. J. Morrill House). Mount Desert, Maine. 1879. William Ralph Emerson. Exterior and plan.

4-18. "Kragsyde" (G. N. Black House). Manchester-by-the-Sea, Massachusetts. 1882–84. Peabody & Stearns. With plans and sketches by E. Eldon Deane.

towns like Marblehead, Newburyport, Nantucket, Edgartown, and, always, Newport, to escape from an environment grown "too large." There they found Colonial houses, mellowed in place as nothing else in America seemed to be. The nostalgia aroused by the Philadelphia Centennial Exhibition of 1876 encouraged the revival, and the photograph of the Colonial Fairbanks House, in Dedham, Massachusetts, which was published in 1881, shows the kind of Colonial architecture the revivalist generation especially admired (*Fig. 4-16*). Out of it, and some English sources as well, the "Shingle

Style" came into being. Surely the first example of it, in this case owing more to English than to American precedent, was Henry Hobson Richardson's Watts Sherman House, at Newport, of 1874; but a house like that at Mount Desert, of 1879, by William Ralph Emerson (*Fig. 4-17*), shows the amalgam complete.[2] Now the freedom in plan is amazing, with several levels of space intersecting around a spacious living hall that is monumentalized by a fireplace and lighted by a wall of windows. Shingles enclose most of the surface, making a shaggy but continuous container for the flowing and continuous

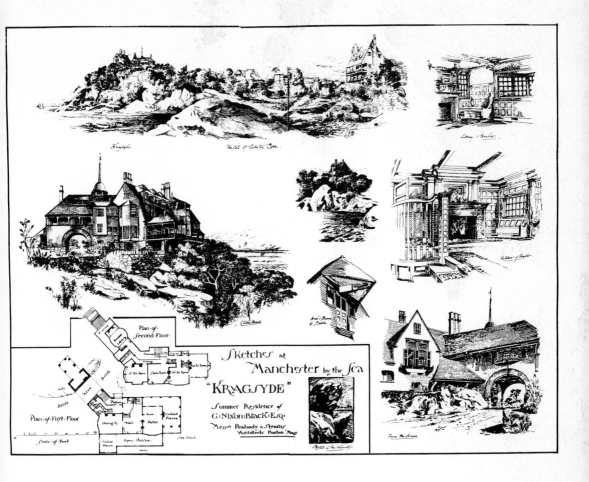

Sketches at Manchester by the Sea

"KRAGSYDE"

Summer Residence of G. Nixon Black Esq.

Mess. Peabody & Stearns Architects Burton Mass.

space inside. "Shingleside," at Swampscott, Massachusetts, by Arthur Little, shows how an early eighteenth-century salt-box type might be blown up in scale, projected by bays, penetrated by the voids of porches, and opened up by a two-storied living hall with its wall of glass (*see Fig. 1-28*). "Shingleside" was published in England in 1882, and I have always felt that it must have had some effect on such architects as C. F. A. Voysey, but the English have consistently denied the connection.

Or again, the G. N. Black House at Manchester-by-the-Sea, Massachusetts, by Peabody & Stearns (Robert Swain Peabody and John Goddard Stearns), shows how architects might put everything together—the Fairbanks House, "Shingleside," and Richardson's Ames Gate House at North Easton, Massachusetts—and come up with a big, ballooning shingle shell that creates a varied interior landscape of room spaces widely open to each other and giving out to Japanese-screened pavilions of porches from which the whole exterior landscape can be viewed (*Fig. 4-18*). A sense of freedom and a desire for the "accommodation" of all varieties of experience release each shape

179

4-19. Victor Newcomb House. Elberon, New Jersey. 1880—81. McKim, Mead & White. Living hall.

4-20. "Kingscote." Dining room added by Stanford White, 1880—81.

to act out its own environment-making potential to the utmost. The general effect is warm, maternal, and protective. Contemporary sketches tell us how such houses were experienced, inside and out, from inglenook, staircase, and sea (*see Fig. 4-18*). Everything runs together; continuity of spatial flow is everywhere desired. That flow is directed from room to room by means of interwoven moldings and screens, which derive from Japanese methods of framing room volumes (*Figs. 4-19 and 4-20*). A Japanese building, well published, had rivaled the popular "Colonial Kitchen" at the Philadelphia Centennial of 1876. Through this system, it is as if the porch itself penetrates the house and reshapes the interior into its own open and interwoven image. How quickly architects in the 1880's developed and refined the method can be seen in three buildings that were designed in rapid succession by the fine young firm of McKim, Mead & White (Charles Follen McKim,

William Rutherford Mead, and Stanford White): the Newport Casino, of 1879–81, the Victor Newcomb House, of 1880–81, and the new dining room in "Kingscote," of the same years. Cubic, static shapings of volume by closed planes with windowed voids have given way to a fluid and kinetic interweaving of horizontally continuous moldings and pierced, in-filling screens.

That instinct toward the interpenetration of elements and for horizontal continuity is crossed by another strong trend during the early 1880's: one toward simple geometric order and single large shapes. Architects like John Calvin Stevens of Portland, Maine, and Wilson Eyre of Philadelphia stretched their houses out laterally in order to unify their spaces and masses along one continuous axis with horizontal window bands (*Figs. 4-21 and 4-22*). Gables and gambrels were stretched to engulf the voids of porches. McKim, Mead & White's Cyrus

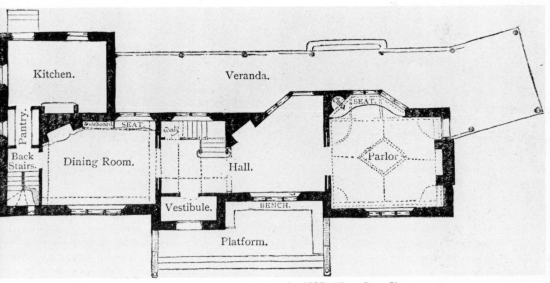

4-21. Charles A. Potter House. Chestnut Hill, Pennsylvania. 1885. Wilson Eyre. Plan.

4-22. C. A. Brown House. Delano Park, near Portland, Maine. 1885–86. John Calvin Stevens.

4-23. Cyrus McCormick House. Richfield Springs, New York. 1880–81. McKim, Mead & White.

McCormick House, for example, employs a stretched gable with horizontally continuous planes that seem to float through it and open it up (*Fig. 4-23*). By the mid-1880's, the movement was toward stricter order and less compromised geometry, as the Low House at Bristol, Rhode Island, of 1887, clearly shows. It was with exactly this kind of design that Frank Lloyd Wright began his domestic work. His own house at Oak Park, of 1889, as I have

shown all too many times before, was closely based upon gabled houses of this type at Tuxedo Park, designed by Bruce Price.

As the architects of the mid-1880's moved toward geometric simplicity and order, it is no wonder that they began to be drawn toward Colonial architecture in its Provincial-Baroque, eighteenth-century aspects, rather than toward, as before, its more medieval, seventeenth-

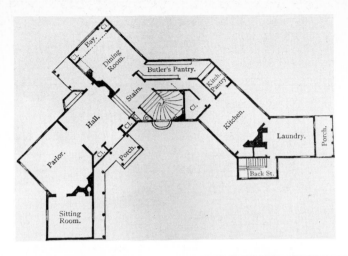

4-24. Misses Appleton House. Lenox, Massachusetts. 1883–84. McKim, Mead & White. Exterior and plan.

century guise. The mellower and usually darker shingles began to be discarded for red or yellow clapboarded surfaces with white-painted Renaissance or Adamesque details. McKim, Mead & White's Appleton House is a beautiful example of an open and inventive set of spaces, controlled by intersecting diagonals, which are housed within thin wooden walls in the new mode, designed like stage flats (*Fig. 4-24*). It was probably White who

consciously, perhaps even ironically, exploited and exaggerated the applied character that such Colonial details had always possessed, tending to look as if they could be sliced off with a razor. One has to await the work of Robert Venturi in the 1960's to find again such expressively melodic groupings of apparently random elements that derive from a common and usually deprecated vernacular condition.

Soon, however, everything tightened

4-25

up. The beautifully dark and compact Villard houses on Madison Avenue, of 1883, were the first masterpieces of that tightening, with their dense, cubical masses and taut Renaissance details. At suburban and more vernacular scale, the H. A. C. Taylor House in Newport, of 1885–86, used a typical eighteenth-century plan, encased in a contained cube of walls (*Fig. 4-25*). In this way the entire colonial system was re-established. The open spaces and the outward-bursting horizontal continuities of the Shingle Style were all discarded. Not freedom but order derived from precedent was now the rule. At the same time, the retraction back into the box was a reasonable way to accommodate millions of houses built together in series, and it was precisely because it offered a solution at once reasonable and precedented that the Colonial "style" became the normal vernacular architecture of the United States right up until World War II. It probably did so successfully because the freedom and individuality which the mass suburb

was presumed to offer—and which its inhabitants had removed there to find—was really a spurious freedom. The inmates were, in fact, tied to the city and to the whole highly engineered system of commercial services upon which they depended. That may be one of the reasons why the saltboxes and so on of the 1930's and 1940's made generally less distressing suburban groups than the nervously articulated, superficially more free and varied, split-levels and ranches do today. Their pretense of freedom in a program fundamentally unfree is probably what renders their gestures so embarrassingly cramped, jerky, and compromised.

But even as they turned toward precedent and order, the architects and clients of the 1880's made one grandiose attempt to break loose into a new scale: that of the millionaire. In his vast "Biltmore," Richard Morris Hunt set out to build a house for George Vanderbilt at the scale of the mountain chain in which it was so grandly set (*Fig. 4-26*). Indeed, "the mountains are in scale with the house,"

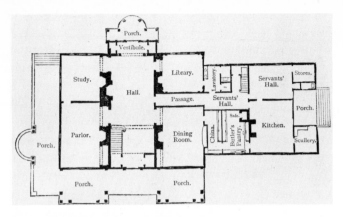

4-25. H. A. C. Taylor House. Newport, Rhode Island. 1885—86. McKim, Mead & White. Exterior and plan.

4-26. "Biltmore." Asheville, North Carolina. 1895. Richard Morris Hunt.

Hunt eventually wrote. At Newport, he threw up a more than Genoese palazzo for another Vanderbilt, to dominate the sea. Why was this not freedom? In a sense it surely was: free choice, enormous resources. Only potency was lacking. There could be no offspring, no family line, because the palaces and their programs were in fact too unique to produce the freedom *en masse* which, deep at the root, under everything, was the century's true dream, and out of which it had itself been born. There were no Medici any more, clearly no Bayards, only millions of persons. The ultimate power lay there, whether one liked it or not, and since architecture is always based on power, and reflects it, the earlier architects, in working with common materials and more moderate programs had, perhaps unconsciously, recognized its source. Hence, the Stick and Shingle styles were able to produce a new vernacular, and the Colonial reaction involved an old one. The palaces tried to break free of all sense of the vernacular; they hoped to cast off the trammels of the people's architecture entirely. So they stand alone and without issue.

In the early twentieth century, a new vernacular was produced for a while in Chicago. Frank Lloyd Wright made it pretty much by himself. Those who followed him and worked around him, the other members of what they liked to call the Prairie School, were gifted vernacular practitioners of a way of making houses that depended in every essential aspect upon the integral reassessment of function and structure that Wright carried out alone. For other buildings, some of those architects were dependent more on Sullivan than on Wright, who had himself, in house architecture, grown directly out of the Shingle Style, as I noted earlier. He began to practice just at the moment when that style had moved toward

stricter order and was just beginning to turn toward the order of precedent. He, too, tested the possibilities of precedent in his earliest works and based one of his designs directly on McKim, Mead & White's Taylor House. He tried other sources as well—French, Academic, Tudor, Japanese, Turkish, and, later, pre-Columbian—as if he were exhausting all at once the whole range of free eclectic choices that had been exercised by the century just coming to a close.

When he finally began to design on his own, his desire for order had already been distilled into abstracted shapes. The Charnley and Winslow houses both have that quality. The Froebel kindergarten-training of Wright's childhood seems to come through. It leads him to design in abstract blocks, bounded and clean, and he calls upon a long Middle Western tradition of bluff brick construction to endow his forms with permanence and solidity. But the Winslow House, with its fine Roman brick, shows that he wants something else as well. He floats the roof above a band of ornament, seeming in this way to cast it free from the flat, sharply windowed planes of the first floor. In the massive Heller House, of 1897, he repeats the ornament and begins to group the windows within it into horizontal bands (*Fig. 4-27*). In the Husser House, of 1899, he still uses the ornament in the same way but opens it out in the true voids of windows around the corners. The box is breaking open, the roof planes riding free. The beginnings of a cross-axial organization can also be seen articulating and extending the as yet unwieldy masses. The Husser House is a graceless brute of a building and a touching one, no longer a self-satisfied burgher like the Heller House but a hulking lumpen trying to break loose.

But in Wright's River Forest Golf Club,

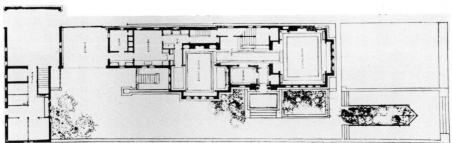

4-27. Isidor Heller House. Chicago. 1897. Frank Lloyd Wright. Exterior and plan.

built of wood frame, a truly suburban summertime suavity takes over (*Fig. 4-29*); one can hear the band in the fire-fly evening and see the Japanese lanterns gleaming on Ernest Hemingway's first brass buttons. The long, low gabled roofs of the golf club ride easily above continuous window bands, and so wholly release the interior spaces as they interpenetrate each other through the liberating cross-axial plan. The horizontal board-and-batten sheathing also insists on the lateral extension, so reversing the emphasis of the old Stick Style on the vertical stud, and, closer in time, denying the over-all surface containment of the Shingle Style (*see Figs. 4-9 and 4-17*). Wright's sheathing is directional. Since we have stepped a little, if not much, outside the suburban domestic program with Wright's Golf Club, we cannot help but contrast at this point Stanford White's

Shingle Style casino, of 1882–83, at Short Hills, New Jersey (*Fig. 4-28*). How ferociously disciplined and uncompromising Wright's design appears by comparison, and how new in its time. Yet White's relaxed accommodations of differences and his ironic ambiguities are much closer to the advanced architectural taste of 1970.

In the Ward Willitts House, of 1902, Wright summed it all up: cross-axial plan around the Colonial fireplace mass (*see Fig. 4-2 d*), interwoven interior spaces, continuous window bands, and intersecting low-hipped roof planes. The stuccoed surface (for which that of Wright's Evans House must stand here), is contained as panels within dark wood stripping that evokes the structural frame and creates an effect eminently Japanese (*see Fig. 4-36*). It has, on the one hand, gotten right away from Europe (Jefferson's col-

4-28. Casino. Short Hills, New Jersey. 1882–83. McKim, Mead & White.

4-29. Golf Club. River Forest, Illinois. 1898–1901. Frank Lloyd Wright. Perspective, 1901.

4-30. Glessner House. Chicago. 1885–87. Henry Hobson Richardson.

umns and dome are gone) and is, on the other hand, wholly integral to and unified in itself (Jefferson's contradictory objectives have also disappeared).

I have written about that sequence of Wright's design so often before that I cannot approach it without apology. But I am convinced that it is the basic sequence through which Wright created an architecture growing directly out of the American past but which must be recognized as wholly new as well. It was a cultural achievement of enormous stature for one man to have pulled off on his own. One would guess that not since Brunelleschi had anything comparable occurred—though Brunelleschi had great sculptors and painters to goad him on, and Wright had none. A comparison between Richardson's fine Glessner House and Wright's Heurtley House (*Figs. 4-30 and 4-31*) shows how the second grows out of the first but completely turns the basis of the design around from one of enclosing walls to one of intersecting planes, through which space is no longer simply contained and lighted by windows but liberated to flow out as if seeking the

light on its own. The masonry is dark and strong, its forms properly very different from those Wright created in wood; yet the space is still all. The masonry, here and in, say, the Martin House, forms planes to lead one through it and beyond (*Figs. 4-32 and 4-33*). True enough, there is a kind of counterdevelopment in Wright's masonry houses, running from such early examples as the Heller (*see Fig. 4-27*) on to the Fricke, Dana, and Heath houses, and perhaps the Booth project in part. In some of the houses of this group, the tendency is toward more upstanding, cubical, somewhat more heavily closed and enclosing forms. Those relate, of course, to monumental structures like Wright's Larkin Building and Unity Temple. Such types are recessive at first in domestic architecture, but they come forward after the break in Wright's career after 1914, and surely have something to do with shaping his concrete-block projects of the 1920's.

Still, it is no wonder that devotees of Wright have tended to become mystical about space. That is surely what his design had to do with, as he himself repeat-

4-31

190

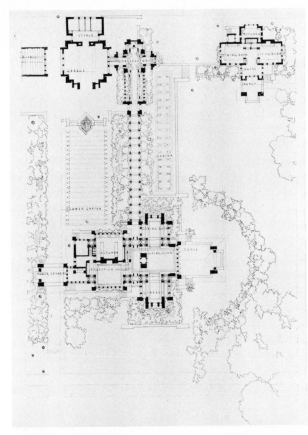

4-31. Heurtley House. Oak Park, Illinois. 1902. Frank Lloyd Wright.

4-32. D. W. Martin House. Buffalo, New York. 1904. Frank Lloyd Wright. Plan.

4-33. D. W. Martin House. Living room.

4-32

4-33

edly affirmed. And it was a space in which the continuity of the Shingle Style tradition, with its interwoven moldings and screens, was more obsessively developed (*see Figs. 4-32 and 4-33*). The great interior of the Martin House—with its cross-axis defined by clumps of piers in fours, which contain utilities—stretches out from the central fireplace mass to the dim but continuous band of light coming through the windows, beyond which the deep overhangs and porches attract the eye. The insistently woven moldings, barely above head height, enforce that lateral extension. The occupant is forced to give way to the releasing environment. The furniture is scaled to it and enforces its orders as well (*see Fig. 4-33*). Integration of the surroundings is everything; the individual is at once relaxed and enslaved

4-34. Isabel Roberts House. River Forest, Illinois. 1908. Frank Lloyd Wright. Living room.

4-35. Avery Coonley House. Riverside, Illinois. 1908. Frank Lloyd Wright. Stair and passage to living room.

by it. How American it is. Those who have contact with the young in 1970 cannot fail to be reminded here of their "Encounter" and "massage" groups, where what they refer to as "wholly competent leaders" can relax them into a physical homogeneity roughly comparable to that of a school of fish. One must ask if this is freedom? One remembers Jefferson's bright columns that stand on their feet and deny the horizontal flow. Wright will never use them. He will often recall the living halls of the Shingle Style (*see Fig. 1-28*) by releasing his space upward, as in the two-storied living rooms of the Roberts and Baker houses (*Fig. 4-34*), but in general, his horizontal strippings get bigger to enforce the horizontal spatial oneness as the decade goes on. In the splendid Coonley House, the separate pavilions are interwoven by long, heavily framed corridors, and the low ceilings sail on seemingly endlessly before the flat faces of the deeply embedded fireplace walls (*Fig. 4-35*). It was a kind of freedom and there being, as it were, no end to it, it was also a kind of death; underneath everything, how great and terrible an architecture it was.

We ask ourselves about the clients. Did they know what they had, or what had swallowed them? Here surely more work needs to be done.[3] What did the clients see here? Why did they want it? They saw peace, surely, and utter calm and dim quietness and warmth, and marvelous functional flexibility despite the general order, and plenty of unexpected discoveries, and even a few witty asides. These things probably induced them to put up

4-36. Robert W. Evans House. Chicago. 1908. Frank Lloyd Wright. Exterior, plan, and dining room.

4-37. W. A. Glasner House. Glencoe, Illinois. 1905. Frank Lloyd Wright. Exterior and plan.

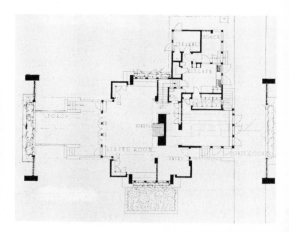

4-37

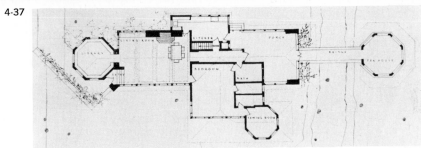

with some feeling of oppression and the occasional real darkness, and the sense of an "utterly competent leader" directing it all. They must also have recognized how masterfully Wright organized the suburban building "lot" which he normally had to work with and which he was to refuse to build on during his later years. But in these early days he was a master of the American grid and its rectangular plots. He controlled them with port-cochères, porches, and even flower pots, and he beautifully provided for driveways, garages, and service yards (*Fig. 4-36 and see Fig. 4-32*). He could take a simple square house and get all that from it, weaving inside and out. The street itself, out there beyond the American lawn, is respected, used, enhanced. Wright's people seemed actively to want to see it as they sat in the protected green darkness of their porches, watching the white dresses come up the sidewalk in the failing light.

The clients were not all rich, either. The Glasner House (*Fig. 4-37*) shows that, and it looks forward in almost every detail to Wright's Usonian Houses of the 1930's, when the rise in building costs no less than the increase in population usually required the building of much smaller houses with fewer rooms than had been the norm in Wright's early years.

We know that some of Wright's clients endured mild forms of that formidable cultural discipline known euphemistically as "kidding" in the Middle West and peculiarly effective in that region. There was already some sense, as there had not been during the Shingle Style years, for example, that the general architectural tradition was wearing out and that its forms had indeed become *outré* in comparison with more remotely precedented types. Some of Wright's clients may have taken pleasure in their difference, especially their difference from the Colonial East. Populism was, after all, in the air in Chicago, even if it was not politically strong in Wright's suburbs. There are in-

4-38. Harold McCormick House. Lake Forest, Illinois. 1907–12. Charles Platt. "Roman Court."

dications that it may have been the more cosmopolitan-minded of Wright's potential clients who first turned against him. In 1907, he lost the grandiose encampment that was his projected McCormick House to the eastern Beaux-Arts architect Charles Platt. This even seems to have had a considerable effect upon Wright's view of himself and his milieu. Hitchcock once described the vividness with which Wright recalled his surprise and shock some thirty-five years later. Why did the client's wife change her mind? Regional snobbery? A desire for a more obvious kind of elegance than Wright could produce? Perhaps, as Platt's rather icily austere and upstanding design *(Fig. 4-38)* suggests, she simply wanted to be left alone—wanted a house as a backdrop rather than a tranquilizer. The result looks forward to the next wave of classicism in the 1950's, as exemplified by the courtyarded houses of Mies and Johnson.

Whatever the case, Wright never forgot his loss, and it may have played some part in his readiness to throw his own entire environment over in 1909 for what he regarded as true love. In the meantime, he built his suburbs' monuments, growing out of the whole suburban domestic tradition that they culminated but abstracting and transcending it in powerful and tragic forms. The Gale House *(Fig. 4-39)* is, after all, already European "International Style" design some twenty years before its time, and it predicts Wright's own masterpieces of thirty years later when he was to find his ultimate, Indian-summer, national clientèle. It is always wonderful to watch Wright gather force and grow. He projects a long, shiplike form in the Tomek House *(Fig. 4-40)*, but it is still a little thin and boxy. In the Robie House, he weighs it all down with brick and still breaks free *(Fig. 4-41)*. The latter

4-39. Mrs. Thomas H. Gale House. Oak Park, Illinois. 1909. Frank Lloyd Wright.

4-40. F. F. Tomek House. Riverside, Illinois. 1907. Frank Lloyd Wright. Exterior and plan.

4-41
4-42

is the domestic monument, mountain, road, and airplane, that culminates the century.

Having accomplished this, Wright then did his best to return to Jefferson. The story of Wright's retreat to Taliesin and the tragedy that struck him there has been told too often to be repeated here. Unlike Jefferson's, his house tried to hug rather than to culminate the hilltop (*Fig. 4-42*); he built himself not a Pantheon but a cavern and a tent on its breast. In 1914, it was burned by a madman and was never to be the same, though twice rebuilt later. Wright's own leap for freedom thus ended in society's, or fate's, revenge upon him. Immediately thereafter—just before his withdrawal in space and time to Meso-America and Japan—he built a proud, tight little fortress in Chicago, bursting with energy all self-contained (*Fig. 4-43*);

4-41. Frederick C. Robie House. Chicago. 1909. Frank Lloyd Wright.

4-42. Taliesin I. Spring Green, Wisconsin. 1911–14. Frank Lloyd Wright.

4-43. Emil Bach House. Chicago. 1915. Frank Lloyd Wright.

4-43

4-44. Bradley House. Woods Hole, Massachusetts. 1912. Purcell & Elmslie.

envy would never be able to peep in those windows. The pavilions flower only above, as in the houses of Arabia. Arson, murder, and revolution could be sat out inside. While making perfectly reasonable sense, the Bach House, at the other level of all great art, is also the epitaph of a social hope passed by.

It is anticlimactic to turn from Wright's work to that of his contemporaries, but the other members of the Chicago School built some memorable houses too.[4] The Bradley House at Woods Hole, by Purcell & Elmslie, comes immediately to mind: splendidly sited, sailing across the Sound

4-45. David B. Gamble House. Pasadena, California. 1908. Charles and Henry Greene.

(*Fig. 4-44*). It puts together the Winslow, Willitts, and Robie houses but covers them all in the old traditional shingles. The fine contemporary work in California is also somewhat anticlimactic, perhaps as the culture of California itself has so far proved something of an anticlimax in the American drama as a whole.[5] It is true that Charles and Henry Greene of Pasadena put together some houses of great sweep, awesomely complicated in detail as they revived and elaborated the skeletal articulation of the mid-century. The Greenes's Gamble House (*Fig. 4-45*) is their most classically Stick Style, the

4-46. R. R. Blacker House. Pasadena, California. 1907. Charles and Henry Greene.

4-47. R. R. Blacker House. Stair hall.

202

Blacker House their most Oriental (*Figs. 4-46 and 4-47*). It is also their most elaborate, but its profiles and intersections are not far from those of the small houses in which Greene & Greene created the last vernacular of the old nineteenth-century kind. The California bungalows that the publications of Gustav Stickley briefly popularized throughout the country derived from their design. By the time of World War I, their vogue had passed. Greene & Greene themselves, like the architects of the Prairie School, hardly functioned thereafter, though they lived long enough to witness the revival of their influence after World War II. The same was, unfortunately, not true of Irving Gill, the Greenes's contemporary. Gill simplified Spanish-Colonial precedent into cast concrete and produced a marvelously lucid and severely rational architecture that was not unconnected with contempo-

4-48. Dodge House. Los Angeles, California. 1916. Irving Gill.

4-49. Dodge House. Stair hall.

rary puritanical polemics in Europe and was thus a double precursor of the International Style of the 1920's (*Figs. 4-48 and 4-49*). Gill's unselfish social conscience, rare among American architects of any period, should also be mentioned, as should his Lewis Courts in Sierra Madre, a highly successful housing project that was prompted by it (*Fig. 4-50*).

Greene & Greene and Gill alike were swamped by the rise of academic, Beaux-Arts design in southern California after 1915, and so was their counterpart, Bernard Maybeck, in the Bay Area, despite the fact that he was Beaux-Arts trained himself. Indeed, Maybeck still seems a sport in American architecture, much more European than American in many ways: an original, a bit of a crank, a true expressionist in design. Maybeck really exercised that individual and captious freedom of thought, behavior, and choice

4-50. Lewis Courts. Sierra Madre, California. 1910. Irving Gill.

4-51. Lawson House. Berkeley, California. 1907. Bernard Maybeck. Exterior and plan of the second floor.

that has normally been more honored in American protestations than in American practice. He was not driven to integrate, or to systematize, as Wright had been. He was a good and practical house architect, and could build in reinforced concrete as well and as appropriately as Gill (*Fig. 4-51*). But his genius also ranged wide, and slyly. His works leaped from theme to theme—Chinese, Baroque, or Gothic—and they distilled out of Maybeck's master, Viollet-le-Duc, much the same kind of inspired fantasy that his similarly trained contemporary, Antonio Gaudí, was producing in Catalonia: halls for Lords of the Ring, houses for hobbits (*Figs 4-52 and 4-53*). From the American nineteenth-century past, and then not in house architecture, only Frank Furness, similarly inspired though much tougher, can be recalled in related terms.

It was Wright who summed up almost everything his great century had most earnestly desired and made a new architecture out of it. His leap for freedom earnestly sought to organize everything and to carry it with him in a very American way. Maybeck, for all his learning, was one of the great innocents, in every age always free.

4-52. "Wyntoon" (a castle for Mrs. William Randolph Hearst). McCloud River, California. 1902. Bernard Maybeck. Living room.

4-53. Goslinksy House. San Francisco, California. 1909. Bernard Maybeck.

Notes

1. The editor has kindly assured me that it does not matter that this account is based upon research which was largely done almost a generation ago but which has not been superseded. It began with my doctoral dissertation, "The Cottage Style," of 1949, which was written with the advice of Henry-Russell Hitchcock, the dean of all scholarship in nineteenth-century architecture. That work itself was published in two parts, Part I in my "Romantic-Rationalism and the Expression of Structure in Wood: Downing, Wheeler, Gardner, and the 'Stick Style,' 1840–1876," *Art Bulletin,* 35 (1953), 121–42; and Part II as a book, *The Shingle Style: Architectural Theory and Design from Richardson to the Origins of Wright,* New Haven, Conn., 1955. Since Part I dealt at length with the work of Andrew Jackson Downing and of the other Pattern Book writers of the mid-century, and since some recent works, including editions of Downing such as that cited below in the Bibliography, do not refer to it at all, it may be well to underscore the fact that it was the first analysis of mid-nineteenth-century architecture to be based upon a consideration of what the people of that period thought and said they were doing. An application of the method to one site resulted in my chapters, "The Stick Style" and "The Shingle Style," in Antoinette F. Downing and Vincent J. Scully, Jr., *The Architectural Heritage of Newport, Rhode Island,* Cambridge, Mass., 1952; new edition, New York, 1967; and a more synoptic view was presented in my "American Villas: Inventiveness in the American Suburb from Downing to Wright," *Architectural Review,* 115 (March, 1954), 168–79. My work on Wright's design owed a considerable debt to earlier scholarship, especially to Henry-Russell Hitchcock's *In the Nature of Materials: The Buildings of Frank Lloyd Wright, 1887-1941,* New York, 1942. My own views were published in my *Frank Lloyd Wright,* New York, 1960, and a very brief general characterization of the period in relation to the development of modern architecture as a whole in my *Modern Architecture,* New York, 1961. I have tried to treat the topic in greater detail and in relation to the general development of American architecture and city planning in my *American Architecture and Urbanism,* New York, 1969. I ask the pardon of those who may have read one or another of those books or articles for whatever repetitions appear here. I have tried to vary the treatment as much as I could in order to reduce such recurrences and to broaden the conceptual base, but the subject has proved recalcitrant to much amendment—at least by me. It still seems to me to demand to be treated more or less in this way.

2. In *The Shingle Style* (p. 83, n. 39), I recorded an erroneous report that this house could not be found and had probably been destroyed in the fire of 1947. The welcome exhibition of Emerson's work, presented in 1969 by the Fogg Art Museum in collaboration with the Carpenter Center for the Visual Arts, Harvard University, corrects that error: *The Architecture of William Ralph Emerson, 1833-1917* (catalogue by Cynthia Zaitzevski, photography by Myron Miller, Cambridge, 1969, pp. 8–9, 79, Fig. 1, and Plate 8). Zaitzevski identifies it as "Redwood," the C. J. Morrill House.

3. Though Manson has given us a welcome amount of such information in his study of Wright's early years: Grant Car-

penter Manson, *Frank Lloyd Wright to 1910: The First Golden Age,* New York, 1958.

4. Recent publication of their work, with many illustrations, should be noted here: H. Allen Brooks, "The Prairie School, the Midwest Contemporaries of Frank Lloyd Wright," *Acts of the Twentieth International Congress of the History of Art,* 4 (Prince-ton, 1963), 22–23; and M. L. Peisch, *The Chicago School of Architecture: Early Followers of Sullivan and Wright,* New York, 1965; also David Gebhard, *A Guide to the Existing Buildings of Purcell and Elmslie,* Roswell, N.M., 1960.

5. Though here should be cited at least: Esther McCoy, *Five California Architects,* New York, 1960.

Selected Bibliography

This bibliography includes books mentioned in the Notes which are most readily available, and some additional titles. Listing is from the general to the specific, according to chronological applicability, with a few sources and anthologies added.

HITCHCOCK, HENRY-RUSSELL. *Architecture: Nineteenth and Twentieth Centuries.* Harmondsworth and Baltimore: Penguin Books, 1958. 3d ed. [Harmondsworth] © 1968.

SCULLY, VINCENT. *American Architecture and Urbanism.* New York: Praeger, 1969.

HAMLIN, TALBOT. *Greek Revival Architecture in America.* New York: Oxford University Press, 1944. Dover paperback, 1964.

HITCHCOCK, HENRY-RUSSELL. *Rhode Island Architecture.* Providence: Rhode Island Museum Press, 1939. DaCapo reprint, 1969.

MUMFORD, LEWIS. *Sticks and Stones.* New York: Boni & Liveright, 1924. Dover paperback, 1955.

DOWNING, ANTOINETTE F., and SCULLY, VINCENT J., Jr. *The Architectural Heritage of Newport, Rhode Island, 1640–1915.* Cambridge, Mass.: Harvard University Press, 1952. 2d ed., rev. New York: Clarkson N. Potter, 1967.

HITCHCOCK, HENRY-RUSSELL. *The Architecture of H. H. Richardson and his Times.* New York: Museum of Modern Art, 1936. M.I.T. paperback, 1965.

SCULLY, VINCENT J., Jr. *The Shingle Style.* New Haven, Conn.: Yale University Press, 1955.

ANDREWS, WAYNE. *Architecture, Ambition, and Americans: A History of American Architecture.* New York: Harper & Bros., 1955. Free Press paperback as *A Social History of American Architecture,* 1964.

HITCHCOCK, HENRY-RUSSELL. *In the Nature of Materials, 1887–1941: The Buildings of Frank Lloyd Wright.* New York: Duell, Sloan & Pearce, 1942.

MANSON, GRANT. *Frank Lloyd Wright to 1910: The First Golden Age.* New York: Reinhold, 1958.

SCULLY, VINCENT, JR. *Frank Lloyd Wright.* New York: Braziller, 1960.

PEISCH, M. L. *The Chicago School of Architecture: Early Followers of Sullivan and Wright.* New York: Random House, 1965.

McCOY, ESTHER. *Five California Architects.* New York: Reinhold, 1960.

DOWNING, ANDREW JACKSON. *Cottage Residences; or a series of designs for rural cottages and cottage villas. And their cottages and grounds.* New York and London: Wiley & Putnam, 1842 (13 issues to 1887).

————. *The Architecture of Country Houses, including designs for cottages, farm houses and villas, with remarks on interiors, furniture, and the best modes of warming and ventilating.* New York: D. Appleton & Co., 1850 (9 issues to 1894). Dover paperback, 1969.

KAUFMANN, EDGAR, and RAEBURN, BEN, eds. *Frank Lloyd Wright: Writings and Buildings.* New York: Horizon Press, 1960.

List of Illustrations

1-22. Eiffel Tower. Paris. 1887–89. Gustave Eiffel. Section of Otis elevator car: Figure 27 in Gaston Tissandier, *The Eiffel Tower,* London, 1889.

1-23. Eccentric Mill Works. New York City, Centre Street. 1848–49. James Bogardus. As published in *Illustrated London News,* April 12, 1851. *Demolished.*

1-24. Jamaica Street Warehouse. Glasgow, Scotland. 1856. John Baird.

1-25. Ritz Hotel. London. Mewès & Davis. 1905–6. As published in *The Architect,* October 19, 1906.

1-26. Project for church and parsonage, Columbus, Ohio. 1872. Henry Hobson Richardson. As published in *The Architect,* October 5, 1872.

1-27. Library. North Easton, Massachusetts. 1877–79. Henry Hobson Richardson. Elevation.

Town Hall. North Easton, Massachusetts. 1879–81. Henry Hobson Richardson. Elevation.

Library. Quincy, Massachusetts. 1880–83. Henry Hobson Richardson. Elevation and plan.

As published in *The British Architect,* January 5, 1883.

1-28. "Shingleside." Swampscott, Massachusetts. 1882. Arthur Little. Plans, elevation, and interiors. As published in *The Building News and Engineering Journal* (London), April 28, 1882. *Altered.*

1-29. Fred White House. London, Queen's Gate. 1887. R. Norman Shaw.

1-30. "Thirlstane" (Mrs. R. B. Scott House). Bar Harbor, Maine. 1881. William Ralph Emerson. Elevation. *Demolished.*

Casino. Elberon, New Jersey. *Ca.* 1885. Peabody & Stearns. Elevation. *Demolished.*

General J. Van Alen House. Newport, Rhode Island. Date uncertain. Clarence S. Luce. Elevation.

As published in *The Builder* (London), December 25, 1886.

1-31. "Lululund" (Sir Hubert von Herkomer House). Bushey (Hertfordshire), England. As remodeled by Henry Hobson Richardson, 1886–94. *Demolished.*

1-32. Electric Works. Stockholm. 1892. Ferdinand Boberg.

1-33. Fire Station. Gävle, Sweden. 1894. Ferdinand Boberg.

1-34. Library. Woburn, Massachusetts. 1877–78. Henry Hobson Richardson. As published in *The Architect,* June 25, 1886.

1-35. House at Suur-Merijoki, near Viborg, Finland. 1903. Eliel Saarinen. Elevation.

1-36. Workers' Clubhouse. Silkeborg, Denmark. 1895. Anton Rosen.

1-37. Savoy Hotel. Copenhagen. 1906. Anton Rosen. Elevation.

1-38. Number 9 Regeringsgaten, Stockholm. 1912. G. A. Nilsson.

1-39. House at Huis ter Heide, near Utrecht, Holland. 1915. Robert van t' Hoff.

1-40. De dubbele Sleutel. Woerden, Holland. 1917. Jan Wils.

1-41. Administration Building. Cologne, Germany. Werkbund Exposition of 1914. Walter Gropius.

1-42. Preliminary project for the plan of Canberra. 1911. Walter Burley Griffin. From a perspective drawing by Marion Mahony Griffin.

1-43. National Radiator Building. London. 1928. Raymond Hood.

1-44. Chile House. Hamburg, West Germany. 1923. Fritz Höger.

1-45. Stumm Konzern (Stahlhaus). Düsseldorf, West Germany. 1922–24. Bonatz & Scholer.

1-46. Krediet Bank. Antwerp, Belgium. 1928–33. J. Van Hoenacker.

1-47. Banque Lambert. Brussels. 1965. Skidmore, Owings & Merrill.

1-48. United States Consulate. Bremen, West Germany. 1956. Skidmore, Owings & Merrill.

1-49. BASF Building. Ludwigshafen on the Main, West Germany. *Ca.* early 1960's. Hentrich & Petschnigg.

2-1. "Dens of Death," Mulberry Bend, New York City. *Ca.* 1872. Photograph by Jacob A. Riis for the Board of Health.

2-2. William Ellery Channing. Statue by Herbert Adams, erected 1903, in the Boston Public Garden.

2-3. Henry Whitney Bellows. Undated photograph.

2-4. All Souls Unitarian Church. New York City. 1853–55. John Wrey Mould. Photograph, 1905. *Demolished.*

2-5. Horace Bushnell, *ca.* 1870.

2-6. Plan for Philadelphia. 1682. William Penn.

2-7. Map of Boston. 1722. John Bonner.

2-8. View of Boston Common, showing the National Lancers with the Reviewing Officers. 1837. C. Hubbard.

2-9. View of Boston, showing the Common and Public Garden. *Ca.* 1850. John Bachmann.

2-10. Public common, Worcester, Massachusetts. 1849.

2-11. Map of New Haven. 1748.

2-12. Map of New Haven. 1837.

2-13. Map of Hartford. 1640.

2-14. Map of Hartford. 1869.

2-15. Frederick Law Olmsted. Photograph, *ca.* 1868.

2-16. Commissioner's plan for New York City. 1807–11.

2-17. View of New Amsterdam. 1660.

2-18. The Battery promenade, New York City. 1851.

2-19. The Elgin Botanic Garden, New York City. *Ca.* 1859.

2-20. View of City Hall Park, New York City. *Ca.* 1850. John Bachmann.

2-21. Plan for Gramercy Park, New York City. 1874. Jacob Weidenmann.

2-22. View of Union Square, New York City. 1849. James Smillie.

2-23. Andrew Jackson Downing. Undated drawing.

2-24. Plan for the Public Grounds, Washington, D.C. 1851. Andrew Jackson Downing.

2-25. Calvert Vaux. Photograph, 1868.

2-26. View of Savannah, Georgia. 1734.

2-27. Plan of Mt. Auburn Cemetery, Cambridge, Massachusetts. 1901.

2-28. Plan of Laurel Hill Cemetery, Philadelphia. 1836–40.

2-29. Plan and views of Greenwood Cemetery, Brooklyn, New York. 1846.

2-30. Outline map of Central Park, New York City, showing transverse roads and differentiated circulation system. *Ca.* 1868. Frederick Law Olmsted and Calvert Vaux.

2-31. Map of Central Park, New York City, illustrating sites for museums of art and natural history. 1873. Detail.

2-32. Design for a proposed historical museum on the site of the Central Park Arsenal, New York City. 1866. Richard Morris Hunt.

2-33. Design for Eastern Parkway, Brooklyn, New York. 1868.

2-34. First section of The American Museum of Natural History. New York City. 1877. J. C. Cady & Co. Photograph, 1879–81.

2-35. The American Museum of Natural History. New York City. Photograph, 1890.

2-36. Central Park Museum, Observatory, and Menagerie. New York City. 1848. Photograph, *ca.* 1870.

2-37. View of Central Park, New York City, from the Belvedere looking southeast. 1869. Drawing by Albert Fitch Bellows, as published in Clarence Chatham Cook, *A Description of the New York Central Park,* New York, 1869.

2-38. The Metropolitan Museum of Art. New York City. 1874–80. Calvert

213

Vaux with John Wrey Mould. Photograph, 1894.

2-39. Design for Prospect Park, Brooklyn, New York. 1868. Olmsted, Vaux & Co.

2-40. Sketch map of Buffalo, New York, showing the relation of the park system to the general plan of the city. 1876. After Frederick Law Olmsted.

2-41. Map of Chicago, showing the boulevard system. *Ca.* 1886.

2-42. Map of Minneapolis, showing the park system as recommended by Horace W. S. Cleveland in 1883.

2-43. Plan of Tower Grove Park, St. Louis. 1867.

2-44. Plan of the Boston Park System. 1887. Detail.

2-45. Jacob A. Riis. Photograph, *ca.* 1910.

2-46. Joseph Lee. Photograph, published 1937.

2-47. Mulberry Bend Park, New York City. Photograph, *ca.* 1890–99.

2-48. Corlears Hook Park, New York City. 1899.

2-49. School playground in the Bronx, New York City. Photograph, *ca.* 1890–99.

2-50. Map of the buildings and grounds of the World's Fair (World's Columbian Exposition). Chicago. 1893.

3-1. Union Trust Building. New York City. 1889–90. George B. Post. *Demolished.*

3-2. American Surety Building. New York City. 1894–95. Bruce Price.

3-3. Woolworth Building. New York City. 1911–13. Cass Gilbert.

3-4. Singer Building. New York City. 1906–8. Ernest Flagg. *Demolished.*

3-5. Metropolitan Tower. New York City. 1909. Napoleon Le Brun & Sons. *Remodeled.*

3-6. Equitable Life Assurance Company Building. New York City. 1868–70. Gilman & Kendall and George B. Post. *Demolished.*

3-7. Tribune Building. New York City. 1873–75. Richard Morris Hunt. *Demolished.*

3-8. Western Union Building. New York City. 1873–75. George B. Post. *Demolished.*

3-9. St. Paul Building. New York City. 1898–99. George B. Post.

3-10. Park Row Building. New York City. 1896–99. Robert H. Robertson.

3-11. Masonic Temple Building. Chicago. 1891–92. Burnham & Root. *Demolished.*

3-12. Home Life Insurance Company Building. Chicago. 1884–85. William Le Baron Jenney. *Demolished.*

3-13. Chamber of Commerce Building. Chicago. 1888–89. Baumann & Huehl. *Demolished.*

3-14. Mutual Life Insurance Company Building. New York City. 1863–65. John Kellum. *Demolished.*

3-15. New York Life Insurance Company Building. New York City. 1868–70. Griffith Thomas. *Demolished.*

3-16. Lord & Taylor. New York City. 1869–70. James H. Giles. *Demolished.*

3-17. Boreel Building. New York City. 1878–79. Stephen Hatch. *Demolished.*

3-18. Morse Building. New York City. 1879. Silliman & Farnesworth. *Demolished.*

3-19. Jayne Building. Philadelphia. 1849–52. William L. Johnston. *Demolished.*

3-20. 241 Broadway scheme. New York City. *Ca.* 1849. Calvin Pollard.

3-21. Haughwout Store. New York City. 1857. John P. Gaynor.

3-22. McCullough Shot Tower. New York City. 1856. James Bogardus. *Demolished.*

3-23. Harper Brothers Building. New York City. 1854. James Bogardus. Section. *Demolished.*

3-24. Mills Building. New York City. 1881–83. George B. Post. *Demolished.*

3-25. Mills Building preliminary scheme. New York City. 1880. George B. Post.

3-26. Produce Exchange. New York City. 1881–84. George B. Post. *Demolished.*

3-27. Auditorium. Chicago. 1887–89. Adler & Sullivan.

3-28. The Rookery. Chicago. 1885–86. Burnham & Root.

3-29. Ames Building. Boston. 1889–91. Shepley, Rutan & Coolidge.

3-30. Hammond Building. Detroit. 1889–90. George H. Edbrooke. *Demolished.*

3-31. Havemeyer Building. New York City. 1891–92. George B. Post. *Demolished.*

3-32. 715–727 Broadway. New York City. 1894. Robert Maynicke.

3-33. Union Trust Company Building. St. Louis. 1892–93. Adler & Sullivan. *Demolished.*

3-34. Marquette Building. Chicago. 1893–94. Holabird & Roche.

3-35. Washington Life Building. New York City. 1897. Cyrus L. W. Eidlitz. *Demolished.*

3-36. Broadway-Chambers Building. New York City. 1899–1900. Cass Gilbert.

3-37. Tower Building. New York City. 1888–89. Bradford Gilbert. *Demolished.*

3-38. Tower Building. Philadelphia. 1855. Samuel Sloan. *Demolished.*

3-39. Design for a twenty-eight-story office building. 1888. Leroy Buffington.

3-40. Odd Fellows' Temple scheme. 1891. Adler & Sullivan.

3-41. Sun Building scheme. 1890. Bruce Price.

3-42. Prudential Life Insurance Building Tower project. 1899. George B. Post.

3-43. The Spreckles Building. San Francisco. 1897. J. W. & M. J. Reid. *Altered.*

3-44. Book Tower. Detroit. 1926. Louis Kamper, Inc.

3-45. Foshay Tower. Minneapolis. 1927–29. Magney & Tusler, Inc.

3-46. 111–115 Broadway. New York City. 1906–7. Francis H. Kimball.

3-47. Equitable Life Assurance Building. New York City. 1913–15. E. R. Graham.

3-48. Rockefeller Center. New York City. 1930–40. Reinhard & Hofmeister; Hood, Godley & Fouilhoux; and Corbett, Harrison & MacMurray.

3-49. West Street Building. New York City. 1906–7. Cass Gilbert.

3-50. Washington Building. New York City. 1882–85. Edward Kendall. *Demolished.*

4-1. Monticello. Charlottesville, Virginia. 1770–1809. Thomas Jefferson.

4-2. a. Monticello. Early plans, with plan by Robert Morris.

b. Kent House. Tuxedo Park, New York. 1885–86. Bruce Price. Plan.

c. Monticello. Plan with porches and bays.

d. Ward Willitts House. Highland Park, Illinois. 1902. Frank Lloyd Wright. Plan.

e. Monticello. Final plan.

4-3. David Sears House (Somerset Club). Boston. *Ca.* 1816. Alexander Parris.

4-4. Hillhouse House. New Haven. 1835. Town & Davis. *Demolished.*

4-5. Ithiel Town House. New Haven. 1830. Town & Davis. Perspective drawing and plans. *Demolished.*

4-6. Edward King House. Newport, Rhode Island. 1845–47. Richard Upjohn.

4-7. "Kingscote." Newport, Rhode Island. 1841. Richard Upjohn.

4-8. Plan of Riverside, Illinois. 1869. Frederick Law Olmsted and Calvert Vaux.

4-9. "Small Bracketted Cottage." Illustration in Andrew Jackson Downing, *The Architecture of Country Houses . . . ,* New York, 1850.

4-10. "Bracketted Veranda from the Inside." Illustration in Andrew Jackson Downing, *The Architecture of Country Houses . . . ,* New York, edition of 1853.

4-11. Boarding house. Madrid, New Mexico. Date uncertain.

4-12. J. N. A. Griswold House. Newport, Rhode Island. 1862. Richard Morris Hunt.

4-13. Sturtevant House. Middletown, Rhode Island. 1872. Dudley Newton.

4-14. "Olana" (Frederic Church House). Hudson, New York. 1870–72, 1888–89. Calvert Vaux.

4-15. "Dumbbell" tenement. Design by James E. Ware, 1879. Plan.

4-16. Fairbanks House. Dedham, Massachusetts. 1636, with eighteenth-century additions. As published in *American Architect,* 1881.

4-17. "Redwood" (C. J. Morrill House). Mount Desert, Maine. 1879. William Ralph Emerson. Exterior and plan, as published in *American Architect,* 1879.

4-18. "Kragsyde" (G. N. Black House). Manchester-by-the-Sea, Massachusetts. 1882–84. Peabody & Stearns. With plans and sketches by E. Eldon Deane.

4-19. Victor Newcomb House. Elberon, New Jersey. 1880–81. McKim, Mead & White. Living hall. *Demolished.*

4-20. "Kingscote." Newport, Rhode Island. 1841. Richard Upjohn. Dining room added by Stanford White, 1880–81.

4-21. Charles A. Potter House. Chestnut Hill, Pennsylvania. 1885 (date of completion; date of *ca.* 1881–82 given in *The Shingle Style,* Fig. 97, on stylistic grounds). Wilson Eyre. Plan.

4-22. C. A. Brown House. Delano Park, near Portland, Maine. 1885–86. John Calvin Stevens.

4-23. Cyrus McCormick House. Richfield Springs, New York. 1880–81. McKim, Mead & White.

4-24. Misses Appleton House. Lenox, Massachusetts. 1883–84. McKim, Mead & White. Exterior and plan.

4-25. H. A. C. Taylor House. Newport, Rhode Island. 1885–86. McKim, Mead & White. Exterior and plan. *Demolished.*

4-26. "Biltmore." Asheville, North Carolina. 1895. Richard Morris Hunt.

4-27. Isidor Heller House. Chicago. 1897. Frank Lloyd Wright. Exterior and plan.

4-28. Casino. Short Hills, New Jersey. 1882–83. McKim, Mead & White.

4-29. Golf Club. River Forest, Illinois. 1898–1901. Frank Lloyd Wright. Perspective, 1901. *Demolished.*

4-30. Glessner House. Chicago. 1885–87. Henry Hobson Richardson.

4-31. Heurtley House. Oak Park, Illinois. 1902. Frank Lloyd Wright.

4-32. D. W. Martin House. Buffalo, New York. 1904. Frank Lloyd Wright. Plan. *Remodeled.*

4-33. D. W. Martin House. Buffalo, New York. 1904. Frank Lloyd Wright. Living room. *Remodeled.*

4-34. Isabel Roberts House. River Forest, Illinois. 1908. Frank Lloyd Wright. Living room. *Remodeled.*

4-35. Avery Coonley House. Riverside, Illinois. 1908. Frank Lloyd Wright. Stair and passage to living room. *Remodeled.*

4-36. Robert W. Evans House. Chicago. 1908. Frank Lloyd Wright. Exterior, plan, and dining room.

4-37. W. A. Glasner House. Glencoe, Illinois. 1905. Frank Lloyd Wright. Exterior and plan.

4-38. Harold McCormick House. Lake Forest, Illinois. 1907–12. Charles Platt. "Roman Court."

4-39. Mrs. Thomas H. Gale House. Oak Park, Illinois. 1909. Frank Lloyd Wright.

4-40. F. F. Tomek House. Riverside, Illinois. 1907. Frank Lloyd Wright. Exterior and plan. *Remodeled.*

4-41. Frederick C. Robie House. Chicago. 1909. Frank Lloyd Wright.

4-42. Taliesin I. Spring Green, Wisconsin. 1911–14. Frank Lloyd Wright. *Demolished.*

4-43. Emil Bach House. Chicago. 1915. Frank Lloyd Wright.

4-44. Bradley House. Woods Hole, Massachusetts. 1912. Purcell & Elmslie.

4-45. David B. Gamble House. Pasadena, California. 1908. Charles and Henry Greene.

4-46. R. R. Blacker House. Pasadena, California. 1907. Charles and Henry Greene.

4-47. R. R. Blacker House. Pasadena, California. 1907. Charles and Henry Greene. Stair hall.

4-48. Dodge House. Los Angeles, California. 1916. Irving Gill. *Demolished.*

4-49. Dodge House. Los Angeles, California. 1916. Irving Gill. Stair hall. *Demolished.*

4-50. Lewis Courts. Sierra Madre, California. 1910. Irving Gill.

4-51. Lawson House. Berkeley, California. 1907. Bernard Maybeck. Exterior and plan of the second floor.

4-52. "Wyntoon" (a castle for Mrs. William Randolph Hearst). McCloud River, California. 1902. Bernard Maybeck. Living room. *Demolished.*

4-53. Goslinsky House. San Francisco, California. 1909. Bernard Maybeck.

PICTURE CREDITS

1-1, 1-2. Courtesy The Netherlands Information Service. 1-3. Photograph: David Hirsch, Brooklyn, N.Y. 1-4. Courtesy Philip Johnson. 1-5. In *Architectural Record*, November, 1968. 1-6. Courtesy Philip Johnson, 1-7. In *Architecture by Albert Kahn Associated Architects and Engineers, Inc.* (New York, 1948). 1-8, 1-9, 1-10. Photograph: Jay Cantor, New York. 1-11. Courtesy Avery Library, Columbia University, New York. 1-12. In Hentrich and Petschnigg & Partner, Architekten, *Bauten, 1953–1969* (n.d.). 1-15. Courtesy of The Royal Institute of British Architects, London. 1-17, 1-18, 1-19. Courtesy of The New-York Historical Society, New York City. 1-20. Author's collection. 1-21. The Lawrence G. Zimmerman World's Fair Collection. 1-22. Photograph: Jay Cantor, New York. 1-23. Courtesy of The New-York Historical Society, New York City. 1-24. Reproduced from Gomme and Walker, *Architecture of Glasgow* (London, [Lund Humphries], 1968). 1-25, 1-26, 1-27, 1-28. Photograph: Jay Cantor, New York. 1-29. In Henry-Russell Hitchcock, *Architecture: Nineteenth and Twentieth Centuries* (Harmondsworth and Baltimore, 1958). 1-30. Photograph: Jay Cantor, New York. 1-31. Author's collection. 1-32, 1-33. In *Progressive Architecture*, March, 1966. 1-34. Photograph: Jay Cantor, New York. 1-35. In *Arkkitehti Arkitekten*, February, 1967. 1-36, 1-37, 1-38. In *Progressive Architecture*, March, 1966. 1-39. Courtesy The Netherlands Information Service. 1-40. In [Wils] *Jan Wils* (Geneva, n.d.). 1-41. In Walter Gropius, *The New Architecture and the Bauhaus* (London, 1956). 1-42. Courtesy Mark Peisch, New York. 1-43. In *Raymond M. Hood* (New York, 1931). 1-44. In *Wasmuth Monatshefte für Baukunst*, XIII, 1924. 1-45. In Friedrich Tamms, *Paul Bonatz, Arbeiten aus den Jahren 1907 bis 1937* (Stuttgart, 1937). 1-46. By courtesy of Kredietbank N.V., Antwerp, Belgium. 1-47, 1-48. Courtesy Skidmore, Owings & Merrill, New York. 1-49. In Hentrich and Petschnigg & Partner, Architekten, *Bauten, 1953–1969* (n.d.). 2-1. The Jacob A. Riis Collection, Museum of the City of New York. Photograph: Jacob A. Riis. 2-2. Courtesy Print Department, Boston Public Library. 2-3. Courtesy Museum of the City of New York. 2-4. Courtesy of The New-York Historical Society, New York City. 2-5. Courtesy Prints Division, The New York Public Library. 2-6, 2-7, 2-8. The I. N. Phelps Stokes Collection, The New York Public Library. 2-9. Courtesy of The New-York Historical Society, New York City. 2-10. In Mildred M. Tymeson, comp., *Worcester Centennial: 1848–1948* (Worcester, Mass., 1948). Courtesy Library of the Graduate School of Design, Harvard University. 2-11. The I. N. Phelps Stokes Collection, The New York Public Library. 2-12, 2-13, 2-14. Courtesy Map Division, The New York Public Library. 2-15. In Frederick Law Olmsted, Jr., and Theodora Kimball, eds., *Forty Years of Landscape Architecture* (New York, 1928), II. Courtesy of The New-York Historical Society, New York City. 2-16. The J. Clarence Davies Collection, Museum of the City of New York. 2-17. The I. N. Phelps Stokes Collection, The New York Public Library. 2-18. Courtesy of The New-York Historical Society, New York City. 2-19. In *D. T. Valentine's Manual*, 1859. 2-20. Courtesy of The New-York Historical Society, New York City. 2-21. S. J. Tilden Papers, package #3, Manuscript Division, The New York Public Library. 2-22. The J. Clarence Davies Collection, Museum of the City of New York. 2-23. In *Records of the Columbia County Historical Society*, Washington, D.C., 27, 1925. Courtesy of The New-York Historical Society, New York City. 2-24. National Archives, F 116, Record Group 77, Records of the Office of the Chief of Engineers. 2-25. Courtesy of The New-York Historical Society, New York City. 2-26. The I. N. Phelps Stokes Collection, The New York Public Library. 2-27. Courtesy Library of the Graduate School of Design, Harvard University. 2-28. Private collection. Photograph: Jay Cantor, New York. 2-29. Courtesy Map Division, The New York Public Library. 2-30. Author's collection. 2-31. Courtesy The Metropolitan Museum of Art, New York. 2-32. Courtesy of The New-York Historical Society, New York City. 2-33. In *Report to the Commissioners of Prospect Park. 8th Annual Report*. 1868. 2-34. Courtesy The American Museum of Natural History, New York. 2-35. Courtesy of The New-York Historical Society, New York City. 2-36. Courtesy Museum of the City of New York. 2-37. Courtesy of The New-York Historical Society, New York City. 2-38. The J. Clarence Davies Collection, Museum of the City of New York. 2-39. Author's collection. 2-40. Courtesy Buffalo Historical Society. 2-41. In A. T. Andreas, *History of Chicago from the Earliest Period to the Present Time* (Chicago, 1886), III. Courtesy The New York Public Library. 2-42. In H. W. S. Cleveland, *Suggestions for a System of Parks and Parkways for the City of Minneapolis* (Minneapolis, 1883). Courtesy The New York Public Library. 2-43. In David H. Macadam, *Tower Grove Park of the City of St. Louis* (St. Louis, 1883). Courtesy The New York Public Library. 2-44. In Julius Fabos, *et al., Frederick Law Olmsted, Sr.* (Amherst, Mass., 1968). Courtesy Library of the Graduate School of Design, Harvard University. 2-45. Courtesy Museum of the City of New York. 2-46. In *Recreation*, December, 1937. 2-47. The Jacob A. Riis Collection, Museum of the City of New York. Photograph: Jacob A. Riis. 2-48. In G. W. Bromley, *Atlas of the City of New York* (Philadelphia, 1899), I. Courtesy of The New-York Historical Society, New York City. 2-49. The Jacob A. Riis Collection, Museum of the City of New York. Photograph: Jacob A. Riis. 2-50. In Julius Fabos, *et al., Frederick Law Olmsted, Sr.* (Amherst, Mass., 1968). Courtesy Library of the Graduate School of Design, Harvard University. 3-1. Courtesy of The New-York Historical Society, New York City. 3-2. In *King's Views of New York* (New York, 1905). 3-3. In Francisco Mujica, *History of the Skyscraper* (New York, 1930). 3-4, 3-5. In *King's Views of New York* (New York, 1911). 3-6. In *New York Illustrated* (New York [Appleton], 1870). 3-7. In *New York Tribune*, April 10, 1875. 3-8. Courtesy Museum of the City of New York. 3-9. In Francisco Mujica, *History of the Skyscraper* (New York, 1930). 3-10. In *King's Views of New York* (New York, 1905). 3-11. In Francisco Mujica, *History of the Skyscraper* (New York, 1930). 3-12. Courtesy Chicago Historical Society. 3-13. In *Industrial Chicago* (Chicago [Goodspeed], 1891), I. 3-14, 3-15. Courtesy of The

New-York Historical Society, New York City. 3-16. In *King's Views of New York* (New York, 1911). 3-17. In *King's Views of New York* (Boston, 1895). 3-18. In *King's Handbook of New York* (Boston, 1893). 3-19. Courtesy Historical Society of Pennsylvania, Philadelphia. 3-20. Courtesy of The New-York Historical Society, New York City. 3-21. In D. D. Badger, *Architectural Iron Works of New York* (New York, 1865). 3-22. In *Harper's Monthly Magazine*, December, 1865. 3-23, 3-24, 3-25. Courtesy of The New-York Historical Society, New York City. 3-26. In *Views of New York* [Hall], 1909). 3-27. In Carl W. Condit, *The Chicago School of Architecture* (Chicago, 1964). Photograph: Chicago Architectural Photo. 3-28. In *Industrial Chicago* (Chicago [Goodspeed], 1891), II. 3-29, In *American Architect and Building News*, July 13, 1889. 3-30. In *American Architect and Building News*, September 7, 1889. 3-31. In Francisco Mujica, *History of the Skyscraper* (New York, 1930). 3-32. In *Both Sides of Broadway* (New York [De Leeuw Riehl], 1910). 3-33. In *American Architect and Building News*, October 12, 1895. 3-34. In *American Architect and Building News*, January 30, 1897. 3-35. In *American Architect and Building News*, October 15, 1898. 3-36. In *American Architect and Building News*, February 24, 1900. 3-37. Courtesy of The New-York Historical Society, New York City. 3-38. Courtesy Historical Society of Pennsylvania, Philadelphia. 3-39. In *The Inland Architect and News Record*, XI, 1888. 3-40. In *Industrial Chicago* (Chicago [Goodspeed], 1891), II. 3-41. In *A History of Real Estate, Building and Architecture in New York City 1868-1893* (New York, 1967). 3-42. Courtesy of The New-York Historical Society, New York City. 3-43. In *American Architect and Building News*, August 25, 1897. 3-44. In W. Hawkins Ferry, *The Buildings of Detroit* (Michigan, 1968). Photograph: Manning Bros. 3-45. Courtesy Minnesota Historical Society. 3-46. In *King's Views of New York* (New York, 1911). 3-47. In Francisco Mujica, *History of the Skyscraper* (New York, 1930). 3-48. Courtesy Rockefeller Center, Inc., New York. 3-49. In Francisco Mujica, *History of the Skyscraper* (New York, 1930). 3-50. In *King's Views of New York* (New York, 1905). 4-1. Author's collection. 4-2 (a) From Robert Morris's *Select Architecture*. In T. T. Waterman, *Mansions of Virginia* (Chapel Hill, N.C., 1945). (b) In G. W. Sheldon, *Artistic Country Seats* (New York, 1886-87). (c) Coolidge Collection, Massachusetts Historical Society. In F. Kimball, *Thomas Jefferson, Architect* (Boston, 1916). (d) Reproduced with the permission of Verlag Ernst Wasmuth, Tübingen, Germany. In C. R. Ashbee, *Frank Lloyd Wright: Ausgeführte Bauten* (Berlin, 1911). (e) In I. T. Frary, *Thomas Jefferson, Architect and Builder* (Richmond, Va., 1931). 4-3. Photograph: Wayne

Andrews, Grosse Pointe, Michigan. 4-4, 4-5. Photograph collection Yale University Art Library. 4-6, 4-7. Courtesy The Preservation Society of Newport County, Newport, R. I. 4-8. Courtesy The New York Public Library. 4-9, 4-10. Photograph: Jay Cantor, New York. 4-11. Author's collection. 4-12. Photograph: Wayne Andrews, Grosse Pointe, Michigan. 4-13. Courtesy The Preservation Society of Newport County, Newport, R. I. 4-14. Photograph: Jinny and Wendy Neefus, Hudson, N.Y. 4-15. In Robert W. de Forest and Lawrence Veiller, eds., *The Tenement House Problem* (New York, 1903), I. Photograph: Jay Cantor, New York. 4-16, 4-17, 4-18, 4-19. In Vincent Scully, *The Shingle Style*, New Haven, 1955. 4-20. Courtesy William King Covell, Newport, R. I. 4-21. In G. W. Sheldon, *Artistic Country Seats* (New York, 1886-87). Photograph: Jay Cantor, New York. 4-22, 4-23. In Vincent Scully, *The Shingle Style*, New Haven, 1955. 4-24, 4-25. In G. W. Sheldon, *Artistic Country Seats* (New York, 1886-87). Photograph: Jay Cantor, New York. 4-26. Photograph collection Yale University Art Library. 4-27. In Henry-Russell Hitchcock, *In the Nature of Materials* (New York, 1942). 4-28. Reproduced with the permission of Verlag Ernst Wasmuth, Tübingen, Germany. In *Ausgeführte Bauten und Entwürfe von Frank Lloyd Wright* (Berlin, 1910). 4-29. In Vincent Scully, *The Shingle Style*, New Haven, 1955. 4-30. Collection Henry-Russell Hitchcock, Northampton, Mass. 4-31, 4-32. In Henry-Russell Hitchcock, *In the Nature of Materials* (New York, 1942). 4-33. Reproduced with the permission of Verlag Ernst Wasmuth, Tübingen, Germany. 4-34, 4-35, 4-36. Photograph: Chicago Architectural Photo Co. 4-37. In Henry-Russell Hitchcock, *In the Nature of Materials* (New York, 1942). 4-38. Photograph collection Yale University Art Gallery. 4-39, 4-40. In Henry-Russell Hitchcock, *In the Nature of Materials* (New York, 1942). 4-41. Photograph: Wayne Andrews, Grosse Pointe, Michigan. 4-42. Courtesy The Museum of Modern Art, New York. 4-43. In Henry-Russell Hitchcock, *In the Nature of Materials* (New York, 1942). 4-44. Photograph: Wayne Andrews, Grosse Pointe, Michigan. 4-45. In Esther McCoy, *Five California Architects* (New York, 1960). Photograph: Marvin Rand, Los Angeles. 4-46. Courtesy Randall L. Makinson, Curator, The Gamble House, Greene and Greene Museum & Library, Pasadena. 4-47, 4-48. Photograph: Marvin Rand, Los Angeles. 4-49. Photograph: Julius Shulman, Los Angeles. 4-50. Collection Esther McCoy, Santa Monica, Calif. Courtesy University of California Art Gallery, Santa Barbara, Calif. 4-51. Courtesy L. Morgan Yost, FAIA, Kenilworth, Ill. 4-52. Architectural Documents Collection, University of California. Courtesy K. H. Cardwell, Berkeley, Calif. 4-53. Photograph: Roy Flamm, San Francisco.

The Rise of an American Architecture

A BOOK AND AN EXHIBITION

The Rise of an American Architecture

A BOOK AND AN EXHIBITION

This book was conceived as counterpart to an exhibition opening under the same name and the same auspices at The Metropolitan Museum of Art in May of 1970.

The book demonstrates current scholarship in the field of American architectural history centered on the critical developments of the nineteenth century. It is evidence of the museum as patron and, indeed, as beneficiary of learned studies.

The exhibition displays the other side of museum work—taking the results of careful scholarship and presenting them in contexts attractive and meaningful to the world at large.

In presenting THE RISE OF AN AMERICAN ARCHITECTURE, one main purpose was to encourage preservation of an inspiring and eminently useful heritage. We aimed to stir the enthusiasm of both the experts and large numbers of museumgoers. The plenitude, the detail, and the subtleties of erudition were allocated to the book, while highlights and the broad sweep of human considerations were assigned to the show.

The exhibition, which will travel to several American cities, gives prominence to nine important, still standing American buildings of the period 1815 to 1915. These are presented in photographs, the principal ones specially taken in color. Texts explain and connect the pictures.

A list of contents and their sequence in the exhibition, and the texts just mentioned, are printed here to indicate the other component of this double program.

EDGAR KAUFMANN, JR.

THE RISE OF AN AMERICAN ARCHITECTURE 1815–1915

EXHIBITION DIRECTOR, Edgar Kaufmann, jr.

ASSISTANT TO THE DIRECTOR, Morrison H. Heckscher

ADVISOR ON PARKS SECTION, Albert Fein

EXHIBITION DESIGNERS, James Stewart Polshek and Arnold Saks

COLOR PHOTOGRAPHS, Elliott Erwitt

FILM SEQUENCE, Cinemakers Inc.

INITIAL SPONSORS: The Metropolitan Museum of Art, National Trust for Historic Preservation, The New York Chapter of The American Institute of Architects

223

Contents of the Exhibition

224

Texts from the Exhibition

INTRODUCTION

Frederick Law Olmsted, Sr., 1822–1903
Henry Hobson Richardson, 1838–1886
Louis Henri Sullivan, 1856–1924
Frank Lloyd Wright, 1867–1959

The development of an American architecture parallels the growth of our country. By 1815, the United States stood firm as a nation that then spread westward to the Pacific Ocean. As its territory grew, a great debate arose over the American way of life, climaxing in the Civil War. When the Union prevailed, it brought the dominance of middle-class virtues, of industry, and of commercial enterprise.

A rich prosperity followed, in which some national ideals were forgotten; nevertheless, first steps had been taken toward equal opportunity for all and toward the organized power of labor. Architecture under these conditions grew strongest where there was least constriction from older, European traditions. In earlier ages, architecture in the Western world was evolved to suit the Church, the State, and the aristocracy. Now, architecture, accompanied by landscape architecture, turned to new tasks:

—buildings for commerce
  —small homes for middle-class families
    —parks and squares to make the cities habitable.

Works designed for these interrelated needs by the four American geniuses mentioned above and works of similar quality are found throughout the United States.

In this exhibition, a handful of important examples illustrate these interrelated developments, leaving many achievements of American architecture and landscaping unmentioned.

More detail will be found in the earlier sections of the present book published to complement the exhibition. If the exhibition and the book arouse interest and respect for some vital accomplishments of this era in our land, two benefits will ensue. Many works of value that could not be considered within the present program will share in the increase of attention, and more of the architectural and landscape treasures of our national heritage will be put to use, actively serving people today.

GREAT BUILDINGS FOR COMMERCE

Preliminary:
Projected Shopping Center,
Berlin, Germany, 1827
Karl Friedrich Schinkel, architect

Commercial architecture advanced rapidly during the period considered in this exhibition—1815 to 1915. The most extraordinary advance was made early, in 1827, by Karl Friedrich Schinkel, chief architect to the king of Prussia, but Schinkel's scheme was not carried out. He suggested replacing antiquated buildings on Unter den Linden, in the heart of Berlin, by a great shopping center that included apartments for tradesmen as well as a large central court with trees, a fountain, and, in summer, an outdoor café. Although Schinkel had made a study of new city-planning ideas and new architectural forms in France and England, there was no precedent for his proposal. In Schinkel's project, the state would have built and owned the edifice, renting space in it to shopkeepers. Two shopping levels were planned, each with apartments above, reached by interior stairs. Ground-floor shops were to be entered directly; those on the upper level could be reached by ample stairs rising in skylit wells, and then by a central corridor made pleasant by more light and air shafts. Within the simple, dignified stone framework, great curtain walls of glass were hung; these were, in fact, double windows, traditional in north-central Europe, and their framing expressed the high ceilings of the shopping floors as well as the lower ones of the apartments. The ceilings were to be vaulted, in fire resistant construction, and many subsidiary stairs were provided for safety. Schinkel's mature grasp of the situation led him to specify many features accepted as essential in a shopping center today; even the mixture of shops and apartments is now considered progressive. Here, as in many of his ideas, Schinkel was well ahead of his times.

THE ARCADE, Providence, Rhode Island, 1828
Warren & Bucklin, architects

Although the Berlin scheme was not built, another form of commercial edifice flourished from the 1780's through the whole nineteenth century. This was called arcade, gallery, or passage, and it provided a convenient assortment of shops and services away from vehicles, sheltered from the weather, sometimes several stories high, and lit and ventilated from above—an interior shopping street. The concept goes far back in history, at least to Roman times. Trajan's market, built around A.D. 110, had shops on a terraced hillside next to his forum. In one corner, a vaulted, multilevel hall, top lit, can still be seen: supposedly, it was used by the state to distribute grain, oil, and wine. Such Roman market halls were developed into the famous *souks* of the Orient.

Later still, from the Middle Ages on, European traders and bankers built handsome exchanges; the larger ones had upper shopping aisles with clerestory lights, and booths let out to tradesmen.

Toward the end of the eighteenth century, as urban populations grew, shopping arcades were built by private investors; they were especially successful in Paris, where they extended in networks at the center of town. It was in Paris that the glass roof was developed for such *passages couverts*. London had a few arcades early in the nineteenth century, and the idea was introduced to the United States by John Haviland, who found clients in Philadelphia and New York; his structures no longer exist. They were followed immediately by the Providence Arcade, still in active use and one of the pleasantest arcades ever designed, thanks chiefly to its stepped-back levels—an American improvement—assuring the best natural light and ventilation and an agreeable space. This stepped-back construction was copied abroad and may be seen in use in one of the largest shopping arcades ever built, now the state department store in Moscow.

The Providence Arcade was first designed for two stories only, with separate basements below each ground-level unit. But the backers, led by Cyrus Butler, decided to increase it by a third public level, and the present ample space was built. At night, the Arcade was lit by gas lamps attached to the slender cast-iron balustrades that, together with the glazed fronts for stores and offices —different at each level—give an air of slender strength to the interior. Uniform, readable signs allow the visitor to find his way easily. The classical street façades of massive granite may echo the forms of Boston's then new market buildings, but at Providence, the end pavilions also served to enclose the principal stairways, for security in case of fire.

Later in the century, grander arcades were built, ingeniously and openly, as in Cleveland, Ohio, or more monumentally, with high vertical walls pierced by rows of interior windows, as in Brussels or Milan. None of these have the character of the

Providence Arcade, with its sense of easy relationships in agreeable surroundings. The Arcade is more than a curious relic; it has miraculously survived in use, a complete and gentle expression of commercial civilization. It seems well worth emulating today.

THE AUDITORIUM BUILDING, Chicago, 1889
Adler & Sullivan, architects

The Auditorium Building was planned around a vast central hall, where everything from grand opera to a national convention could be housed appropriately and conveniently. In the mid-1880's, some private citizens of Chicago, led by Ferdinand W. Peck, decided to sponsor a civic monument for these purposes, but they were determined to avoid the recurrent expenses and inconveniences that characterized the then new Metropolitan Opera House of New York. The Chicagoans had selected a remarkable site in the midst of the busy city, facing Lake Michigan. They chose local architects whose ability in theater design had been demonstrated, the young firm of Adler & Sullivan. The resulting building was a practical success and an architectural triumph.

The auditorium hall itself was embedded in a shell of income-producing areas: stores and offices in one section—including the tower—and, in the other, a luxury hotel with unusual services, forty baths for four hundred bedrooms! Despite the differences between the 1890's and the 1970's, the Auditorium Building still pulls its weight. It is now owned and actively used for teaching and administration by Roosevelt University, a pioneer in integrated higher education. Only recently, thousands of Chicagoans contributed funds to restore the main room itself as an independently operated concert hall and theater. After long years of neglect, the Auditorium—an American masterwork —is again an effective entity.

The idea of a central space for public gatherings surrounded by a hive of smaller units was institutionalized in Roman amphitheaters. Later, similar relationships were temporarily realized when courtyards of castles and palaces were used for jousts and masques—the windows and arcades surrounding the courts became the loges for onlookers. Only with the spread of commerce after the Industrial Revolution were these practices transformed into community programs with income-producing possibilities. Such a scheme—hotel and theater combined—was proposed at the end of the eighteenth century for Richmond, Virginia, by one of the new country's most alert architects, Benjamin Latrobe. His designs, never carried out, expressed the separate characters of each part. During the next century, throughout the West, commodity and financial exchanges were built containing offices and large halls where open competitive bidding took place, as in the New York Stock Exchange today—a building designed by George B. Post. Post had designed one of the best of these structures in 1884, the New York Produce Exchange. When this was demolished in 1957, its daring iron structure and accomplished architectural design were again noticed and admired.

The New York Produce Exchange was studied by Adler & Sullivan in preparation for their Auditorium commission. Not only the bold iron frame interested them but also the over-all massing, with a prominent tower and windows grouped within arcading, and even the use of brick, with its crisp profiling. The backers of the Chicago venture were much impressed by a new building in their city, a warehouse for Marshall Field by Henry Hobson Richardson. The dignity of its granite exterior and the proud reticence of its detailing were assimilated into the Adler & Sullivan design to the satisfaction of all. But the extra weight of the stone and, furthermore, the repeated increases of facilities required by the enthusiastic committee of investors, made the construction of the Auditorium Building on the soggy soil of the lake shore something of a grand opera in its own right, especially in terms of engineering. The backers finally commissioned a work that cost more than double their original proposal to the architects.

227

The great central space—the Auditorium proper—was designed with remarkable ingenuity. It could pleasantly house an audience as small as 2,500 or be opened up for an assembly as large as 7,000, thanks to adjustable floor levels, movable proscenium screens, and gallery sections masked or put to use at will. Throughout these changes, the acoustics and conditioned air remained so excellent that they were soon world famous. The incorporation of the latest novelty, electric lighting, together with the sumptuous over-all ornament (some of it detailed by Sullivan's young assistant Frank Lloyd Wright) made the Auditorium an almost magically exciting place when it opened. The public rooms of the Auditorium Hotel were also among the handsomest interiors of their day.

This one building, then, united American ingenuity in structural, mechanical, and electrical engineering with the architectural genius of Louis Sullivan influenced by Henry Hobson Richardson and abetted by Frank Lloyd Wright. This masterwork was elicited by the courage and enterprise of a few civic-minded, farsighted businessmen in the 1880's. Few European palaces or cathedrals could claim brighter records. And the Auditorium Building still serves its community well and with the glamour of architectural greatness.

THE FLATIRON BUILDING, New York City, 1903
Daniel H. Burnham & Company, architects

Skyscrapers are acknowledged to be the most striking American innovation in architecture. Today, they are built all over the world, symbols of the push and power of modern civilization.

What is a skyscraper? It is a building so tall that it can be recognized from afar, while from nearby it rises to invisible heights. A skyscraper imposes by sheer verticality, no matter where it is located or what is next to it or what activities it houses. Tallness is its essence. How did this idea begin? Tall structures have always symbol-ized greatness. From the ziggurats of Babylon to the spires of Strasbourg and the steeples of Wren's London churches, tall towers have linked man to the greatness of his gods. Towers have also served as citadels of human might; the ultimate strength of ancient fortresses lay in their tower-keeps.

When, in turn, the modern world began to demand expression in architecture, men conceived of towers to celebrate the greatness of commercial prosperity and of technological progress. At first, the dreams outstripped reality, but soon, improvements in metals and in structural methods reshaped the skeleton; thin, light materials changed the skin; elevators permitted vertical circulation unimpeded; perimeter heating and a handful of lesser ingenuities made the skyscraper habitable.

A good deal of detective work has been done on the origins of the practical procedures of skyscraper construction, particularly metal framework (including ways of resisting the pressure of high winds), and devices that led from walls of brick or stone to lightweight screens carried, one floor at a time, by the framework. Improvements that transformed iron into steel were important; so, too, was an understanding of fireproofing, a knowledge bought at the price of tragedy in the days before testing laboratories. But these technological advances were required for something more than mere function— they served to make the skyscraper a symbol of the powers of modern man.

It has been said that skyscrapers arose because land in the business districts of big cities became so expensive that ways had to be found to make it more "productive" by piling more people—executives and office workers—onto each lot. Yet the technological skills that made the skyscrapers feasible also revolutionized communications. In sober fact, only a portion of those who work in business districts need to be so near one another. People are employed in skyscrapers in order to make good, practical use of buildings constructed in the first place to proclaim the glory of the chief tenants. Thus, the architecture of skyscrapers, like the architecture of churches, palaces, government buildings, and so on, is centered on symbolic expression, not on technologies or economics.

There have been a few master images that ruled the architecture of skyscrapers. These may be called the tower, the column, and the slab (single or clustered). The tower, whether it rises directly from the earth or is attached to a bulkier building block, is characteristically symmetrical, equal on all sides. The slab is typically broad on two sides and narrow on the others; it, too, may be linked to a lower mass. These two forms tend to display walls that are essentially alike from top to bottom, with only modest features to indicate ground level, mechanical levels, and building tops. The remaining image, on the contrary, aims to differentiate a beginning, a middle, and an end in the high rise of a skyscraper. These main parts may be called, by analogy with a classical column: base, shaft, and capital. Though only very rarely were skyscrapers designed to look like columns, for a considerable length of time the tripartite "columnar" division was considered the most mature approach to skyscraper architecture.

The greatest American architect of business buildings during the years covered by this exhibition was Louis Sullivan of Chicago; unfortunately, his boldest designs for skyscrapers were not built. The same can be said of two New Yorkers whose talents were only slightly less than his, George Post and Bruce Price. Sullivan, Post, and Price believed in three-part design for skyscrapers. So did a close competitor of theirs, Daniel H. Burnham, another Chicagoan and one of the busiest architects of his day.

Burnham's superbly coherent and refined design for the Flatiron Building, the Fuller Construction Company's headquarters in New York was realized in 1903. This was at that time the tallest habitable building in the world, and it commanded wide attention for both structural ingenuity and architectural sophistication. The inflection of its surfaces in shallow, rhythmic bays, the balanced proportions of its three chief zones, and the deft texturing of its specially made bricks all radiate architectural elegance of a high order, suiting the proud isolation of its site. The triangular site, exceptional in New York City, is entirely filled by the building, and the resulting wedge-shaped mass soon was called the "Flatiron." Few early skyscrapers were as well designed, and the Flatiron is probably the handsomest survivor of its kind. The whole world builds skyscrapers, yet the Flatiron, neglected and shabby, stands as a great, largely forgotten landmark in the rise of a distinctively American architecture.

SMALL FAMILY HOMES
Preliminary:
"Sunnyside," Tarrytown, New York, 1836
Washington Irving, designer

"Sunnyside" was the home of Washington Irving, the first American author to gain fame and acceptance abroad as well as in the United States. The house, perfectly restored, stands on the banks of the Hudson River just north of New York City. In its design, European precedent was modified to meet the independent ideas and special conditions of North America. Andrew Jackson Downing, the mid-nineteenth century landscape architect, wrote of it, "there is scarcely a building or place more replete with interest in America than [this] cottage."

After long years of productive work and travel in Europe, in 1835 Irving bought a small farm with an old house once belonging to the Van Tassel family, whom he had mentioned in his famous story *Rip Van Winkle*. He remodeled the house into a picturesque villa, such as he had known abroad. Like many educated men of those times, after asking the advice of friends, Irving acted as his own designer. The result was a lively assemblage of warm-hued, angular masses nestled in the landscape. Irving's visitors and neighbors could find references to his books and sojourn abroad in the features of "Sunnyside." Early settlers along the Hudson were associated with the Dutch stepped-gables, and weather vanes from old New York buildings recalled local civic history. The romantic garden, somewhat in Downing's taste, contained a pond called "Little Mediterranean," after an area dear to Irving; he was U.S. Minister to Spain in the early 1840's. So many visitors sought out Irving that, in 1847, he built an annex in the form of a pagoda-like tower. Eventually, he suffered the fate of many modern exurbanites: Progress caught up with him. His last eight years were disturbed by a railway constructed between his home and the Hudson. Today, honoring Irving's unique place in American letters and life, an unstinting restoration has brought back the flavor of "Sunnyside" as Irving knew and loved it. Few old homes anywhere show as well as this one how greatly a proper restoration enriches life in the present.

EVERGREEN HAMLET, Millvale, Pennsylvania, 1852
William Shinn, promoter

It was a remarkable cultural coincidence that a new concept of the American home took shape toward the middle of the nineteenth century in the Hudson River valley just when this area was made famous by a national school of landscape painters. The architectural trend was spread widely by books and periodicals, chiefly those of Andrew Jackson Downing, a successful practitioner of building, horticulture, and landscaping. Through Calvert Vaux (who worked with them both), Downing was linked to Frederick Law Olmsted, Sr. some of whose great city parks are displayed later in this exhibition.

The "cottages, farm houses, and villas" in Downing's books were derived from picturesque European types but much transformed in plan, elevation, and materials. The new American homes were carefully proportioned and conveniently arranged; in a modest house, as a rule, a wood frame was neatly wrapped in vertical boards and battens. Downing wrote, "The majority of such cottages in this country are occupied not by tenants, dependents or serfs, as in many parts of Europe, but by industrious and intelligent mechanics and working men, the bone and sinew of the land, who own the ground upon which they stand, build them

for their own use, and arrange them to satisfy their own peculiar wants and gratify their own tastes."

No work of this kind survives exactly as depicted by Downing. But a group of houses stands near Pittsburgh, Pennsylvania, completed according to Downing's precepts in 1852 (the very year of his death, at the early age of thirty-seven, in a river-boat explosion on the Hudson). Evergreen Hamlet, as it is still called, was founded in 1851 as a rural retreat from city bustle. Several families of comfortable means acquired eighty-five acres, which they laid out with plank roads, farming areas, and a school. Farm and school were common responsibilities, one acre and a house designed to suit was owned by each family separately. Construction was undertaken for the entire project by one firm, and within a year, the whole was ready for use. A jointly owned carriage made connections between the hilltop site and the nearest railway station. The idea of a small, planned community with shared responsibilities and facilities is as noteworthy as the advanced and logical architecture; Evergreen Hamlet is one of the remarkable survivals from its era. The homes are individually and privately owned today, cared for and appreciated as at first.

The leading spirit of this venture was a lawyer, William Shinn, and it is his house that is given prominence in the exhibition, since it is exceptionally close to Downing's more innovative designs. Two other Evergreen homes share with the Shinn house the vertical board-and-batten surfacing that Downing says was "generally practised" in his day along with horizontal siding. Downing preferred the vertical because it was more durable and "the main timbers which enter into the frame of a wooden house and support the structure, are vertical, and hence the vertical boarding properly signifies to the eye a wooden house."

If domestic architecture in America has a single native source, it is Downing, and nowhere is it possible to come closer to experiencing his ideals than in this small Pennsylvania enclave.

230

REV. PERCY BROWNE'S HOUSE, Marion,
Massachusetts, 1881–82
Henry Hobson Richardson, architect

Richardson was the first American architect
whose genius was recognized during his life-
time on both sides of the Atlantic. This
fame arose from his great buildings in
stone: churches, city halls, libraries, and
stores like the one for Marshall Field in
Chicago. When Richardson collaborated
with his friend Olmsted, the superb stone
bridge in Boston's Fenway resulted.

After architectural training in France,
young Richardson (a grandson of the Rev.
Joseph Priestley, discoverer of oxygen) returned to the United States at the close of
the Civil War. He soon worked his way to
the top of his profession, tempering the
latest ideas from France and England with
the realities of American clients, workmen,
and materials. In time, he developed a broad
and noble architecture. Each work began
with a strong unitary concept; this he
formed and refined in free sketches, explor-
ing the building masses and how they sat
on the land. Even on the building site, Richardson continued to clarify his expression.
"The architect acts on his building," Richardson would say, "but his building reacts
on him—helps to build itself. His work . . .
cannot be fully judged except in concrete
shape and color, amid actual lights and
shadows and its own particular surroundings." (Quoted from Richardson's biography
by his friend Marianna Griswold van
Rensselaer.)

Richardson also brought his intensity of
creative power to bear on small houses of
wood; one of his earlier ones was built for
the Rev. Browne and his family. Its architectural brilliance was recognized by Mrs. van
Rensselaer and by the chief later commen-
tators on Richardson's work, Henry-Russell
Hitchcock and Vincent Scully. The house
has been only partially presented in pictures before this show.

Mrs. van Rensselaer wrote:

Its foundations follow with delightful
frankness the variations of the ground
upon which it stands. . . . It explains
itself at once as a gentleman's summer
home, but with a simplicity which does
not put the humblest village neighbor
out of countenance. Inside, the planning
gives an unexpected amount of comfort
and air of space. The doorways are very
wide, and are so arranged as to afford a
diagonal instead of a straight perspective.
The windows are carefully placed . . . ,
the rear views toward woods and sunset
being as much considered as those which
show the sea. . . . Outside, the only touch
of ornament is given by the varied shaping of the shingles, and inside, pleasant
tints alone relieve the plainness of the
woodwork, and good outlines the severity
of the chimney-pieces. It has sometimes
been said that Richardson took so much
interest in great problems that he had
none left to give to small ones. But no
one could have more carefully studied
a little house like this, the cost of which,
exclusive of foundations, barely exceeded
twenty-five hundred dollars.

The house sits on hilly land, approached by
a rising driveway and flights of steps. En-
twined with porches, the main floor is open
in plan except for the minister's study at
one end and the services at the other. Above,
an ample bedroom floor is lit by dormers
strung along the sloping roof in an accented
band. The shingles have long since lost their
stain and are weathered silver gray. Neat, ret-
icent trim around the openings was painted
dark green, which Richardson preferred to
the more usual white. In his shingle houses,
Richardson made use of several New England precedents—both early and immediate.
Like Downing, Richardson presented the
modest, wood-framed house within a continuous weathertight skin of wood; unlike
Downing, he absorbed minor elements into
a unit whose articulation depended not on
detail but on rhythmical massing and on
gathered openings. In the small Browne
house, Richardson achieved a concentrated
purity of expression unsurpassed in his own
or any other architecture.

FRANK J. BAKER'S HOUSE, Wilmette, Illinois, 1909
Frank Lloyd Wright, architect

Frank Lloyd Wright followed Richardson as the most gifted inheritor and glorifier of Downing's cottage ideal. This theme in Wright's work appeared early, as part of his Prairie Style in the first decade of the twentieth century. The name signified Wright's desire to relate houses to the flat Middle Western terrain by reiterated architectural horizontals—the house form echoing the prairie line. Wright felt that vertical contrast was desirable but should be treated with caution. About sixty of his prairie houses were built, some large, some small, and all were explicit about their timber framing, stucco or board exteriors, earthy coloring quiet against the foliage, and ingenious heating and ventilating. These four features had been recommended by Downing, and fifty years after his time they were so generally approved that Wright could easily have been unaware of his debt to the earlier man.

Wright wrote of his first houses, "all architecture worthy of the name is growth in accord with natural feeling and industrial means to serve actual needs. . . . The chimney in hot weather ventilates [as do] circulating air spaces beneath the roofs, fresh air entering beneath the eaves through openings easily closed in winter." He went on to discuss open spouts for rain water discharging into ground-level receptacles without unsightly downspouts. "By means of [hot water heating at the perimeter—a device developed for skyscrapers] buildings may be more completed articulated with light and air on several sides. . . . The walls may be opened with a series of windows to the outer air, the flowers and trees, the prospect, and one may live as comfortably as formerly, less shut in." In his mind, economy, convenience, and environment were inextricably intertwined with architecture in these small houses.

An often admired variant of the prairie house was built in 1908 to Wright's design for Isabel Roberts, one of the drafters in his office. It was a compact house with a two-story living room; a big bay window dominated the front. The cross-shaped ground floor centered on chimney and stairs. Living and dining areas were at right angles to each other, the remaining arms held service rooms and porch. Bedrooms extended along a single axis, above. A double-height main room had already been proposed by Wright in designs published by the *Ladies' Home Journal* early in 1901, but the Roberts house plan was more deft and appealing. The same plan was built in 1909, with awkward changes; this house was altered beyond recognition, and the Roberts house has suffered drastic changes to walls and windows.

In 1909, Wright revised the Roberts theme in a design more expressive and elegant; this was used for the Baker house in Wilmette. It still stands, far less changed. Here the forms were freely extended in space, and the site permitted a simple distribution of secondary rooms. The central features retained their dominance. Every aspect of the house was made more poetic than in the precedent—in the framing of the front bay and the high window-strips separating roof from side walls in the living room. The balcony, too, which formed an inglenook for the fireplace and allowed access to some upper windows, was less self-conscious than the Roberts version. The Baker house scheme was reused, minus the upper window-strips, in a house built in Buffalo, also in 1909 (recently reconditioned). Then, in 1916, a small beach house for summer use was built to the same basic design, though this time the main bedrooms were at ground level, the great window encompassed the whole front of the living room, and the interior balcony was carried outside in an interesting interpenetration of forms.

In all these houses, the roof overhung the south front bay emphatically, and flower-boxes were placed beneath this extended roof. Inside, the flower-box was paralleled by a built-in window seat that—in the year-round houses—incorporated a sizable radiator behind simple grilles. This grouping of features in an orderly composition was in accord with Wright's desire to use comforts and facilities as elements of architecture rather than as addenda. Built-in lighting in his houses was treated in the same way.

Frank Lloyd Wright took the general approach of Downing—based in human convenience, common sense of a high order, and respect for the economy of middle-class life—and carried it forward with the help of more sophisticated techniques into a thoroughly original, creative architecture.

He continued to design modest homes throughout a long career. A later one, the Pope-Leighy house of 1940, has been conserved by the National Trust for Historic Preservation and can be visited on the outskirts of Washington, D.C.

THE AMERICAN PARK TRADITION

Preliminaries:
The English Garden, Munich, Germany, 1792
Benjamin Thompson (Baron Rumford), designer

In the late eighteenth century, public parks began to be established in the Western world. Frequently, gardens and hunting reserves were donated to the citizenry, as towns grew larger, by kings and noblemen. In fact, ancient custom often had allowed some public use of these lands even before the change of ownership. Grand avenues (cut through the woods for huntsmen), ornamented springs of water, pavilions for music and repose, and sports grounds were usually already on the land; sometimes, more elaborate plantings and embellishments existed as well.

At this time, military installations—parade grounds, bulwarks, bastions, and avenues for the quick deployment of troops—were partially (or, if obsolete, wholly) dedicated to public leisure. Moreover, city squares left open wherever people congregated—around spring houses and market stalls, in front of churches and palaces—were given fresh greenery, converting them to more parklike semblances.

Besides such adaptations of old facilities, there were some new parks. The growth of cities had led to housing developments, and in England, at least, these might include park areas, fenced and gated and thus limited to use by adjacent households.

These many forms of parks, public and semipublic, were developed to meet a practical need for open green spaces. However, by the end of the eighteenth century, a new park began to be conceived that would help to realize the ideals of the Enlightenment and of Human Rights. A most remarkable early example of this park concept survives, the English Garden in Munich, Germany. This was opened to the public in 1792; it had been designed by an American expatriate, Benjamin Thompson of Woburn, Massachusetts, knighted by the king of England and made Count Rumford of the Holy Roman Empire by the king of Bavaria. Thompson's international fame came from his successful attacks on unemployment, malnutrition, and inefficient management of fuels in cooking and heating.

His only venture into the design of parks was characteristically bold, successful, and renowned. The English Garden comprised 600 acres salvaged from marshy wasteland along Munich's Isar River. In two short years, it was transformed into a romantic Elysium of hillocks and streams, ponds and plantations, complete with paths, grottoes, outdoor theater, concert hall, racecourse, café, experimental farms for stock-breeding and crop improvements, and a thatched icehouse, as well as ornamental pavilions—all expressly for the delight, instruction, and relaxation of ordinary citizens. Created by the king's fiat and at his expense, it was a working demonstration of the good life, a model of what men could make of their world. As such, it became an important influence on the design of parks, first in Britain, then in Thompson's native country.

Olmsted and American Parks

During the nineteenth century, American city parks developed new forms. As happened with business buildings and small homes, the earlier efforts were close to

European precedents; then, gradually, an approach to parks evolved that was suited to the practical conditions and social goals of the United States.

Three stages of park design can be distinguished in the course of years from 1815 to 1915: (a) the park embellished the city as a special feature; (b) the park fulfilled the city as its necessary counterpart; (c) the park guided the growing city as an arm of regional planning. An American way of urban life worthy of respect required the park to complement the small home and the office tower. One of them without the others was a phenomenon, a curiosity; but as a trio, these developments spoke for a central sector of city life. Some severe problems of cities today are closely related to the decay of this three-sided achievement and the failure to develop it after a healthy start, to extend it to more citizens.

If this claim seems to offer too simple an explanation of complex evils, it is because a great vision has been forgotten, the vision of the park as the fulfillment of the city. This remarkable concept of a partnership, so to speak, between city and park was refined and tested by an admirable (and today little-known) band of men who centered around an authentic genius, Frederick Law Olmsted, Sr.

Olmsted was a personal friend of Richardson during the same years that brought the growth of the skyscrapers. Similarly, Sullivan's closest assistant was Frank Lloyd Wright. Burnham was one of Wright's earliest admirers, and an associate of Olmsted. In fact, much of American progress in the design of commercial buildings, small homes, and city parks, was the work of men who knew and respected each other, often as old friends.

Olmsted knew the work of Thompson in Munich, as he knew about the Utopian planners (like Fourier and Owen) of the early nineteenth century and about the reforming planners (like Chadwick and Howard) in his own times. Though his extended tour of Europe was taken in 1850, just before the great reshapings of Paris and Vienna, he knew well the English precedents on which they were based. Olmsted had his own point of view, rooted in American conditions. He believed in taking the modern city whole, on its own terms, in guiding it by example and supplementing its shortcomings wherever necessary, until a new and healthier environment had been evolved. It was an approach inconceivable in the metropolises of Europe but apt in the United States.

Olmsted's first and stormy venture into the world of city parks, undertaken in the late 1850's in the company of Calvert Vaux, who had been Downing's partner, was Central Park in New York City. Earlier, while writing dispatches for the *New York Times* on life in the Southern states, Olmsted had visited Savannah, Georgia, where he could appreciate at its best the older concept of small, inner-city parks. He, himself, preferred to plan on an ampler scale. Olmsted's initial landscape accomplishments were Central and Prospect Parks in New York City and Brooklyn. These two large parks differ in many ways one from the other, but both were designed and still function as many-faceted fulfillments of city life.

Toward the end of an exceptionally productive career, Olmsted led a vanguard of farsighted civic leaders, planners, and architects to the idea of parkways, park systems, and regional plans. The Chicago lake shore is a grand example of this development. Respect for the environment was the golden rule behind these concepts, so that modern man and nature could interact productively.

Today, scientists recognize the importance of this interaction:

> There is an increasing evidence suggesting that mental health and emotional stability of populations may be profoundly influenced by frustrating aspects of an urban, biologically artificial environment. . . . It seems likely that we are genetically programmed to a natural habitat of clean air and a varied green landscape, like any other mammal. . . . The specific physiological reactions to natural beauty and diversity, to the shapes and colors of nature, especially to green, to the motions

and sounds of other animals, we do not comprehend and are reluctant to include in studies of environmental quality. Yet it is evident that in our daily lives nature must be thought of not as a luxury to be made available if possible, but as part of our inherent indispensable biological need. . . . We need . . . a balance of social structures with . . . natural environment. [from Iltis, Loucks, and Andrews, "Criteria for an Optimum Environment," in *Science and Public Affairs,* January, 1970.]

Olmsted is an almost forgotten prophet, and his vision, the often missing ingredient of a truly modern, American urbanity.

THE PARK SQUARES, Savannah, Georgia, 1733–ca. 1833
General James E. Oglethorpe, original designer

In the 1730's, the English general James Oglethorpe was planning a capital port city for the newly created colony of Georgia, in North America. He was interested in an ideal setting for a better way of life and in the need to defend his settlement from attacks by Indians, Frenchmen, and Spaniards. Both requirements seemed met by a city high on a bluff, layed out to a gridiron plan with rectangular areas kept open at certain evenly spaced street-crossings. These open areas were to serve as market and meeting places, and they also could be used in case of attack as temporary camping grounds within the stockade for settlers farming outlying country.

Plans with numerous squares had been proposed for London after the Great Fire of 1666 and, before that, in the books of Italian Utopian planners—though with no defensive needs in mind. A rather conventional modification of this scheme with a central square had been used for Philadelphia, and the Savannah plan was occasionally reused for smaller communities in its neighborhood. But only at Savannah was the scheme carried out systematically, all the open areas about equal in size and regularly spotted through the town. Remark-

ably, the idea was continued as the city grew, so that by the end of the eighteenth century, quite free from the fear of attack, Savannah had the unique amenity of multiple civic spaces reserved from exploitation and speculation.

With the nineteenth century, Savannah's squares began to be surrounded by good architecture, public and private, and embellished with generous plantings, as well as fountains and ornaments. These improvements in gentle, provincial "Regency" taste gave Savannah unequaled charm. Thus, from purely practical and theoretical beginnings, Savannah in the nineteenth century developed a city spangled with delightful small parks. Olmsted, visiting there in 1853, saw these parks at the peak of their maturity.

One of the heartening evidences of American cultural awareness is that, in recent decades, the citizens of Savannah have struggled successfully to preserve the quality of their city from inconsiderate and unnecessary change. What began spontaneously developed into a model of civic grace and now deservedly has found conscious champions.

CENTRAL PARK, New York City; PROSPECT PARK, Brooklyn, New York, 1860's
Olmsted and Vaux, designers

These two great ventures into landscaping, the first undertaken by Olmsted and Vaux, were epic undertakings, interrupted by the Civil War, obstructed by municipal politics and personal chicanery, publicly attacked again and again, but finally accomplished with loyal support from leading citizens and fellow workers.

New York City had been planned at first with a great central parade ground. In 1811, the particularly unimaginative and constricting gridiron plan had been imposed on Manhattan Island; then the parade ground had been reduced to almost a third of its size and the rest sold off for building sites. Yet, the city required a great park and a variety of public educational museums if it were to grow suitably to its position as the leading city of the country. William Cullen Bryant of the *New York Post,* Washington Irving, and Andrew Jackson Downing, among others, were talking of this from the mid-1840's onward.

To the north of the city, a shanty town had grown up in a swampy hollow. This truly metropolitan slum, it was felt, had to go. Olmsted and Vaux saw their opportunity. The shore of the island could not be salvaged from the gridiron with its salable slivers of real estate, but the very center of Manhattan, obviously the future heart of the city itself, might be drained and restored by planting to become an internal pleasure garden for the people, walled by the city's buildings yet scaled to the city's size, linked to the city's vital transportation system, and adorned with civic institutions of knowledge —a weather station, popular museums of natural and local history and of the arts fine and applied. From New York's shame to New York's pride, that was the vision of what is now Central Park; but it was to be achieved only at the price of fanatical perseverance.

Across the river in Brooklyn, Olmsted and Vaux grasped a very different opportunity. There, an expanding urban center was linked by a great avenue—Flatbush— to outlying, semirural settlements. A city park was planned on both sides of the avenue. When Olmsted was approached, he counseled selling the land reserved to the northeast of the traffic artery for the use of public institutions—a library, botanical gardens, a museum, and the like—then preempting a larger area to the southwest. Here, unlike in Manhattan, unspoiled countryside still existed with majestic rolling vistas of water, landscape, and human habitation. It asked only to be put to advantageous use.

Thus, at the start of Olmsted's career in landscaping, the New York port area provided him with rare opportunities to create great public parks, one internal and one peripheral. His programs for them were based on certain basic precepts. These were: *first,* taking careful stock of the natural features and conditions of the site in order to utilize them to full advantage by careful improvements and adaptations to human requirements; *second,* separating traffic into commercial, private and pedestrian, each independent of the others; *third,* assuring the best quality of materials and workmanship in manmade constructions—walls, bridges, roads, paths, arbors, fountains, and service structures—as examples of good craftsmanship to set standards for the community; *fourth,* utilizing every opportunity for public self-education available to each citizen at his own convenience through:

- —a variety of sports and recreation facilities
- —the air, light, and vistas so lacking in city life
- —plants, especially those native to the area, on view and identified clearly, as well as exotic animals
- —the best of human culture, the arts and sciences, displayed and explained in museums and libraries open to the public, the park as a self-service university
- —facilities for special occasions and celebrations, public holidays and ceremonies, seasonal music and theater outdoors, the park as a center of happenings.

With such aims, Olmsted saw the park as the fulfillment of urban existence, the counterbalance to the artificiality, the social and physical constraints of cities. Olmsted knew there was no way back to an agricultural Eden and that industry and urbanization were the conditions of modern life. He fought to complete them to form a community worthy of mankind. As early as the 1860's, Olmsted saw New York and Brooklyn as part of a great conurbation, and he dreamed of a parkway uniting and extending Central Park and Prospect Park into a regional park system.

THE LAKE SHORE AND PARKS, Chicago, Illinois, 1833–1893
Olmsted, Burnham, and others, designers

When the city of Chicago was founded in 1833, it adopted a motto: *Urbs in Hortus,* the city in a garden. For years, the idea lay dormant, though eventually a system of city parks was envisaged. The idea was pursued with varying enthusiasm, until Chicago recovered from its disastrous fire of 1871. Booming, and equipped with new buildings of every kind, the city proposed a World's Fair to mark the four-hundredth anniversary of Columbus's landing in the New World.

The 1893 exhibition was planned by America's foremost architects and landscapers; they created a vision of grand urbanistic effects that was immensely popular. The architectural components, pompous and gross, influenced public building in the United States for the next half century. The landscape planning was generously scaled, adapted to its natural setting, and sensitively detailed. It influenced city park systems and regional plans throughout the continent.

As chief coordinator for design of the fair, the Chicago architect of the Flatiron Building, Daniel H. Burnham, called on Frederick Law Olmsted, Sr. to coordinate the overall plan. Later, Burnham called Olmsted "first in the heart and confidence of American artists. . . . our best advisor and our common mentor. In the highest sense he is the planner of the Exposition." It was assumed that, after the fair, Chicago would inherit the new parks linked to those already existent, as well as the public educational buildings, thus lifting the city to its proper dignity as the capital of the Middle Western area of the country. Today, this remains one of the most ample and comprehensive civic park systems in use, and it is used to great advantage. As long as it prevailed, control over the pollution of Lake Michigan allowed thousands of Chicago office workers to take a midday swim in the torrid summer months —an advantage rare indeed in the northern hemisphere!

Olmsted and Vaux, and, later, Olmsted with other partners, planned parks and park systems for Buffalo, Montreal, Detroit, Boston, Bridgeport, Rochester, Philadelphia, Knoxville, Louisville, San Francisco, and other communities. Horace W. S. Cleveland, Olmsted's most active contemporary, made similar park plans, the most admirable perhaps being that for Minneapolis and St. Paul. Kansas City, Missouri, benefited from an exceptional park plan by George Kessler. If American cities are to keep pace with the future, these magnificent parks, with their facilities and institutions, must be revitalized and carried forward. Without adequate and well-maintained park systems, the most skillfully engineered skyscrapers and the most livable family homes will not suffice. American life still needs the three-way support that its designers developed for it in the years 1815–1915.

Index

Gaynor, John P., 20, 130, 158
Gesellius, Herman, 32
Giedion, Sigfried, 46n.
Gilbert, Bradford, 142, 143
Gilbert, Cass, 117, 141, 147, 155, 158, 159, 166
Gilbert, E.-J., 19, 46n.
Giles, James H., 126
Gill, Irving, 204, 205
Gilman & Kendall, 119, 125, 158
Glover, J. G., 145
Godkin, Edward L., 80
Godwin, Parke, 85
Graham, E. R., 150, 151
Greene, Charles, 201, 202, 204
Greene, Henry, 201, 202, 204
Greenough, Horatio, 57–59
Griffin, Walter Burley, 39
Griscom, John H., 80
Griswold, J. N. A., 175
Gropius, Walter B., 29, 37, 38

Hale, Edward Everett, 60
Hall, William Hammond, 96
Harrison, Abramovitz & Abbe, 154, 159
Harrison & Abramovitz, 153
Hastings, Thomas, 149
Hatch, Stephen, 127, 132
Hausen, Marika, 31
Haussmann, Baron, 87
Haviland, John, 15, 17
Hawthorne, Nathaniel, 60
Hentrich & Petschnigg, 43, 44
Herkomer, Sir Hubert von, 29
Hilberseimer, Ludwig, 153
Hildreth, Richard, 80
Hitchcock, Henry-Russell, 122, 208n.
Höger, Fritz, 39
Holabird & Roche, 34, 140, 158, 159
Holme, Thomas, 59
Holmes, Oliver Wendell, 60
Hood, Godley & Fouilhoux, 152, 158
Hood, Raymond, 38, 39, 40
Howard, Ebenezer, 109n.
Howard, John, 81
Howells & Hood, 147, 158, 159
Hume, Joseph, 84, 108n.
Hunt, Richard Morris, 22, 86, 120, 143, 158, 174, 175, 184, 185

J. C. Cady & Company, 88
J. E. Carpenter & Associates, 158, 159
Jacobus, John, 46n.
Jarves, James Jackson, 85
Jeanneret, Charles Edouard (see˙ Le Corbusier)
Jefferson, Thomas, 79, 164, 165
Jenney, William Le Baron, 21, 123, 158
Jenney & Mundie, 159
John Portman & Associates, 153, 158
Johnson, Philip, 4, 5, 6, 154, 158, 159, 196
Johnson & Burgee, 153
Johnston, William L., 128, 143, 158
Jones, Inigo, 9

Kahn, Albert, 8
Kahn, Moritz, 45n.
Kamper, Louis, 146, 147, 159
Kellum, John, 124, 159
Kendall, Edward, 156, 157
Kensett, John F., 90
Kessler, George E., 100
Kiesler, Frederick, 9
Kimball, Francis H., 150
King, Moses, 153

Le Brun, Napoleon, 25, 116, 158
Le Corbusier, 6, 41, 153
Lecointe, J. F. J., 46 n.
Lee, Joseph, 100
Leggett, William, 108n.
L'Enfant, Pierre Charles, 73, 85
Lindgren, A. E., 32
Little, Arthur, 26
Livingston, Edward, 80
Loos, Adolf, 32
Loudon, John Claudius, 81
Luce, Clarence, 5, 28, 29

McCagg, Ezra B., 94
McEntee, Jervis, 90
McIntire, Samuel, 168
McKim, Charles Follen, 181
McKim, Mead & White, 26, 180, 181, 182, 183, 184, 186, 188
Magney & Tusler, Inc., 148
Mangin, Joseph, 68
Mann, Horace, 80
Maybeck, Bernard, 206, 207
Maynicke, Robert, 138
Mead, William Rutherford, 181
Mengelson, Charles F., 127, 132, 158, 159
Mewès & Davis, 25
Meyer, Adolf, 37
Mies van der Rohe, Ludwig, 4, 5, 6, 19, 29, 35, 39, 43, 45n., 48n., 153, 154, 158, 159, 196
Moltke, J. W. von, 45n.
Morrison, Hugh, 138
Moseley Brothers, 20
Motley, John L., 84
Mould, John Wrey, 56, 92
Mujica, Francisco, 122, 125, 149, 153
Mumford, Lewis, 104
Murphy, C. F. (see C. F. Murphy & Associates)

Napoleon Le Brun & Sons, 118, 158
Nash, John, 81, 84
Newton, Dudley, 174
Nicholson, Peter, 13
Nilsson, G. A., 34
Norton, Charles E., 94
Nyrop, Martin, 33

Oglethorpe, James E., 77, 85
Olbrich, J. M., 32
Olmsted, Frederick Law, 51, 54, 64, 67, 75, 77, 78, 79, 80, 81, 83–84, 85, 87, 88, 93, 94, 95, 96, 99, 100, 104, 107n., 109n., 110n., 172, 173